The
SEVEN
PRINCIPLES
for
MAKING
MARRIAGE
WORK

ALSO BY JOHN GOTTMAN

And Baby Makes Three
with Julie Gottman

What Makes Love Last?
with Nan Silver

Meta-Emotion:
How Families Communicate Emotionally
with Lynn Katz and Carole Hooven

Raising an Emotionally Intelligent Child: The Heart of Parenting
with Joan DeClaire

The Analysis of Change

The Mathematics of Marriage
with James Murray and students

Why Marriages Succeed or Fail
with Nan Silver

What Predicts Divorce?

The Science of Trust

The Mathematics of Marriage

The SEVEN PRINCIPLES *for* MAKING MARRIAGE WORK

A PRACTICAL GUIDE FROM THE COUNTRY'S
FOREMOST RELATIONSHIP EXPERT

John M. Gottman, Ph.D.,
and Nan Silver

HARMONY

BOOKS · NEW YORK

Library of Congress Cataloging-in-Publication Data
Gottman, John Mordechai.
The seven principles for making marriage work / by John Gottman, and Nan Silver.—
Second edition.
pages   cm
1. Marriage. 2. Married people—Psychology. 3. Communication in marriage.
4. Man-woman relationships. I. Silver, Nan. II. Title.
HQ734.G7136 2014
306.81—dc23
2014034168

ISBN 978-0-553-44771-2
eBook ISBN 978-1-101-90291-2

Printed in the United States of America

Cover design: Kalena Schoen
Cover image: Juk86/Shutterstock

20

Second Edition

To my beautiful and brilliant girls, Julie and Moriah Gottman.
     J.G.

In honor of my devoted parents, Blanche and Murray Silver,
and their sixty-year marriage.
     N.S.

Acknowledgments

First and foremost, I need to acknowledge the brave gift that several thousand volunteer research couples have contributed to my understanding. Their willingness to reveal the most private aspects of their personal lives has opened a hitherto closed door that has made it possible to construct these Seven Principles for making marriages work.

This book was based on research that received continuous support from the National Institute of Mental Health, the Behavioral Science Research Branch. Of great assistance was the dedicated guidance of Molly Oliveri, Della Hahn, and Joy Schulterbrandt.

This book was also made possible by a number of important collaborations that have been a joyful part of my life. These include the main collaboration that has graced my life for the past thirty-eight years with Professor Robert Levenson of the University of California, Berkeley. Friendship and laughter have always been the heart of our collaboration. Also important to me have been my collaboration with the late Neil Jacobson of the University of Washington and my work with Laura Carstensen of Stanford University.

I have been blessed with rich associations inside my laboratory and with the Gottman Institute, particularly Etana and Alan Kunovsky, and David Penner.

My wife, Dr. Julie Schwartz Gottman, provided great love, wonderful friendship, motivation, intellectual camaraderie, support, and conceptual organization. Julie brought her wisdom and enormous clinical acumen and great spirit to our joint work. After many productive and heated arguments lasting decades (arguing is Jewish love), the Sound Relationship House Theory is totally the product of our mutual collaboration; detached scientist and empathic clinician have met and learned from each other. She has also been my teacher and guide in practicing psychotherapy. She made doing the couples' and parents' workshops an exciting creative experience. While Julie and I are busy with our full-time jobs, Alan and Etana Kunovsky capably run the Gottman Institute with great spirit, imagination, and attention to detail, and they also help facilitate our communication. Linda Wright helps us keep the couples' enterprise very warm and human—she is unusually gifted in talking to desperate couples.

I have recently been blessed with excellent students and staff, including Kim Buehlman, Jim Coan, Melissa Hawkins, Carole Hooven, Vanessa Kahen, Lynn Katz, Michael Lorber, Kim McCoy, Jani Driver, Eun Young Nahm, Sonny Ruckstahl, Regina Rushe, Kimberly Ryan, Alyson Shapiro, Amber Tabares, Tim Stickle, Beverly Wilson, and Dan Yoshimoto. Jim Coan's recent work on relationships and the brain is a great source of inspiration.

I need to acknowledge the intellectual heritage upon which I draw. As Newton once wrote, "If I have seen further it is by standing on the shoulders of giants." For me these shoulders begin with the impressive work of Susan Johnson on emotionally focused marital therapy. Susan Johnson led the way, and she showed us what to focus on. Not only that, but she also combined her great intuition and empathy with the relentless and steadfast work of the objective scientist. No one in our field can come close to her enormous contribution. I want to acknowledge Bob Weiss's scholarly work on many concepts, including sentiment overrides; Cliff Notarius's work on many concepts, including sentiment override and couple efficacy; Howard Markman and Scott Stanley's faith in preventive intervention; psychiatrist Jerry Lewis's work focusing on the balance of autonomy and connectedness in marriage; and the persistent work of my late colleague Neil Jacobson, who was the first gold standard for honest marital therapy research. I am also indebted to Jacobson's more recent work with Andy Christensen, on acceptance in marital therapy. I also wish to acknowledge the contributions of William Doherty on rituals of connection, Peggy Papp, and Pepper Schwartz, as well as the work of Ronald Levant and Alan Booth on men in families.

I must also mention Dan Wile's brilliant work on marital therapy, with its superb focus on process. I love Wile's writing; his thinking is a great inspiration. His writing, entirely from a clinical perspective, is (amazingly, I think) prescient and entirely consistent with many of my research findings. I think that Wile is a genius . . . I am blessed to have been able to exchange ideas with him. He is a great therapist.

I wish to acknowledge the work of Irvin Yalom and Victor Frankl on existential psychotherapy. Yalom has provided a great faith in the therapeutic process itself and in the human force toward growth. Frankl holds a special place in my heart. He and my beloved cousin Kurt Ladner were both residents and survivors of the Dachau concentration camp. Both found meaning in the context of intense suffering, tyranny, and dehumanization. Julie and I have brought their existential search for meaning into the relationship context. Doing so can turn conflict into a new experience of revealing and honoring life dreams, finding shared meaning, and reaffirming the couple's friendship.

I have come to the conclusion that many insightful writers in the relationship field are basically correct. I hope my contribution will be to honor them all, adding a bit of precision and integration to the struggle to understand what makes close relationships work.

J.G.

Contents

Introduction

When we sat down to write the first edition of this book, we were excited to share the results of laboratory research into relationships but we knew we'd face some skepticism. Could scientific study of something as intangible, idiosyncratic, and personal as romantic love deliver useful advice to couples in the real world? Well, more than fifteen years and millions of readers later we are happy to report that *The Seven Principles for Making Marriage Work* has done just that. Countless readers across the globe tell us that the book's strategies have enhanced, shielded, or saved their relationship. We have received thank-yous from every imaginable type of couple, including newlyweds, traditional spouses, two-career partners, devoutly religious spouses, military couples, cohabitants, same-sex partners, not-yet-marrieds, divorced people looking toward the future, and counselors who work with all of the above.

It is a great source of satisfaction and pride that we have been able to help so many people. We're also gratified that research continues to confirm what these readers consistently tell us: *The Seven Principles* can have a powerfully positive effect on your relationship. In fact, a randomized clinical study by John and his co-researchers (Julia Babcock, Kim Ryan, and Julie Gottman) found that married couples who simply read *The Seven Principles* and worked through the quizzes and exercises on their own (but received no additional professional aid) were significantly happier in their relationship, and these effects lasted when assessed a year later. Simply reading this book proved so successful that it actually bollixed the research: the original experiment had been designed to use these "book-only" couples as a control group to test marital therapy techniques!

Considering the current book's great track record, you may

wonder why we've chosen to revise it. The answer is simple: John's research and work with couples have progressed since he first "crunched the numbers" on what makes marriages thrive and how to predict and prevent divorce. There are now forty-two years of longitudinal data on the importance of marital friendship. There is also a growing body of statistics on marital outcomes among diverse populations, including low-income families, partners who have recently become parents, same-sex couples, and those from diverse ethnic backgrounds. This work has confirmed the universality of the Seven Principles and advanced our understanding of why they are so powerful and how couples can best utilize them.

Perhaps most notably, in the years since *The Seven Principles* was first published, John and his wife, therapist Dr. Julie Gottman, have put these research findings to work through the Gottman Institute. This organization offers direct support to couples through seminars and therapy and also trains professionals in providing counseling based on John's research. Thanks to the Institute, classes on the Seven Principles are taught worldwide. The Institute's therapeutic and educational work has a synergetic relationship with laboratory research—it both benefits from the scientific findings and helps the Gottmans apply the theory to couples in need. A growing body of controlled studies has demonstrated the positive impact of this approach. For example, in a randomized clinical trial, unhappy couples who participated in a combination of Gottman workshops on conflict resolution and marital friendship, in conjunction with nine sessions of Gottman Method Couples Therapy based on *The Seven Principles*, showed the greatest lasting benefit and least relapse when assessed a year later.

Another area of great success for the Gottman Institute has been in supporting couples after the birth of their first child, a stressful time in most marriages. (About 67 percent of couples experience a large drop in marital satisfaction in the three years after the birth of their first baby.) The Bringing Baby Home workshop uses the Seven Principles approach to address the specific concerns of new parents. In a randomized clinical trial, unhappy couples who participated in the two-day program significantly reversed the drop in their marital satisfaction. The program also reduced postpartum depression and hostility between spouses, and improved both of the parents' interaction with the baby and the child's emotional and language development. Hospital-based studies in Australia and Iceland have shown similar results.

This new edition is an opportunity to share with readers all that we have learned from the Love Lab and the Gottman Institute's work. Throughout, you'll find clarifications and important additions and revisions that address the pressures and tensions that modern couples face. We've also expanded and updated the interactive nature of *The Seven Principles*: For each Principle you'll find questionnaires (with high reliability and validity) so you can assess its status in your own relationship, and new or revised exercises to enhance it. The exercises have been thoroughly vetted by numerous participants in the Gottman Institute's workshops and those in couples therapy with Institute-trained practitioners.

One of the strengths of *The Seven Principles* approach is its versatility in addressing all stages of a relationship. This book is for you if you're single and looking to "road test" your relationship before making a permanent commitment. It is also for you if you've already committed and want to bolster and protect what you have. If you and your partner are facing dramatic life changes or challenges, *The Seven Principles* will help you keep connected. Following the guidance in the pages ahead may also rescue a marriage that is already in deep danger.

Of course, no relationship guide can salvage every marriage, nor is it true that every match "should" be saved. Sometimes negativity and betrayal so consume a relationship that it has really already died by the time the couple seek support. But the right form of assistance can repair far more relationships and offer a greater degree of hope than the divorce statistics would suggest. Anyone who works with or studies couples is left humbled and awed by the tenacity, resourcefulness, and grit of people who love each other and are determined to make their marriages work. We wrote this book to be a fitting companion for their journey.

Much has changed in the fifteen-plus years since the arrival of the first edition of *The Seven Principles*, but one fact has held constant: a romantic and sexual long-term committed relationship with another human remains the greatest gift life can offer. We hope this new edition of *The Seven Principles* safeguards and strengthens your relationship—and helps you add purpose and meaning to the life you build together.

The
SEVEN
PRINCIPLES
for
MAKING
MARRIAGE
WORK

1

Inside the Seattle Love Lab: The Truth About Happy Marriages

*I*t's a surprisingly cloudless Seattle morning as newly-weds Mark and Janice sit down to breakfast. Outside the apartment's picture window, the waters of Mont-lake cut a deep-blue swath, while runners jog and geese waddle along the lakeside park. Mark and Janice are enjoying the view as they munch on their French toast and share the Sunday paper. Later Mark will probably switch on the football game while Janice chats over the phone with her mom in St. Louis.

All seems ordinary enough inside this studio apartment—until you notice the three video cameras bolted to the wall, the micro-phones clipped talk-show style to Mark and Janice's collars, and the Holter monitors strapped around their chests. Mark and Jan-ice's lovely studio with a view is really not their apartment at all. It's a laboratory at the University of Washington in Seattle, where for sixteen years I spearheaded the most extensive and innovative research ever into marriage and divorce.

As part of one of these studies, Mark and Janice (as well as forty-nine other randomly selected couples) volunteered to stay overnight in a fabricated apartment, affectionately known as the Love Lab. Their instructions were to act as naturally as possible, despite my team of scientists observing them from behind the one-way kitchen mirror, the cameras recording their every word and facial expression, and the sensors tracking bodily signs of stress or relaxation, such as how quickly their hearts pounded. (To preserve basic privacy, the couples were monitored only from 9 a.m. to 9 p.m. and never while in the bathroom.) The apartment came equipped with a foldout sofa, working kitchen, phone, TV, and music player. Couples were told to bring their groceries, books, laptops, needlepoint, hand weights, even their pets—whatever they would need to experience a typical weekend.

Our goal was nothing more ambitious than to uncover the truth about marriage—to finally answer the questions that have puzzled people for so long: Why is marriage so tough at times? Why do some lifelong relationships click, while others just tick away like a time bomb? And how can you prevent a marriage from going bad—or rescue one that is already in trouble?

Predicting Divorce with 91 Percent Accuracy

Thanks to decades of research, these questions can finally be answered. In fact, I can predict with great precision whether a couple will stay happily together or lose their way after listening to them interact for as little as fifteen minutes! Over seven separate studies, my accuracy rate in making such predictions has averaged 91 percent. In other words, in 91 percent of the cases where I predicted that a couple's marriage would eventually either fail or succeed, time proved me right. I don't think my success in foretelling divorce earns me any bragging rights because it isn't due to some superhuman perception or intuition. Instead, it rests solely on the *science*: the decades of data my colleagues and I accumulated.

At first you might be tempted to shrug off our research results as just another in a long line of newfangled theories. Skepticism is certainly called for when someone tells you they've figured out what really makes marriages last and can show you how to rescue or divorce-proof your own. Plenty of people consider themselves to be experts on marriage—and are more than happy to give you their opinion of how to form a more perfect union. But that's the key word—*opinion*. Before the breakthroughs our research provided, point of view was pretty much all that anyone trying to help couples had to go on. And that included just about every qualified, talented, and well-trained marriage counselor out there. Usually a responsible therapist's approach to helping couples was (and often still is) based on his or her professional training and experience, intuition, family history, perhaps even religious conviction. But the one thing it was not based on was hard scientific evidence. Because there really hadn't been any rigorous scientific data about why some marriages succeeded and others collapsed.

Predicting divorce makes for great headlines, but sometimes the statistics can be confusing. I've heard people dismiss the scientific approach to assessing marriage by pointing out that, with the divorce rate at about 50 percent, even random guessing would lead to a pretty good prediction rate. But that interpretation is based on a misunderstanding of what we are analyzing. That widely cited 50 percent rate is a general estimate of divorce over forty years of marriage. Our studies predict divorce over a much shorter time frame. For example, in a study of 130 newlywed couples, we determined which fifteen of them would divorce over the next seven years, based on our analysis of their interactions. In fact, seventeen couples divorced (including our fifteen), making our prediction rate for that study 98 percent.

Over the years, other laboratories using methods we pioneered have also tallied impressive successes at prediction, thus confirming that our long-term findings were stable scientific results, not anomalies. For example, the labs headed by Rand Conger at Iowa State University and Tom Bradbury at the University of California, Los Angeles have both made highly accurate predictions of a marriage's fate by analyzing a couple's physiological responses while they discussed a single conflict. In another landmark study of newlyweds, psychologist Janice Kiecolt-Glaser, her husband Ron Glaser, and their colleagues at The Ohio State University were able to measure the levels of the stress-related hormone adrenaline in the blood of newlywed couples while they argued. Ten years later the researchers determined that, compared with the couples who remained happily married, those who ended up unhappy or divorced had secreted 34 percent higher levels of adrenaline while arguing as newlyweds. These researchers also found that another stress hormone, ACTH, was twice as high in the newlywed wives who ended up in troubled marriages or divorced ten years later compared with the happily married women. In other words, these researchers were able to predict the fate of newlywed couples *ten years later* just by measuring hormone levels in their blood during their first year of marriage!

Although the ability to predict divorce through laboratory research has made for great advances in the study of long-term relationships, I don't think it is this project's most significant contribution. Instead, I think my most rewarding discovery has been the Seven Principles, which aren't just about predicting divorce but also about *preventing* it. Unlike so many other approaches to helping couples, ours is based on knowing what makes marriages succeed rather than on what makes them fail. We no longer have to guess about why some couples stay so happily married. Thanks to years of scientific data and analysis, we really can identify what makes happily married couples different from everybody else.

Emotionally Intelligent Marriages

What can make a marriage work is surprisingly simple. Happily married couples aren't smarter, richer, or more psychologically astute than others. But in their day-to-day lives, they have hit upon a dynamic that keeps their negative thoughts and feelings about each other (which all couples have) from overwhelming their positive ones. Rather than creating a climate of disagreement and resistance, they embrace each other's needs. When addressing a partner's request, their motto tends to be a helpful "Yes, and . . ." rather than "Yes, but . . ." This positive attitude not only allows them to maintain but also to increase the sense of romance, play, fun, adventure, and learning together that are at the heart of any long-lasting love affair. They have what I call an emotionally intelligent marriage.

I can predict whether a couple will divorce after watching and listening to them for just fifteen minutes.

Emotional intelligence has become widely recognized as an important predictor of a child's success later in life. The more in touch with feelings and the better able a child is to understand and get along with others, the sunnier that child's future, whatever his or her academic IQ. The same is true for spouses. The more emotionally intelligent a couple—the better able they are to understand, honor, and respect each other and their marriage—the more likely that they will indeed live happily ever after. Just as parents can teach their children emotional intelligence, this is also a skill that couples can learn. As simple as it sounds, developing this ability can keep husband and wife on the positive side of the divorce odds.

Why Save Your Marriage?

One of the saddest reasons a marriage dies is that neither spouse recognizes its value until it is too late. Only after the papers have been signed, the furniture divided, and separate apartments rented do the exes realize how much they really gave up when they gave up on each other. Too often a good marriage is taken for granted rather than given the nurturing and respect it deserves and desperately needs. Some people may think that getting divorced or languishing in an unhappy marriage is no big deal—they may even consider it a simple fact of modern life. But there's now plenty of evidence documenting just how harmful both divorce and an unhappy relationship can be for all involved.

Thanks to the work of researchers Lois Verbrugge and James

House, both of the University of Michigan, we now know that an unhappy marriage can increase your chances of getting sick by roughly 35 percent and even shorten your life by an average of four to eight years. The flip side: people who are happily married live longer, healthier lives than either divorced people or those who are unhappily married. Scientists know for certain that these differences exist, but we are not yet sure why.

Part of the answer may simply be that in an unhappy marriage people experience chronic, diffuse physiological arousal—in other words, they feel physically stressed and usually emotionally overwrought as well. This puts added wear and tear on the body and mind, which can present itself in any number of physical ailments, including high blood pressure and heart disease, and in a host of psychological troubles, including anxiety, depression, substance abuse, psychosis, violence, and suicide.

Not surprisingly, happily married couples have a far lower rate of such maladies. They also tend to be more health-conscious than others. Researchers theorize that spouses keep after each other to have regular checkups, take medicine, eat nutritiously, and so on.

People who stay married live four to eight years longer than people who don't.

But there is growing evidence that a good marriage may also keep you healthier by directly benefiting your immune system, which spearheads the body's defenses against illness. Researchers have known for about two decades that divorce can depress the immune system's function. Theoretically, this decline in the system's ability to fight foreign invaders could leave you open to more infectious diseases and cancers. Now we have found that the opposite may also be true. Not only do happily married people avoid this drop in immune function, but their immune systems may even be getting an extra boost.

When we assessed the immune-system responses of the fifty couples who stayed overnight in the Love Lab, we found a striking difference between those who were very satisfied with their marriages and those whose emotional response to each other was neutral or who were unhappy. Specifically, we used blood samples from each subject to test the response of certain of their white blood cells—the immune system's major defense weapons. In general, happily married men and women showed a greater proliferation of these white blood cells when exposed to foreign invaders than did the other subjects.

Researchers Janice Kiecolt-Glaser and Ron Glaser tested the effectiveness of other immune-system warriors: the natural killer cells, which, true to their name, destroy body cells that have been damaged or altered (such as infected or cancerous ones) and are also known to limit the growth of tumor cells. Again, subjects who were satisfied with their marriage had more effective natural killer cells than did the others.

It will take more study before scientists can confirm that this boost in the immune system is one of the mechanisms by which a good marriage benefits your health and longevity. But what's most important is that we know for certain that a good marriage does offer these advantages. I often think that if fitness buffs spent just 10 percent of their weekly workout time—say, twenty minutes a day—working on their marriage instead of their bodies, they would get three times the health benefits they derive from exercise class or the treadmill.

When a marriage goes sour, husband and wife are not the only ones to suffer—the children do, too. In a study I conducted of sixty-three preschoolers, those being raised in homes where there was great marital hostility had chronically elevated levels of stress hormones compared with the other children studied. We don't know what the long-term repercussions of this stress will be for their health. But we do know that this biological indication of extreme stress was echoed in their behavior. We followed them through age fifteen and found that, compared with other children their age, these kids suffered far more from truancy, depression, peer rejection, behavioral problems (especially aggression), low achievement at school, and even school failure.

One important message of these findings is that it is not wise to stay in a bad marriage for the sake of your children. It is clearly harmful to raise kids in a home that is consumed by hostility. A peaceful divorce is preferable to endless marital warfare. Unfortunately, many divorces are not peaceful. Too often there is mutual enmity between the parents that continues after the breakup. For that reason, children of divorce often fare just as poorly as those caught in the crossfire of a miserable marriage.

Innovative Research, Revolutionary Findings

When it comes to saving a marriage, the stakes are high for everybody in the family. And yet despite the documented importance of marital satisfaction, the amount of scientifically sound research into keeping marriages stable and happy is shockingly small. When I first began researching marriage more than forty years ago, you could probably have held all of the good scientific data on marriage in one hand. By "good" I mean findings that were collected using scientific methods as rigorous as those used by medical science. For example, many studies of marital happiness were conducted solely by having husbands and wives fill out questionnaires. This approach is called the self-report method, and although it has its uses, it is also quite limited. How do you know a wife is happy just because she checks the "happy" box on some form? Women in physically abusive relationships, for example, score very high on questionnaires about marital satisfaction. Only if the woman being abused feels safe and is interviewed alone does she reveal the truth.

To address this paucity of quality research, my colleagues and I supplemented traditional approaches to studying marriage with more extensive and innovative methods. We tracked the fates of seven hundred couples in seven different studies. We didn't just look at newlyweds but also at long-term couples who were first assessed while in their forties or sixties. In addition, we analyzed couples who had just had their first baby and couples parenting preschoolers and teenagers. We have examined the relationships of couples from diverse socioeconomic, racial, and ethnic groups and sexual orientations.

Most of my long-term studies have entailed extensive interviews in which the spouses detailed for me the history of their marriage, their philosophy about relationships, and how they viewed the marriages of others, including their parents. I videotaped them talking to each other about how their day went, discussing areas of continuing disagreement in their marriage, and also conversing about joyful topics. And to get a physiological read of how stressed or relaxed they were feeling, I measured their heart rate, blood velocity, sweat output, respiration, and endocrine and immune function throughout these taped interactions. In all of these studies, I played back the tapes to the couples and asked them for an insiders' perspective of what they were thinking and feeling when, say, their heart rate or blood pressure suddenly surged during a marital discussion. Then I kept track of the couples, checking in with them at least once a year till the study's end to see how their relationship was faring.

Couples who attend my workshop have a relapse rate that's about half that from standard marital therapy.

My colleagues and I were the first researchers to conduct such an exhaustive observation and analysis of married couples. Our data offered the first real glimpse of the inner workings—the *anatomy*—of marriage. These results, not my own opinions, form the basis of my Seven Principles for making marriage work. These principles, in turn, are the cornerstones of the remarkably effective short-term therapy for couples that I developed along with my wife, clinical psychologist Dr. Julie Gottman.

Thousands of couples have now attended our programs. Almost all of them came to us because their marriage was in deep distress—some were on the verge of divorce. Many were skeptical that a simple workshop based on the Seven Principles could turn their relationship around. Fortunately, their skepticism was unfounded. Our findings indicate that these workshops have made a profound and powerful difference in these couples' lives.

When it comes to judging the effectiveness of marital therapy, it seems that the one-year mark is a pivotal point. Usually by then the couples who are going to relapse after therapy already have. Those who retain the benefits of therapy through the first year tend to continue them long-term. So we put our workshops to the test by doing an extensive twelve-month follow-up of 640 couples. I'm happy to report a success rate of about 75 percent. I'm even happier to report a very low relapse rate of 20 percent. (The nationwide relapse rate for standard behavioral marital therapy is 30 to 50 percent.) More specifically, we found that at the beginning of our workshops, 27 percent of the couples were at very high risk for divorce, but at our twelve-month follow-up, after nine sessions, that proportion had dropped to 7 percent. The rate plummeted to 4 percent for struggling couples who also underwent nine additional sessions of our couples' therapy. Furthermore, we found that *prevention* workshops, in which couples worked on their relationship before conflict began to take its toll, were even three times more effective than our workshops designed for couples who were already troubled.

Why Most Marriage Therapy Fails

In recent years other laboratories have obtained similar findings to ours and have also developed techniques both for improving couples' therapy and preventing relationship problems. But despite the gradual increase in useful and hopeful approaches, the majority of marriage therapists are still offering treatment that does not get to the heart of what makes a long-term relationship last. In order to achieve the next level of understanding about how to keep our relationships thriving, we need to throw out some long-hallowed beliefs about marriage and divorce.

If you've had or are having trouble in your relationship, you've probably gotten lots of advice. Sometimes it seems like everybody who has ever been married or knows anyone who has ever been married thinks he or she holds the secret to guaranteeing endless love. But most of these notions, whether intoned by a psychologist on TV or by a wise manicurist at the local mall, are wrong. Many such ideas, even those initially espoused by talented theorists, have been long discredited—or deserve to be. But they have become so firmly entrenched in the popular culture that you'd never know it.

Perhaps the biggest myth of all is that communication—and more specifically, learning to resolve your conflicts—is the royal road to romance and an enduring, happy marriage. Whatever a marriage therapist's theoretical orientation, whether you opt for short-term therapy or long-term therapy, or regularly read relationship advice blogs, the message you'll get is pretty uniform: learn to communicate better. The sweeping popularity of this approach is easy to understand. When most couples find themselves in a conflict (whether it gets played out as a short spat, an all-out screaming match, or stony silence), they each gird themselves to win the fight. They become so focused on how hurt they feel, on proving that they're right and their spouse is wrong, or on keeping up a cold shoulder, that the lines of communication may be overcome by static or shut down altogether. So it seems to make sense that calmly and lovingly listening to each other's perspective would lead couples to find solutions and regain their marital composure. Indeed, there is an important place for listening skills and problem-solving techniques in building and maintaining a relationship. But too often these approaches are considered *all* that couples need to succeed. And couples who don't problem-solve "well" are considered doomed to fail. Neither of these beliefs is true.

The most common method recommended for resolving conflict—used in one guise or another by most marital therapists—is called active listening. For example, a therapist might urge you to try some form of the listener-speaker exchange. Let's say Rick is upset that Judy works late most nights. The therapist asks Rick to state his complaints as "I" statements that focus on what he's feeling rather than hurling accusations at Judy. Rick will say, "I feel lonely and overwhelmed when I'm home alone with the kids at night while you're working late," rather than, "It's so selfish of you to always work late and expect me to take care of the kids by myself."

Next, Judy is asked to paraphrase both the content and the feelings of Rick's message, and to check with him if she's got it right. (This shows she is actively listening to him.) She is also asked to validate his feelings—to let him know she considers them legitimate, that she respects and empathizes with him even if she doesn't share his perspective. She might say, "It must be hard for you to watch the kids by yourself when I'm working late." Judy is being asked to suspend judgment, not argue for her point of view, and to respond nondefensively. "I hear you" is a common active-listening buzzword. "I feel your pain" may be the most memorable.

By forcing couples to see their differences from each other's perspective, problem solving is supposed to take place without anger. This approach is often recommended whatever the specific issue—whether your conflict concerns the size of your grocery bill or major differences in your life goals. Conflict resolution is touted not only as a cure-all for troubled marriages but as a tonic that can prevent good marriages from faltering.

Where did this approach come from? The pioneers of marital therapy adapted it from techniques used by the renowned psychotherapist Carl Rogers for *individual* psychotherapy. Rogerian psychotherapy had its heyday in the 1960s and is still practiced in varying degrees today. His approach entails responding in a nonjudgmental and accepting manner to all feelings and thoughts the patient expresses. For example, if the patient says, "I just hate my wife, she's such a nagging bitch," the therapist nods and says something like, "I hear you saying your wife nags you and you hate that." The goal is to create an empathetic environment so the patient feels safe exploring inner thoughts and emotions and confiding in the therapist.

Since marriage is also, ideally, a relationship in which people feel safe being themselves, it makes sense to train couples in this sort of unconditional understanding. Conflict resolution is certainly easier if each party expresses empathy for the other's perspective.

The problem is that therapy that focuses solely on active listening and conflict resolution doesn't work. A Munich-based marital therapy study conducted by Kurt Hahlweg and associates found that even after employing active-listening techniques the typical couple was still distressed. Those few couples who did benefit relapsed within a year.

When we began our research, the wide range of marital therapies based on conflict resolution shared a very high level of relapse. In fact, the best of this type of marital therapy, conducted by Neil Jacobson, had only a 35 to 50 percent success rate. In other words, his own studies showed that only 35 to 50 percent of couples saw a meaningful improvement in their marriages as a result of the therapy. A year later, less than half of that group—or just 18 to 25 percent of all couples who entered therapy—retained these benefits. A while ago, *Consumer Reports* surveyed a large sample of its members on their experience with all kinds of psychotherapists. Most therapists got very high customer-satisfaction marks—except for the marital ones, who received very poor ratings. Though this survey did not qualify as rigorous scientific research, it confirmed what most professionals in the field already knew: in the long run, marital therapy did not benefit the majority of couples.

When you really think about it, it's not difficult to see why counseling that relies solely on active listening to rescue relationships so often fails. Judy might do her best to listen thoughtfully to Rick's complaints. But she is not a therapist listening to a patient whine about a third party. The person her husband is trashing behind all of those "I" statements is her! There are some people who can be magnanimous in the face of such criticism—the Dalai Lama comes to mind. But it's unlikely that you or your spouse is married to one of them. (Even in Rogerian therapy, when the client starts complaining about the therapist, the therapist switches from empathy to other therapeutic approaches.) Active listening asks couples to perform Olympic-level emotional gymnastics even if their relationship can barely walk.

I'm not suggesting that validation, active listening, and "I statements" are useless. They can be enormously helpful when attempting to resolve conflicts. In fact, I often recommend them to couples in a modified format with specific guidelines, as you'll see later in the book. But here's the catch: even if they do make your fights "better" or less frequent, these strategies are not enough to save your marriage. You need all Seven Principles.

Even happily married couples can have screaming matches—loud arguments don't necessarily harm a marriage.

After studying some seven hundred couples and tracking the fate of their marriages for up to twenty years, I now understand that the standard approach to counseling doesn't work, not just because it's nearly impossible for most couples to do well but, more important, because successful conflict resolution isn't what makes marriages succeed. One of the most startling findings of our research is that couples who have maintained happy marriages rarely do anything that even partly resembles active listening when they're upset.

Consider one couple we studied, Belle and Charlie. After more than forty-five years of marriage, Belle informed Charlie that she wished they had never had children. This clearly rankled him. What followed was a conversation that broke all the active-listening rules. This discussion doesn't include a lot of validation or empathy—they both jump right in, arguing their point.

CHARLIE: You think you would have been better off if I had backed you in not having children?
BELLE: Having children was such an insult to me, Charlie.
CHARLIE: No. Hold on a minute.
BELLE: To reduce me to such a level!
CHARLIE: I'm not redu—
BELLE: I wanted so much to share a life with you. Instead, I ended up a drudge.

CHARLIE: Now wait a minute, hold on. I don't think not having children is that simple. I think that there's a lot biologically that you're ignoring.

BELLE: Look at all the wonderful marriages that have been childless.

CHARLIE: Who?

BELLE: The Duke and Duchess of Windsor!

CHARLIE (*deep sigh*): Please!

BELLE: He was the king! He married a valuable woman. They had a very happy marriage.

CHARLIE: I don't think that's a fair example. First of all, she was forty. That makes a difference.

BELLE: She never had children. And he fell in love with her not because she was going to reproduce.

CHARLIE: But the fact is, Belle, that there is a real strong biological urge to have children.

BELLE: That's an insult to think that I'm regulated by biology.

CHARLIE: I can't help it!

BELLE: Well, anyway, I think we would have had a ball without children.

CHARLIE: Well, I think we had a ball with the kids, too.

BELLE: I didn't have that much of a ball.

Charlie and Belle may not sound like the Couple of the Year, but they have been happily married for over four decades. They both say they are extremely satisfied with their marriage and devoted to each other.

No doubt they have been having similar in-your-face discussions for years. But they don't end angrily. In this conversation they go on to discuss why Belle feels this way about motherhood. Her major regret is that she wasn't more available to spend time with Charlie. She wishes she hadn't always been so cranky and tired. There's a lot of affection and laughter as they hash this out. The bottom line of what Belle is saying is that she loves Charlie so much, she wishes she had had more time with him. Clearly, there's something very positive going on between them that overrides their argumentative style. Whatever that "something" is, marriage counseling that only focuses on "good" fighting doesn't begin to help other couples tap into it.

Exploding More Myths About Marriage

The notion that you can save your relationship just by learning to communicate more sensitively is probably the most widely held misconception about happy marriages—but it's hardly the only one. Over the years, I've found many other myths that are not only false but potentially destructive. They are dangerous because they can lead couples down the wrong path or, worse, convince them that their marriage is a hopeless case. Among these common myths:

Neuroses or personality problems ruin marriages. Research has found only the weakest connection between run-of-the-mill neuroses and failing at love. The reason: We all have issues we're not totally rational about. We call these triggers "enduring vulnerabilities," a term we borrowed from Tom Bradbury of UCLA. They don't necessarily interfere with marriage if you learn to recognize and avoid activating them in each other. For example, Sam has a problem dealing with authority—he hates having a boss. If he were married to a controlling partner, the result would be disastrous. But instead he is happily married to Megan, who treats him like an equal and doesn't try to dominate him.

Contrast them with another couple who do run into marital problems. Jill has a deep-seated fear of abandonment. Her husband, Wayne, flirts shamelessly at parties despite being fully devoted to her. When she complains, he insists she lighten up and let him enjoy this harmless pleasure. But the threat Jill perceives from his flirtations—and his unwillingness to stop—drives them to separate and eventually divorce. The point is that neuroses don't have to ruin a marriage. If you can accommodate each other's "crazy" side and handle it with caring, affection, and respect, your marriage can thrive.

Of course, a severe mental illness is another matter. You're not a bad person if you end a relationship with a partner who is grappling with severe psychopathology and is unable to think and function independently. What's tricky for many couples, however, is navigating the middle ground: What do you do about mental health issues that are extremely challenging but that some relationships could possibly accommodate? This category includes addiction, clinical depression, phobias, post-traumatic stress disorder, and severe personality or mood disorders. If any of this sounds familiar, don't rely on this book alone to make decisions about your future. Seek the additional advice and support of a knowledgeable and experienced mental health professional.

Common interests keep you together. That all depends on how you interact while pursuing those interests. If a husband and wife who love kayaking are able to glide smoothly down the water together, their mutual hobby enriches and deepens their fondness and interest in each other. But if their travels are punctuated with "That's not the way to do a J-stroke, you idiot!" then pursuing this common interest is hardly benefiting their marriage.

You scratch my back and . . . Some researchers believe that what distinguishes good marriages from failing ones is that in good marriages spouses respond in kind to each other's positive overtures. When one helps out with a chore, the other intentionally reciprocates, and so on. In essence, the couple function with an unwritten agreement to offer recompense for each kind word or deed. In bad marriages, this contract has broken down so that anger and resentment fill the air. By making the floundering couple aware of the need for some such "contract," the theory goes, their interactions could be repaired.

But needing to keep a running tally of who has done what for whom is really a sign of trouble in a marriage. Among happy spouses, one doesn't load the dishwasher just as payback because the other cooked but out of overall positive feelings about the partner and relationship. If you find yourself keeping score about some issue with your spouse, that suggests it's an area of tension in your marriage.

Avoiding conflict will ruin your marriage. Plenty of life-long relationships happily survive even though they sidestep confrontation. Never in forty years of marriage have Allan and Betty sat down to have a "dialogue" about their relationship. Neither could tell you what a "validating" statement is. When Allan gets annoyed at Betty, he turns on ESPN. When Betty is upset with him, she heads for the mall. Then they go on as if nothing happened. Yet they declare that they are very satisfied with their marriage and love each other deeply, hold the same values, love to fish and travel together, and wish for their children as happy a married life as they have shared.

Couples simply have different styles of conflict. Some avoid fights at all costs, some argue a lot, and some are able to talk out their differences and find a compromise without ever raising their voices. No one style is necessarily better than another—as long as the style works for both people.

Affairs are the root cause of divorce. In most cases, it's the other way around. Problems in the marriage that send the couple on a trajectory to divorce also send one (or both) of them looking for intimate connection outside the marriage. Trysts are usually not about sex but about seeking friendship, support, understanding, respect, attention, caring, and concern. In one of the most reliable surveys ever done on divorce, by Lynn Gigy and Joan Kelly from the Divorce Mediation Project in Corte Madera, California, 80 percent of divorced men and women said their marriage broke up because they gradually grew apart and lost a sense of closeness, or because they did not feel loved and appreciated. Only 20 to 27 percent of couples said an extramarital affair was even partially to blame.

Men are not biologically "built" for marriage. A corollary to the notion that affairs cause divorce, this theory holds that men are philanderers by nature and are therefore ill suited for monogamy. But whatever natural laws other species follow, among humans the frequency of extramarital affairs does not depend on gender so much as on opportunity. Now that many women work outside the home, their rate of extramarital affairs has skyrocketed. According to research by British sociologist Annette Lawson, formerly of the University of California, Berkeley, since women have entered the workplace in massive numbers, the number of extra-marital affairs of young women now slightly exceeds those of men.

Men and women are from different planets. According to a rash of bestselling books, men and women can't get along because males are "from Mars" and females "from Venus." However, *happily* married heterosexual couples are also "aliens" to each other. Gender differences may contribute to marital problems, but they don't cause them.

The determining factor in whether wives feel satisfied with the sex, romance, and passion in their marriage is, by 70 percent, the quality of the couple's friendship. For men, the determining factor is, by 70 percent, the quality of the couple's friendship. So men and women come from the same planet after all.

I could go on and on. The point is not just that there are plenty of myths out there about marriage but that the false information they offer can be disheartening to couples who are desperately trying to make their marriage work. If these myths imply one thing, it's that marriage is an extremely complex, imposing institution that most of us just aren't good enough for. I'm not suggesting that marriage is easy. We all know it takes courage, determination, and resilience to maintain a long-lasting relationship. But once you understand what really makes a marriage tick, saving or safeguarding your own will become simpler.

2

What *Does* Make Marriage Work?

*T*he advice I used to give couples earlier in my career was pretty much what you'd hear from virtually any marital therapist at the time—nothing but the same old pointers about conflict resolution and communication skills. But after looking squarely at my own data, I had to face the harsh facts: getting couples to disagree more "nicely" might reduce their stress levels while they argued, but frequently it wasn't enough to pump life back into their marriages.

The right course for these couples became clear only after I analyzed the interactions of spouses whose marriages sailed smoothly through troubled waters. Why was it that these marriages worked so well? Were these master couples more intelligent and stable, or simply more fortunate than the rest? Could whatever they had be taught to others?

It soon became apparent that these happy marriages were never perfect unions. Some couples who said they were very satisfied with each other still had significant differences in temperament, interests, and family values. Conflict was not infrequent. They argued, just as the unhappy couples did, over money, jobs, kids, housekeeping, sex, and in-laws. The mystery was how they so adroitly navigated their way through these difficulties and kept their marriages happy and stable.

It took studying hundreds of couples to uncover the secrets of these emotionally intelligent marriages. No two marriages are the same, but the more closely my research team and I looked at happy marriages, the more evident it became that they were alike in seven telltale ways. Happily married couples may not be aware that they follow these Seven Principles, but they all do. Unhappy marriages always came up short in at least one of these seven areas—and usually in many of them. By mastering these Seven Principles, you can ensure that your own marriage will thrive. You'll learn to identify which of these components are weak spots, or potential weak spots, in your relationship, and to focus your attention where you most need it. In the chapters ahead, we'll fill you in on all the secrets to maintaining (or regaining) a happy marriage, and hold your hand as you apply the techniques to your own relationship.

Friendship Versus Fighting

At the heart of the Seven Principles approach is the simple truth that happy marriages are based on a deep friendship. By this I mean a mutual respect for and enjoyment of each other's company. These couples tend to know each other intimately—they are well versed in each other's likes, dislikes, personality quirks, hopes, and dreams. They have an abiding regard for each other and express this fondness not just in the big ways but through small gestures day in and day out.

Take the case of hardworking Nathaniel, who is employed by an import business and works very long hours. In another marriage, his schedule might be a major liability. But he and his wife, Olivia, have found ways to stay connected. They talk or text frequently throughout the day. When she has a doctor's appointment, he remembers to call to see how it went. When he has a meeting with an important client, she'll check in to see how it fared. When they have chicken for dinner, she gives him drumsticks because she knows he likes them best. When he makes blueberry pancakes for the kids on Saturday morning, he'll leave the blueberries out of hers because he knows she doesn't like them. Although he's not religious, he accompanies her to church each Sunday because it's important to her. And although she's not crazy about spending a lot of time with their relatives, she has pursued a friendship with Nathaniel's mother and sisters because family matters so much to him.

If all of this sounds humdrum and unromantic, it's anything but. In small but important ways, Olivia and Nathaniel are maintaining the friendship that is the foundation of their love. As a result, they have a marriage that is far more passionate than do couples who punctuate their lives together with romantic vacations and lavish anniversary gifts but have fallen out of touch in their daily lives.

Friendship fuels the flames of romance because it offers the best protection against feeling adversarial toward your spouse. Because Nathaniel and Olivia have kept their friendship strong despite the inevitable disagreements and irritations of married life, they are experiencing what is known technically as "positive sentiment override," or PSO, a concept first proposed by University of Oregon psychologist Robert Weiss. This means that their positive thoughts about each other and their marriage are so pervasive that they tend to supersede their negative feelings. It takes a much more significant conflict for them to lose their equilibrium as a couple than it would otherwise. Their positivity causes them to feel optimistic about each other and their marriage, to have positive expectations about their lives together, and to give each other the benefit of the doubt.

Here's a simple example. Olivia and Nathaniel are getting ready to host a dinner party. Nathaniel calls, "Where are the napkins?" and Olivia yells back edgily, "They're in the cupboard!" Because their marriage is founded on a firm friendship, he shrugs off her tone of voice and focuses instead on the information Olivia has given him—that the napkins are in the cupboard. He attributes her anger to some fleeting problem that has nothing to do with him—like she's feeling time-pressured and can't get the cork out of the wine bottle. However, if their marriage were troubled, he would be more likely to sulk or yell back, "Never mind, *you* get them!"

One way of looking at this positive override is similar to the "set point" approach to weight loss. According to this popular theory, the body has a "set" weight that it tries to maintain. Thanks to homeostasis, no matter how much or how little you diet, your body has a strong tendency to hover at that weight. Only by resetting your body's metabolism (say, by exercising regularly) can dieting really help you lose pounds for good. In a marriage, positivity and negativity operate similarly. Once your marriage gets "set" at a high degree of positivity, it will take far more negativity to harm your relationship than if your "set point" were lower. And if your relationship becomes overwhelmingly negative, it will be more difficult to repair.

Most marriages start off with such a high set point that it's hard for either partner to imagine their relationship derailing. But far too often this blissful state doesn't last. Over time, irritation, resentment, and anger build to the point that the friendship becomes more and more of an abstraction. The couple may pay lip service to it, but it is no longer their daily reality. Eventually they end up in "*negative* sentiment override." Everything gets interpreted in an increasingly negative manner. Words said in a neutral tone of voice are taken personally. The husband says, "You're not supposed to run the microwave without any food in it." The wife sees this as an attack, so she says something like, "Don't tell me what to do. I'm the one who actually reads manuals!" Another battle begins.

Building Your Sound Relationship House

In the years since this book was first published, my colleagues and I have thoroughly explored the anatomy of marital friendship and furthered our understanding of why it is so critical to relationship success. The positive feelings that engulf happy couples such as Nathaniel and Olivia come courtesy of their mutual understanding of each other on a core emotional level. I call this connection *attunement*. The more highly skilled at achieving it that partners become, the more resilient their friendship and the more solid and promising their future. Some couples are naturals at attunement. But others (most of us!) need to work at it somewhat. It is well worth the effort.

As partners increasingly come to know and bond with each other, they build what I call their Sound Relationship House. The Seven Principles comprise the Sound Relationship House's many floors or levels. These principles are intricately connected to *trust and commitment*, which form the house's protective, weight-bearing walls.

The importance of trust and commitment to success in love seems so self-evident that you might assume that studying these qualities scientifically would be of little added benefit. But it turns out that is not the case. Thanks to the Love Lab's data, I've been able to dissect what it really means to commit to a partner and relationship. In fact, using the precepts of Game Theory (a well-known mathematical approach to analyzing conflict) I've been able to develop formulas that can determine whether partners have a high trust level or are likely to face infidelity of some sort in the future. (Our book *What Makes Love Last?* delves deeply into this research on trust and deceit and how to prevent or recover from cheating.) Among these equations is what I call a couple's trust metric—an indication of the partners' faith in each other.

Imagine two couples who are assessed in the Love Lab as newlyweds. At first glance, they seem equally adept at building a Sound Relationship House. But when my team codes and analyzes the nitty-gritty of their conversations, the results expose striking differences. At the positive end of the spectrum are Dennis and Jackie. Like Nathaniel and Olivia, they already appear to be experts at having a long-term relationship. They assume the best about each other and their relationship. They are able to acknowledge each other's perspective, at least to some extent, even when they strongly disagree. When they review a videotape of themselves interacting in the lab, they each report feeling distressed when the other seems unhappy or hurt. Their biological readouts of heart rate, blood pressure, etc., confirm this. Their happiness is contingent on their partner's feelings. They are attuned to each other's emotions, share an abiding empathy, and have a high degree of trust. When I do the math, this couple's trust metric is in the upper reaches. In all, they are doing an excellent job of building their Sound Relationship House.

At the other end of the newlywed trust spectrum we find Tina and Matt. Unlike Dennis and Jackie, these two are really struggling with emotional connection and commitment. While conversing in the Love Lab, they demonstrate a lack of mutual understanding or faith in their relationship. Tina's moods are not at all linked to her husband's emotions. For example, she rates her feelings as "neutral" when he expresses regret over not getting a promotion at work. Nor do her bio readouts point to signs of increased stress, such as elevated blood pressure or heart rate. Her husband's reactions display a similar disconnection to her feelings. Clearly, this couple has a low trust metric. If nothing between them changes, their ability to share a rich emotional and sexual life will be greatly hampered. They will also be far less able to extricate themselves from arguments and other negative interactions.

It's no surprise to find that Tina and Matt's marriage is marked by *negative* sentiment override, which will interfere with their ability to build a mutually supportive relationship. In fact, they assume the worst about each other to such a pervasive degree that they become trapped in an absorbing state of negativity that I call the Roach Motel for Lovers. This horrible place is marked by endless conflict and bad feelings. Couples "check in" to it and then discover they can't get out. When couples become trapped in the Roach Motel, they each come to believe that their partner must be fundamentally selfish. Their minds fill with thoughts like, "He doesn't care how I feel" and "All that matters to her is getting her way." Each becomes increasingly convinced that the other isn't on their side and doesn't have their back. The relationship devolves into a zero-sum game in which one partner's victory is perceived as the other's defeat. In the presence of this chronic distrust, the sense of safety vanishes. The Sound Relationship House cannot stand. The walls are ripped apart, leaving the relationship unguarded from the lure of outside forces.

What does the future hold for Tina and Matt? Without intervention they are likely headed for betrayal. Although we tend to think of infidelity in sexual terms, an extramarital physical affair is only one type of disloyalty that threatens a couple once their Sound Relationship House falls. Betrayal is, fundamentally, any act or life choice that doesn't prioritize the commitment and put the partner "before all others." Nonsexual betrayals can devastate a relationship as thoroughly as a sexual affair. Some common forms of deceit include being emotionally distant, siding with a parent against one's mate, disrespecting the partner, and breaking significant promises. The truth is that most of us are guilty of faithlessness from time to time. But when either spouse consistently shortchanges the marriage, danger follows. In fact, the Love Lab research indicates that *betrayal lies at the heart of every failed relationship.*

Most couples are neither as stuck in distrust as Matt and Tina nor as masterful at living together as Dennis and Jackie. The majority of long-term relationships fall somewhere between these two extremes. That's good news because it means partners don't have to achieve a perfect relationship to succeed at love. The key is learning how to better attune to each other and make friendship a top priority. As the Seven Principles guide you in moving toward these goals, you're likely to notice an improvement in the quality of your day-to-day interactions. While you may still disagree, your conflicts will become far less destructive. There's a specific reason why this occurs, and it is one of the most important of the Love Lab's findings.

Repairs: A Happy Couple's Secret Weapon

Rediscovering or reinvigorating friendship doesn't prevent couples from arguing, but it does give them a secret weapon that ensures their quarrels don't get out of hand. For example, here's what happens when Olivia and Nathaniel disagree. As they plan to move from the city to the suburbs, tensions between them are high. Although they see eye to eye on which condo to choose and how to decorate it, they are locking horns over buying a new car. Olivia thinks they should join the suburban masses and opt for a minivan. To Nathaniel nothing could be drearier—he wants a Jeep. The more they talk about it, the higher the decibel level gets. If you were a fly on the wall of their bedroom, you would have serious doubts about their future together. Then all of a sudden, Olivia puts her hands on her hips and, in perfect imitation of their four-year-old son, sticks out her tongue. Since Nathaniel knows that she's about to do this, he sticks out his tongue first. Then they both start laughing. As always, this silly contest defuses the tension between them.

In our research, we have a technical name for what Olivia and Nathaniel are doing. We say they are using a *repair attempt*. This term refers to any statement or action—silly or otherwise—that prevents negativity from escalating out of control. Repair attempts are a secret weapon of emotionally intelligent couples—even though many of these couples aren't aware that they are employing something so powerful. When a couple have a strong friendship, they naturally become experts at sending each other repair attempts and at correctly reading those sent their way. But when couples are in negative override, even a repair attempt as blunt as "Hey, I'm sorry" may have a low success rate.

The success or failure of a couple's repair attempts is one of the primary factors in whether their marriage is likely to flourish or flounder. And again, what determines the success of their repair attempts is the strength of their marital friendship. If this sounds simplistic or obvious, you'll find in the pages ahead that it is not. Strengthening your marital friendship isn't as basic as just being "nice." Even if you feel that your friendship is already quite solid, you may be surprised to find there is room to strengthen it all the more. Most of the couples who participate in our workshops are relieved to hear that almost everybody messes up during marital conflict. What matters is whether their repairs succeed.

The Purpose of Marriage

In the strongest marriages, husband and wife share a deep sense of meaning. They don't just "get along"—they also support each other's hopes and aspirations and build a sense of purpose into their lives together. That is really what I mean when I talk about honoring and respecting each other. Very often a marriage's failure to do this is what causes husband and wife to find themselves in endless, useless rounds of argument or to feel isolated and lonely in their marriage. After watching countless videotapes of couples fighting, I can guarantee you that most quarrels are really not about whether the toilet lid is up or down or whose turn it is to take out the trash. There are deeper, hidden issues that fuel these superficial conflicts and make them far more intense and hurtful than they would otherwise be.

Once you understand this, you will be ready to accept one of the most surprising truths about marriage: *most marital arguments cannot be resolved*. Couples spend year after year trying to change each other's mind—but it can't be done. This is because most of their disagreements are rooted in fundamental differences of lifestyle, personality, or values. By fighting over these differences, all they succeed in doing is wasting their time and harming their marriage. Instead, they need to understand the bottom-line difference that is causing the conflict—and to learn how to live with it by honoring and respecting each other. Only then will they be able to build shared meaning and a sense of purpose into their marriage.

It used to be that couples could achieve this goal only through their own insight, instinct, or blessed luck. But now the Seven Principles make the secrets of marital success available to *all* couples. No matter what the current state of your relationship, following these Seven Principles can lead to dramatic, positive change.

The first step toward improving or enhancing your marriage is to understand what happens when the Seven Principles are *not* followed. This has been well documented by extensive research into couples who were not able to save their marriages. Learning about the failures can prevent your marriage from making the same mistakes—or rescue it if it already has made them. Once you come to understand why some marriages fail, and how the Seven Principles could prevent such tragedies, you'll be on the way to improving your own marriage forever.

3

How I Predict Divorce

*D*ara and Oliver sit face-to-face in the Love Lab. Both in their late twenties, they have volunteered to take part in my study of newlyweds. In this extensive research, 130 couples have agreed to put their marriages not only under the microscope but in front of the camera as well. Dara and Oliver are among the fifty who are observed during an overnight stay at the Love Lab "apartment."

Dara and Oliver say their lives are hectic but happy. She attends nursing school at night, and he works long hours as a software engineer. Like many couples, including those who remain content as well as those who eventually divorce, Dara and Oliver acknowledge that their marriage isn't perfect. But they say they love each other and are committed to staying together. They positively beam when they talk about the life they plan to build.

I ask them to spend fifteen minutes in the lab trying to resolve an ongoing disagreement they are having while I videotape them. As they speak, sensors attached to their bodies gauge their stress levels based on various measurements of their circulatory system, such as how quickly their hearts beat.

I expect that their discussion will be at least somewhat negative. After all, I have asked them to quarrel. While some couples are capable of resolving disagreements with understanding words and smiles, more often there's tension. Dara and Oliver are no exception. Dara thinks Oliver doesn't do his share of the housekeeping, and he thinks she nags him too much, which makes him less motivated to do more.

After listening to them talk about this problem, I sadly predict to my colleagues that Dara and Oliver will see their marital happiness dwindle. And sure enough, four years later they report they are on the verge of divorce. Although they still live together, they are leading lonely lives. They have become like ghosts, haunting the marriage that once made them both feel so alive.

I predict their marriage will falter not because they argue—after all, I asked them to. Anger between husband and wife doesn't itself predict marital meltdown. Other couples in the newlywed study argue far more during the fifteen minutes of videotaping than do Dara and Oliver. Yet I predict that many of these couples will remain happily married—and they do. The clues to Dara and Oliver's future breakup are in the *way* they argue, which leaves them vulnerable to increasing negativity and distrust.

The First Sign: Harsh Start-Up

The most obvious indicator that this discussion (and this marriage) is not going to go well is the way it begins. Dara immediately becomes negative and accusatory. When Oliver broaches the subject of housework, she's ready to be sarcastic. "Or lack thereof," she says. Oliver tries to lighten things up by cracking a joke: "Or the book we were talking about writing: *Men Are Pigs.*" Dara sits poker-faced. They talk a bit more, trying to devise a plan to make sure Oliver does his share, and then Dara says, "I mean, I'd like to see it resolved, but it doesn't seem like it is. I mean, I've tried making up lists, and that doesn't work. And I've tried letting you do it on your own, and nothing got done for a month." Now she's blaming Oliver. In essence, she's saying the problem isn't the housekeeping, it's him. Dara may have legitimate reasons to feel deep frustration toward her husband. But the way she expresses herself will be a major roadblock to resolving their differences.

When a discussion leads off this way—with criticism and/or sarcasm, which is a form of contempt—it has begun with a "harsh start-up." Although Dara talks to Oliver in a very soft, quiet voice, there's a load of negative power in her words. After hearing the first minute or so of their conversation, it's no surprise to me that by the end Dara and Oliver haven't resolved their differences at all. The research shows that if your discussion begins with a harsh start-up, it will inevitably end on a negative note, even if there are a lot of attempts to "make nice" in between. Statistics tell the story: 96 percent of the time you can predict the outcome of a conversation based on the *first three minutes* of the fifteen-minute interaction! A harsh start-up simply dooms you to failure. So if you begin a discussion that way, you might as well pull the plug, take a breather, and start over.

The Second Sign: The Four Horsemen

Dara's harsh start-up sounds the warning bell that she and Oliver may be having serious difficulty. Now, as their discussion unfolds, I continue to look out for particular types of negative interactions. Certain kinds of negativity, if allowed to run rampant, are so lethal to a relationship that I call them the Four Horsemen of the Apocalypse. Usually these four horsemen clip-clop into the heart of a marriage in the following order: Criticism, Contempt, Defensiveness, and Stonewalling.

Horseman 1: Criticism. You will always have some complaints about the person you live with. But there's a world of difference between complaint and criticism. A complaint focuses on a specific behavior or event. "I'm really angry that you didn't sweep the kitchen last night. We agreed that we'd take turns. Could you please do it now?" is a complaint. Like many complaints, it has three parts: (1) Here's how I feel ("I'm really angry"); (2) About a very specific situation ("you didn't sweep *last night*"); (3) And here's what I need/want/prefer ("Could you do it now?"). In contrast, a criticism is global and expresses negative feelings or opinions about the other's character or personality: "Why are you so forgetful? I hate having to always sweep the kitchen floor when it's your turn. You just don't care." Statements that contain complaints are soft start-ups, while those that criticize are harsh start-ups. Two very common forms of criticism are statements that contain "you always" or "you never." But you can turn any complaint into a criticism just by inserting my "favorite" line: "What is wrong with you?"

You can see how quickly Dara's complaint turns into criticism (and a harsh start-up) in this snippet of her conversation with Oliver:

DARA: I mean, I'd like to see it resolved, but it doesn't seem like it is. (*simple complaint*) I mean, I've tried making up lists and that doesn't work. And I've tried letting you do it on your own, and nothing got done for a month. (*Criticism. She's implying the problem is his fault. Even if it is, blaming him will only make it worse.*)

Here are some other examples that show the difference between complaint and criticism.

Complaint. There's no gas in the car. I'm upset that you didn't fill it up like you said you would. Could you please deal with it tomorrow?

Criticism. Why can't you ever remember anything? I told you a thousand times to fill up the tank, and you didn't. You're always so careless.

Complaint. I wish you had told me earlier that you're too tired to make love. I'm really disappointed, and I feel a little embarrassed. Please just let me know when you're not in the mood for sex. I really am fine with a "no."

Criticism. Why are you always so cold and selfish? It was really nasty of you to lead me on. What is your problem? Are you frigid?

Complaint. I need you to check with me before inviting anyone over for dinner. I wanted to spend time alone with you tonight. I want us to schedule a romantic evening this week.

Criticism. Why do you keep putting your friends ahead of me? I always come last on your list. Are you avoiding spending time alone with me?

If you hear echoes of yourself or your spouse in these criticisms, you have plenty of company. The first horseman is very common in relationships. So if you find that you and your spouse are critical of each other, don't assume you're headed for divorce court. The problem with criticism is that when it becomes very frequent, it paves the way for the other, far deadlier horsemen.

Horseman 2: Contempt. The second horseman arises from a sense of superiority over one's partner. It is a form of disrespect. Its arrival is heralded when Dara literally sneers at her husband's suggestion that they keep a list of his chores on the refrigerator to help him remember. She says, "Do you think you work really well with lists?" Next, Oliver tells her that he needs fifteen minutes to relax when he gets home before starting to do chores. "So if I leave you alone for fifteen minutes, then you think you'll be motivated to jump up and do something?" she asks him, still sneering.

"Maybe. We haven't tried it, have we?" Oliver asks.

Dara has an opportunity here to soften up, but instead she comes back with sarcasm. "I think you do a pretty good job of coming home and lying around or disappearing into the bathroom," she says. And then she adds challengingly, "So you think that's the cure-all, to give you fifteen minutes?"

Dara's sarcasm and cynicism are types of contempt. So are name-calling, eye-rolling, mockery, and hostile humor. In whatever form, contempt is poisonous to a relationship because it conveys disgust. It's virtually impossible to resolve a problem when your partner is getting the message you're disgusted with him or her. Inevitably, contempt leads to more conflict rather than to reconciliation.

Peter was a master at contempt, at least when it came to his wife. Listen to what happens when he and Cynthia try to discuss their conflicting views about spending money. He says, "Just look at the difference in our vehicles and our clothes. I think that says a lot for who we are and what we value. I mean, you tease me about washing my truck, and you go and pay to have somebody wash your car. We're paying through the nose for your car, and you can't be bothered to wash it. I think that's outrageous. I think that's probably the most spoiled thing that you do." This is a text-book example of contempt. He's not merely pointing out that they spend their money differently. He is accusing his wife of a moral deficiency—of being spoiled.

Cynthia responds by telling him that it's physically difficult for her to wash her car herself. Peter dismisses this explanation and continues to take the high moral ground. "I take care of my truck because if I take care of it, it'll last longer. I don't come from the mentality of 'Ah, just go out and buy a new one' that you seem to."

Still hoping to get Peter on her side, Cynthia says, "If you could help me to wash my car, I'd really love that. I'd really appreciate it." But instead of grabbing this chance at reconciliation, Peter wants to do battle.

"How many times have you helped me wash my truck?" he counters.

Cynthia tries again to reconcile. "I will help you wash your truck if you will help me wash my car."

Peter's goal is not to resolve this issue but to dress her down. So he responds, "That's not my question. How many times have you helped me?"

"Never," says Cynthia.

"See?" says Peter. "That's where I think you have a little respon-sibility, too. It's like, you know, if your dad bought you a house, would you expect him to come over and paint it for you, too?"

"Well, will you always help me wash my car if I always help you wash your truck?"

"I'm not sure that I'd want you to help me," Peter says, laughing.

"Well, will you always help me wash my car, then?" Cynthia asks.

"I will help you when I can. I won't give you a blanket guarantee for life. What are you gonna do, sue me?" asks Peter. And he laughs again.

Listening to this discussion, it becomes clear that Peter's main purpose is to demean his wife. His contempt comes in the guise of assuming the high moral ground, as when he says: "I think that says a lot for who we are and what we value" or "I don't come from the mentality of 'just go out and buy a new one.'"

Couples who are contemptuous of each other are more likely to suffer from infectious illnesses (colds, flu, and so on) than other people.

Contempt is fueled by long-simmering negative thoughts about the partner. You're more likely to have such thoughts if your differences are not resolved. No doubt, the first time Peter and Cynthia argued about car-washing, he wasn't so disrespectful. He probably offered a simple complaint like, "I think you should wash your own car. It costs too much to always have someone else wash it." But as they kept disagreeing about this, his complaints turned to global criticisms, such as: "You always spend too much money." And when the conflict continued, he felt more and more disgusted and fed up with Cynthia, a change that affected what he said when they argued.

Belligerence, a close cousin of contempt, is just as deadly to a relationship. It is a form of aggressive anger because it contains a threat or provocation. When a wife complains that her husband doesn't come home from work in time for dinner, a belligerent response would be "Well, what are you going to do about it?" When Peter says to Cynthia, "What are you going to do, sue me?" he thinks he's making a joke, but he's really being belligerent.

Horseman 3: Defensiveness. It's no surprise, considering how nasty her husband is being, that Cynthia defends herself. She points out that she doesn't get her car washed as often as he thinks. She explains that it's more difficult physically for her to wash her car herself than it is for him to wash his truck. Although it's under-standable that Cynthia would defend herself, research shows that this approach rarely has the desired effect. The attacking spouse does not back down or apologize. This is because defensiveness is really a way of blaming your partner. You're saying, in effect, "The problem isn't me, it's you." One common form of defensiveness is the "innocent victim" stance, which often entails whining and sends the message: "Why are you picking on me? What about all the good things I do? There's no pleasing you."

Defensiveness in all its guises just escalates the conflict, which is why it's so deadly. When Cynthia tells Peter how hard it is for her to wash her car, he doesn't say, "Oh, now I understand." He ignores her excuse—he doesn't even acknowledge what she's said. He climbs farther up his high moral ground, telling her how well he takes care of his vehicle and implying that she's spoiled for not doing the same. Cynthia can't win—and neither can their marriage.

Criticism, contempt, and defensiveness don't always gallop into a home in strict order. They function more like a relay match—handing the baton off to each other over and over again if the couple can't put a stop to it. You can see this happening as Oliver and Dara continue their discussion about cleaning their house. Al-though they seem to be seeking a solution, Dara becomes increas-ingly contemptuous—mocking Oliver in the guise of questioning him and tearing down every plan he devises. The more defensive he becomes, the more she attacks him. Her body language signals condescension. She speaks softly, her elbows resting on the table, her intertwined fingers cradling her chin. Like a law professor or a judge, she peppers him with questions just to see him squirm.

DARA: So you think that's the cure-all, to give you fifteen minutes? (*sneering*)

OLIVER: No, I don't think that's the cure-all. I think, combined with writing up a list of weekly tasks that have to get done. Why not put a calendar on the fridge? Hey, I'll see it right then and there.

DARA: Just like when you input "to do" lists into your phone it gets done? (*mocking him; more contempt*)

OLIVER: I don't always have a chance to look at lists during the day. But at home . . . (*defensive*)

DARA: So you think you'll look at a calendar, then?

OLIVER: Yeah. At any point in time, if I'm not up to speed, you should ask me about it. But when that happens now, it's not you asking, it's you telling me, "You haven't done this and you haven't done that." Instead say, "Is there any reason why you haven't done this or that?" Like, I mean, when I stayed up and did your résumé that one night. Stuff like that happens all the time, and you just don't take that into account at all. (*defensive*)

DARA: And I don't just all of a sudden do things for you, either? (*defensive*)

OLIVER: No, you do. . . . I think you need to relax a little bit.

DARA (*sarcastic*): Hmm. Well, that sounds like we solved a lot.

Obviously, Dara and Oliver have resolved nothing, thanks to the prevalence of criticism, contempt, and defensiveness.

Horseman 4: Stonewalling. In marriages where discussions begin with a harsh start-up, where criticism and contempt lead to defensiveness and vice versa, eventually one partner tunes out. This trumpets the arrival of the fourth horseman.

Think of the husband who comes home from work, gets met with a barrage of criticism from his stay-at-home wife, and responds by turning on the TV. The less responsive he is, the more she yells. Eventually he gets up and leaves the room. Rather than confronting his wife, he disengages. By turning away from her, he is avoiding a fight, but he is also avoiding his marriage. He has become a stonewaller. Although both husbands and wives can stonewall, research indicates that this behavior is far more common among men in all kinds of marriages, for reasons we'll see later.

During a typical conversation between two people, the listener gives plenty of cues to the speaker that he's paying attention. He may use eye contact, nod his head, and say something like "Yeah" or "Uh-huh." But a stonewaller doesn't give this sort of casual feedback. He tends to look away or down without uttering a sound. He sits like an impassive stone wall. The stonewaller acts as though he couldn't care less about what you're saying, if he even hears it.

Stonewalling usually arrives later in the course of a marriage than the other three horsemen. That's why it's less common among newlywed husbands such as Oliver than among couples who have been in a negative spiral for a while. It takes time for the negativity created by the first three horsemen to become overwhelming enough that stonewalling becomes an understandable "out." That's the stance that Mack takes when he and his wife, Rita, argue about each other's behavior at parties. She says the problem is that he drinks too much. He thinks the bigger problem is her reaction: she embarrasses him in front of his friends. Here they are, already in the middle of an argument:

RITA: Now I've become the problem, again. I started off with the complaint, but now I am the problem. That always seems to happen.

MACK: Yeah, I do that, I know. (*pause*) But your tantrums and childishness are an embarrassment to me and my friends.

RITA: If you would control your drinking at parties, puhleez . . .

MACK: (*Looks down, avoids eye contact, says nothing—he's stonewalling.*)

RITA: Because I think (*laughs*) for the most part, we get along pretty well, really. (*laughs*)

MACK: (*Continues to stonewall. Remains silent, makes no eye contact, head nods, facial movements, or vocalizations.*)

RITA: Don't you think?

MACK: (*no response*)

RITA: Mack? Hello?

The Third Sign: Flooding

It may seem to Rita that her criticism and contempt have no effect on Mack. But nothing could be further from the truth. Usually people stonewall as a protection against feeling psychologically and physically overwhelmed, a sensation we call *flooding*. It occurs when your spouse's negativity is so intense and sudden that it leaves you shell-shocked. You feel so defenseless against this sniper attack that you learn to do anything to avoid a replay. The more often you feel flooded by your spouse's criticism or contempt, the more hypervigilant you are for cues that your spouse is about to "blow" again. That's why all Mack can think about is protecting himself from how awful Rita's onslaught makes him feel. And the way he does that is to disengage emotionally from the relationship. Sadly, Mack and Rita are now divorced.

Another husband, Paul, was quite up front about why he stonewalls when his wife, Amy, gets negative. In the following discussion, he articulates what all stonewallers are feeling.

AMY: When I get mad, that's when you should step in and try to make it better. But when you just stop talking, it means, "I no longer care about how you feel." That just makes me feel one inch tall. Like my opinion or feelings have absolutely no bearing on you. And that's not the way a marriage should be.

PAUL: What I'm saying is, if you wanna have a serious conversation, you're gonna do it without yelling and screaming all the time. You start saying things that are hurtful.

AMY: Well, when I'm hurt, mad, and I wanna hurt you, I start saying things. And that's when we should both stop. I should say, "I'm sorry." And you should say, "I know that you wanna talk about this. And I really should make an effort to talk instead of just ignoring you."

PAUL: I'll talk when—

AMY: It fits your purpose.

PAUL: No, when you're not yelling and screaming and jumping up and down stomping.

Amy kept telling Paul how it made her feel when he shut down. But she did not seem to hear him tell her why he shuts down: he can't handle her hostility. This couple also divorced.

A marriage's meltdown can be predicted, then, by habitual

harsh start-up and frequent flooding brought on by the relentless presence of the four horsemen during disagreements. Although each of these factors alone can predict a divorce, they usually co-exist in an unhappy marriage.

The Fourth Sign: Body Language

Even if I could not hear the conversation between Mack the stone-waller and his wife, Rita, I would be able to predict their divorce simply by looking at his physiological readings. When we monitor couples for bodily changes during a tense discussion, we can see just how physically distressing flooding is. One of the most apparent of these physical reactions is that the heart speeds up—pounding away at more than 100 beats per minute—even as high as 165. (In contrast, a typical heart rate for a man who is about 30 is 76, and for a woman the same age, 82.) Hormonal changes occur, too, including the secretion of adrenaline, which kicks in the "fight or flight response." Blood pressure also mounts. These changes are so dramatic that if one partner is frequently flooded during marital discussions, it's easy to predict that, unless the dynamic between them changes, they will end up divorced.

Recurring episodes of flooding lead to divorce for two reasons. First, they signal that at least one partner feels severe emotional distress when dealing with the other. Second, the physical sensations of feeling flooded—the increased heart rate, sweating, and so on—make it virtually impossible to have a productive, problem-solving discussion. When your body goes into overdrive during an argument, it is responding to a very primitive alarm system we inherited from our prehistoric ancestors. All those distressful reactions, like a pounding heart and sweating, occur because on a fundamental level your body perceives your current situation as dangerous. Even though we live in the age of in vitro conception, organ transplants, and gene mapping, from an evolutionary standpoint not much time has passed since we were cave dwellers. So the human body has not refined its fear reactions—it responds the same way, whether you're facing a saber-toothed tiger or a contemptuous spouse demanding to know why you can never remember to put the toilet seat back down.

When a pounding heart and all the other physical stress reactions happen in the midst of a discussion with your mate, the consequences are disastrous. Your ability to process information is reduced, meaning it's harder to pay attention to what your partner is saying. Creative problem solving and your sense of humor go out the window. You're left with the most reflexive, least intellectually sophisticated responses in your repertoire: to fight (act critical, contemptuous, or defensive) or flee (stonewall). Any chance of resolving the issue is gone. Most likely, the discussion will just worsen the situation.

Men and Women Really Are Different

In 85 percent of heterosexual marriages, the stonewaller is the husband. This is not because of some lack on the man's part. The reason lies in our evolutionary heritage. Anthropological evidence suggests that we evolved from hominids whose lives were circumscribed by very rigid gender roles, since these were advantageous to survival in a harsh environment. The females specialized in nurturing children, while the males specialized in cooperative hunting and protection.

As most nursing mothers can tell you, the amount of milk you produce is affected by how relaxed you feel, which is related to the release of the hormone oxytocin in the brain. So natural selection would favor a female who could quickly soothe herself and calm down after feeling stressed. Her ability to remain composed could enhance her children's chances of survival by optimizing the amount of nutrition they received. But in the male, natural selection would reward the opposite response. For these early cooperative hunters, maintaining vigilance was a key survival skill. So males whose adrenaline kicked in quite readily and who did not calm down so easily were more likely to survive and procreate.

To this day, the male cardiovascular system remains more reactive than that of the female and slower to recover from stress. For example, if a man and woman suddenly hear a very loud, brief sound, like a blowout, most likely his heart will beat faster than hers and stay accelerated for longer, according to research by Robert Levenson and his student Loren McCarter. The same goes for their blood pressure—his will become more elevated and stay higher longer. Psychologist Dolf Zillmann at the University of Alabama has found that when male subjects are deliberately treated rudely and then told to relax for twenty minutes, their blood pressure surges and stays elevated until they get to retaliate. But when women face the same treatment, they are able to calm down during those twenty minutes. (It's interesting that a woman's blood pressure tends to rise again if she is pressured into retaliating!) Since marital confrontation that activates vigilance takes a greater physical toll on the male, it's no surprise that men are more likely than women to attempt to avoid it.

It's a biological fact: men are more easily overwhelmed by marital conflict than are their wives.

This gender difference in how physiologically reactive our bodies are also influences what men and women tend to think about when they experience marital stress. As part of our experiments, we asked couples to watch themselves arguing on tape and then tell us what they were thinking when our sensors detected they were flooded. Their answers suggest that men have a greater tendency to have negative thoughts that maintain their distress, while women are more likely to think soothing thoughts that help them calm down and be conciliatory. Men, generally, either think about how righteous and indignant they feel ("I'm going to get even," "I don't have to take this"), which tends to lead to contempt or belligerence, or think about themselves as an innocent victim of their wife's wrath or complaint ("Why is she always blaming me?"), which leads to defensiveness.

Obviously, these rules don't hold for every male and every female, and the notion that men are more easily overwhelmed by marital conflict than are their wives is still somewhat controversial. But after forty-two years of research, I have noted that the majority of heterosexual couples do follow these gender differences in physiological and psychological reactions to stress. Because of these dissimilarities, most marriages (including healthy, happy ones) follow a comparable pattern of conflict in which the wife, who is constitutionally better able to handle the stress, brings up sensitive issues. The husband, who is not as able to cope with it, will attempt to avoid getting into the subject. He may become defensive and stonewall. Or he may even become belligerent or contemptuous in an attempt to silence her.

If a marriage follows this common pattern, it doesn't mean the couple are headed for divorce. In fact, you'll find examples of all the horsemen and even occasional flooding in some stable marriages. But when the four horsemen take up permanent residence, when either partner begins to feel flooded routinely, the relationship is in serious trouble. Frequently feeling flooded leads almost inevitably to emotional distancing, which in turn leads to feeling lonely. Without help, the couple will end up divorced or living in a dead marriage in which they maintain separate, parallel lives in the same home. They may go through the motions of togetherness—attending their children's plays, hosting dinner parties, taking family vacations. But emotionally they no longer feel connected to each other. They have given up.

The Fifth Sign: Failed Repair Attempts

It takes time for the four horsemen and the flooding that comes in their wake to overrun a marriage. And yet divorce can so often be predicted by listening to a single conversation between newlyweds. How can this be? The answer is that by analyzing any disagreement a couple has, you get a good sense of their pattern, which is unlikely to change unless they receive the right sort of help. A crucial part of a couple's pattern is whether their repair attempts succeed or fail. Repair attempts, as I described on page 27, are efforts the couple makes ("Let's take a break," "Wait, I need to calm down") to de-escalate the tension during a touchy discussion—to put on the brakes so that they can prevent flooding.

Repair attempts save marriages not just because they decrease emotional tension between spouses, but because by lowering the stress level they also prevent your heart from racing and making you feel flooded. When the four horsemen rule a couple's communication, repair attempts often don't even get noticed. Especially when you're feeling flooded, you're not able to hear a verbal white flag.

In unhappy marriages, a feedback loop develops between the four horsemen and the failure of repair attempts. The more contemptuous and defensive the couple are with each other, the more flooding occurs, and the harder it is to hear and respond to a repair. And since the repair is not heard, the contempt and defensiveness just get heightened, making flooding more pronounced, which makes it more difficult to hear the next repair attempt, until finally one partner withdraws.

That's why I can often predict a divorce by hearing only one discussion between a husband and wife. The failure of repair attempts is an accurate marker for an unhappy future. The presence of the four horsemen alone predicts divorce with an 82 percent accuracy rate. But when you add in the failure of repair attempts, the accuracy rate reaches into the 90s. This is because some couples who trot out the four horsemen when they argue are also successful at repairing the harm the horsemen cause. Usually in this situation—when the four horsemen are present but the couple's repair attempts are successful—the result is a satisfying marriage. In fact, 84 percent of the newlyweds who were high on the four horsemen but repaired effectively were in stable, happy marriages six years later. But if there were no repair attempts—or if the attempts were not able to be heard—the marriage faced serious danger.

In emotionally intelligent marriages, I hear a wide range of successful repair attempts. Each person has his or her own approach. Olivia and Nathaniel stick out their tongues; other couples laugh or smile or say they're sorry. Even an irritated "Hey, stop yelling at me" or "You're getting off the topic" can defuse a tense situation. All such repair attempts keep a marriage stable, because they prevent the four horsemen from moving in for good.

Whether a repair succeeds or fails has very little to do with how eloquent it is and everything to do with the state of the marriage. One happily married couple who taught me this lesson were Hal and Jodie. Because of the nature of his research, Hal, a chemist, would often find out at the last minute that he wouldn't be home for dinner. Although Jodie, who also worked full-time, knew Hal couldn't control his hours, the dinner situation frustrated her. When they discussed the problem in our lab, she pointed out to him that the kids always refused to eat dinner till he got home, so they were often having their dinner very late, which she didn't like. So Hal suggested that she give them a snack to tide them over. Incredulous, Jodie snapped at him: "What do you think I have been doing all along?"

Hal realized that he had screwed up. He had displayed a significant lack of awareness about what went on in his own home and, worse, had insulted his wife's intelligence. In an unhappy marriage, this could easily be grounds for some major-league sniping. I waited to see what would happen next. Since all other evidence suggested they were happily married, I anticipated that Hal would use some very skillfully wrought repair attempt. But Hal just gave Jodie a really goofy smile. Jodie burst out laughing, and they went on with their discussion.

Hal's quick grin worked because their marriage was working. But when Oliver tried to soften up Dara by chuckling during their conversation about housekeeping, he got nowhere. In marriages in which the four horsemen have moved in for good, even the most articulate, sensitive, well-targeted repair attempt is likely to fail abysmally.

Ironically, we see more repair attempts between troubled couples than between those whose marriages are going smoothly. The more that repair attempts fail, the more these couples keep trying. It can be poignant to hear a partner offer up one repair after another, all to no avail. What makes the difference? How do you improve the odds that your attempts will work? In the chapters ahead, you'll learn to increase the success rate by enhancing the quality of your underlying friendship.

The Sixth Sign: Bad Memories

When a relationship gets consumed by negativity, it's not only the couple's present and future life together that are put at risk. Their past is in danger, too. When I interview couples, I usually ask about the history of their marriage. I have found over and over that couples who are deeply entrenched in a negative view of their spouse and their marriage often rewrite their past. Based on their answers to questions about their early courtship, their wedding, their first year together, I can predict their chances of divorce, even if I'm not privy to their current feelings.

Most couples enter marriage with high hopes and great expectations. In a happy marriage, couples tend to look back on their early days fondly. Even if the wedding didn't go off perfectly, they are likely to remember the highlights rather than the low points. The same goes for each other. They remember how positively they felt early on, how excited they were when they met, and how much admiration they had for each other. When they talk about the tough times they've had, they glorify the struggles they've been through, drawing strength from the adversity they've weathered together.

But when a marriage is not going well, history gets rewritten—for the worse. Now she recalls that he was thirty minutes late getting to the wedding ceremony. Or he focuses on all that time she spent talking to his best man at the rehearsal dinner—or "flirting" with his friend, as it seems to him now. Another sad sign is when either or both partners find the past difficult to remember—it has become so unimportant or painful that they've let it fade away.

Peter and Cynthia didn't always spend their days arguing about car washing and other money matters. No doubt if you looked at their photo album, you would find plenty of happy pictures from their early days together. But those pictures have long faded from their minds. When asked to describe their history, they do a good job of telling the facts of their courtship and marriage, but nothing more. Cynthia recounts that they met at a café where she was a barista. She got his name and number from his credit card receipt and called him up to see if gloves left in the lost and found belonged to him. Their first date followed.

Cynthia says that she was attracted to Peter at first because he was going to college and was interesting to talk to and nice-looking. "I think it was the fact that I had a charge card," Peter slips in, a snide reference to their current fights over money. He himself seems to have a hard time remembering what attracted him to her when they first met. He says, "Uh . . . (*long pause*) I honestly don't know. I never tried to pin it down to one thing. I think for me that would be pretty dangerous."

When they're asked about the kinds of activities they enjoyed back then, they have a hard time remembering. "Didn't we go on picnics or something?" Cynthia asks, and he shrugs. The same blank feeling is there when they discuss their decision to marry. "I thought it would solidify the relationship. It seemed like a logical progression—that's basically the main reason," says Peter. He recalls that he proposed to her at a restaurant by tying the ring to a white ribbon wrapped around a bunch of white roses. That sounds promising, until he adds with a sad chuckle, "I'll never forget this. She saw the ring. She started shaking a little bit, and she asked me, 'I suppose you want an answer?' That's kind of not the reaction I was looking for." He turns to his wife. "You weren't smiling or laughing or anything when you said it—you were just deadpan, like, 'You idiot.'"

"Oh nooo," Cynthia says limply.

The picture doesn't get any better when they recall the wedding itself. Cynthia remembers feeling hurt because many guests left right after dinner. Peter recounts that everyone kept banging on their glasses with spoons to make him and Cynthia kiss. "I was getting really annoyed." His main memory was being in the limo after the party with Cynthia and his best man. His friend turned on the stereo, and the Mötley Crüe song "Same Old Ball and Chain" came blasting out. To sum up their wedding day, he says, "It was your basic tragedy." Cynthia smiles wanly in agreement.

Peter and Cynthia have such distorted memories because the negativity between them has become so intense, it's been cast in stone. When the four horsemen overrun a home, impairing the communication, the negativity mushrooms to such a degree that everything a spouse does—or ever did—is recast in a negative light.

In a happy marriage, if the husband promises to pick up the wife's dry cleaning but forgets, she is likely to think, "Oh well, he's been under a lot of stress lately and needs more sleep." She considers his lapse to be fleeting and caused by a specific situation. In an unhappy marriage, the same circumstance is likely to lead to a thought like "He's just always so inconsiderate and selfish." By the same token, in a happy marriage a loving gesture, like a wife greeting her husband with a passionate kiss at the end of the workday, is seen as a sign that the spouse is loving and thoughtful. But in an unhappy marriage, the same action will lead the husband to think, "What does she want out of me?"

This distorted perception explains why one husband we studied, Mitch, saw ulterior motives whenever his wife, Leslie, bought him a gift, hugged him, or even called him on the phone. Over time he had rewritten the history of their marriage, creating a very negative script. Whenever a conflict arose, he was all set to feel self-righteous and indignant. His negative thoughts about Leslie helped maintain his distress. He'd get flooded as soon as they had a confrontation. Negative expectations of her and their relationship became the norm for him. Eventually they divorced.

The End Draws Near

When a marriage gets to the point where the couple have rewritten their history, when their minds and bodies make it virtually impossible to communicate and repair their current problems, their relationship is almost bound to fail without the right help.

The partners find themselves constantly on red alert. Because they always expect to do combat, the marriage becomes a torment. The understandable result: they withdraw from the relationship.

Sometimes a couple at this end stage of marriage will come for counseling. On the surface, it may seem like nothing much is wrong because they don't argue, act contemptuous, or stonewall. The four horsemen are completely absent. Instead, they talk calmly and distantly about their relationship and their conflicts. An inexperienced therapist could easily assume that their problems don't run very deep. But actually, one or both of them has already disengaged emotionally from the marriage. Our lab studies indicate that these emotionally distant couples do divorce—but they split after an average of 16 years, compared with 5.6 years for couples whose conflict discussions are overrun by the four horsemen.

Some people leave a marriage literally, by divorcing. Others do so by staying together but leading parallel lives. Whatever the route, there are four final stages that signal the death knell of a relationship.

1. The couple see their marital problems as severe.
2. Talking things over seems useless. Partners try to solve problems on their own.
3. The couple lead parallel lives.
4. Loneliness sets in.

When a couple get to the last stage, one or both partners may have an affair. But this betrayal is usually a symptom of a dying marriage, not the cause. The end of that marriage could have been predicted long before either spouse strayed. Too often, couples begin to seek help for their marriage after they've already hit troubled waters. The warning signs were almost always there early on if they had known what to look for. You can see the seeds of trouble in (1) what partners actually say to each other (the prevalence of harsh start-up, the four horsemen, and the unwillingness to accept influence), (2) the failure of their repair attempts, (3) physiological reactions (flooding), or (4) pervasive negative thoughts about their marriage. Any of these signs suggests that, unless there is change in how the couple interact, emotional separation and, in most cases, divorce may only be a matter of time.

But It's Not Over till It's Over

As bleak as this sounds, I am convinced that far more marriages can be saved than currently are. Even a marriage that is about to hit bottom can be revived with the right intervention. Sadly, most marriages at this stage get the wrong kind of help. Well-meaning therapists will deluge the couple with advice about negotiating their differences and improving their communication. At one time, I would have done the same. At first, when I figured out how to predict divorce, I thought I had found the key to saving marriages. All that was necessary, I presumed, was to teach people how to argue without being overridden by the four horsemen and without getting flooded. Then their repair attempts would succeed, and they could work out their differences.

But like so many experts before me, I was wrong. I was not able to crack the code to saving marriages until I started to analyze what went *right* in happy marriages. After tracking the lives of happily married couples for as long as twenty years, I now know that the key to reviving or divorce-proofing a relationship is not simply how you handle your disagreements but how you engage with each other when you're not fighting. So although my Seven Principles will also guide you in coping with conflict, the basis of my approach, which forms the first three principles, is to strengthen the friendship and trust that are at the heart of any marriage.

Bolstering your friendship is so critical in large part because it fuels the romance, passion, and great sex that we all hope marriage will provide. In fact, when a couple come to me complaining that sex has become routine, infrequent, or virtually nonexistent, I don't start by handing them a sex manual. Instead, I guide them through the first three principles so that they can reinforce and rediscover the camaraderie that brought them together in the first place. The strength of a couple's friendship not only stokes the fire but also foretells the relationship's future because it is the fundamental ingredient of positive sentiment override. As we've seen, PSO is like an insurance policy—it dramatically increases the odds that repair attempts will regularly work and defuse tension. So whatever the current state of your marriage, it will benefit enormously if you support, reinvigorate, or, if necessary, resuscitate your friendship. The first step in this process is to take a look at how much you really (still) know about each other, the topic of my first principle.

4

Principle 1:
Enhance Your Love Maps

*R*ory was a pediatrician who ran an intensive care unit for babies. He was beloved at the hospital, where everybody called him Dr. Rory. He was a reserved man but capable of great warmth, humor, and charm. He was also a workaholic who slept in the hospital an average of twenty nights a month. He didn't know the names of his children's friends, or even the name of the family dog. When he was asked which room led to the house's back door, he turned to ask his wife, Lisa.

His wife was upset over how little she saw of Rory and how emotionally disconnected he seemed to be. She frequently tried to make little gestures to show him she cared, but her attempts just annoyed him. She was left with the sense that he simply didn't value her or their marriage.

To this day, I'm struck by the story of this couple. Here was an intellectually gifted man who didn't even know the name of the family dog or how to find the back door! Of the many problems their relationship faced, perhaps the most fundamental was Rory's shocking lack of knowledge about his home life. He had become so caught up in his work that there was little space left over in his brain for the basics of his wife's world.

As bizarre as Rory's rampant ignorance may sound, I have

found that many married couples fall into a similar (if less dramatic) habit of inattention to the details of their spouse's life. One or both partners may have only the sketchiest sense of the other's joys, likes, dislikes, fears, stresses. The husband may love modern art, but his wife couldn't tell you why or who his favorite artist is. He doesn't remember the names of her friends or the coworker she fears is constantly trying to undermine her.

In contrast, emotionally intelligent couples are intimately familiar with each other's world. I call this having a richly detailed *love map*—my term for that part of your brain where you store all the relevant information about your partner's life. Another way of saying this is that these couples have made plenty of cognitive room for their marriage. They remember the major events in each other's history, and they keep updating their information as the facts and feelings of their spouse's world change. When she orders him a salad, she knows what kind of dressing he likes. If she works late, he'll think to record her favorite TV show. He could tell you how she's feeling about her boss and exactly how to get to her office from the elevator. He knows that religion is important to her but that deep down she has doubts. She knows that he fears being too much like his father and considers himself a "free spirit." They know each other's life goals, worries, and hopes.

Without such a love map, you can't really know your spouse. And if you don't really know someone, how can you truly love them? No wonder the biblical term for sexual love is to "know."

In Knowledge There Is Strength

From knowledge springs not only love but the fortitude to weather marital storms. Couples who have detailed love maps of each other's world are far better prepared to cope with stressful events and conflict. Take, for example, one of the major causes of marital dissatisfaction and divorce: the birth of the first baby. Sixty-seven percent of couples in our newlywed study underwent a precipitous drop in marital satisfaction the first time they became parents. But the remaining 33 percent did not experience this decline—in fact, about half of them saw their marriages improve.

What separated these two groups? You guessed it: the couples whose marriages thrived after the birth had detailed love maps from the get-go, according to a study of fifty couples by my student Alyson Shapiro. These love maps protected their marriages in the wake of this dramatic upheaval. Because husband and wife were already in the habit of keeping up to date and were intently aware of what each other was feeling and thinking, they weren't thrown off course. But if couples don't start off with a deep knowledge of each other, it's easy for a marriage to lose its way when lives shift so suddenly and dramatically.

Maggie and Ken knew each other only a short time when they married and decided to have a family. But what their relationship lacked in longevity, they made up for in intimacy. They were in touch not just with the outlines of each other's lives—their favorite hobbies, sports, and so on—but with each other's deepest longings, beliefs, and fears. No matter how busy they were, they made each other their priority—always taking the time to catch up on each other's day. And at least once a week, they'd go out for dinner and just talk—sometimes about politics, sometimes about the weather, sometimes about their own marriage.

When their daughter Alice was born, Maggie decided to give up her job to stay home with the baby. She herself was surprised by the decision, since she had always been very career driven. But when she became a mother, her fundamental sense of meaning in life changed. She found she was willing to undergo great sacrifices for Alice's sake. Now she wanted the savings they had earmarked for a motorboat to go into a college fund. What happened to Maggie happens to many new parents—the experience of having a child is so profound that your whole notion of who you are and what you value gets reshuffled.

At first, Ken was confused by the changes in his wife. The woman he thought he knew was transforming before his eyes. But because they were in the habit of staying deeply connected, Ken was able to keep up to date on what Maggie was thinking and feeling. Too often when a new baby comes, the husband gets left behind. (More on this and ways of dealing with it in chapter 10.) He can't keep up with his wife's metamorphosis, which he may not understand or be happy about. Knowing Maggie had always been a priority to Ken, so he didn't do what too many new fathers do—he didn't back away from this new charmed circle of mother and child. As a result, they went through the transformation to parenthood together, without losing sight of each other or their marriage.

Having a baby is just one life event that can cause couples to lose their way if they don't have a detailed love map. Any major change—from a job shift to a move to illness or retirement—can have the same effect. Just the passage of time can do it as well. The more you know and understand about each other, the easier it is to keep connected as life swirls around you.

LOVE MAPS QUESTIONNAIRE

By giving honest answers to the following questions, you will get a sense of the quality of your current love maps. For the most accurate reading of how your marriage is doing on this first principle, both of you should complete the following.

Read each statement, and circle T for "true" or F for "false."

1. I can name my partner's best friends. **T F**
2. I can tell you what stresses my partner is currently facing. **T F**
3. I know the names of some of the people who have been irritating my partner lately. **T F**
4. I can tell you some of my partner's life dreams. **T F**
5. I am very familiar with my partner's religious beliefs and ideas. **T F**
6. I can tell you about my partner's basic philosophy of life. **T F**
7. I can list the relatives my partner likes the least. **T F**
8. I know my partner's favorite music. **T F**
9. I can list my partner's three favorite movies. **T F**
10. My spouse is familiar with my current stresses. **T F**
11. I know the three most special times in my partner's life. **T F**

12. I can tell you the most stressful thing that happened to my partner as a child. **T F**
13. I can list my partner's major aspirations and hopes in life. **T F**
14. I know my partner's major current worries. **T F**
15. My spouse knows who my friends are. **T F**
16. I know what my partner would want to do if he or she suddenly won the lottery. **T F**
17. I can tell you in detail my first impressions of my partner. **T F**
18. Periodically I ask my partner about his or her world right now. **T F**
19. I feel that my partner knows me pretty well. **T F**
20. My spouse is familiar with my hopes and aspirations. **T F**

Scoring: Give yourself 1 point for each "true" answer.

10 or higher: This is an area of strength for your marriage. You have a fairly detailed map of your spouse's everyday life, hopes, fears, and dreams. You know what makes your spouse "tick." Based on your score, you'll probably find the love map exercises that follow easy and gratifying. They will serve as a reminder of how connected you and your partner are. Try not to take for granted this knowledge and understanding of each other. Keeping in touch in this way ensures you'll be well equipped to handle any problem areas that crop up in your relationship.

Below 10: Your marriage could stand some improvement in this area. Perhaps you never had the time or the tools to really get to know each other. Or perhaps your love maps have become outdated as your lives have changed over the years. In either case, by taking the time to learn more about your spouse now, you'll find your relationship becomes stronger.

There are few greater gifts a couple can give each other than the joy that comes from feeling known and understood. Getting to know each other shouldn't be a chore. That's why the first love map exercise below is actually a game! While you're having fun playing, you'll also be expanding and deepening your knowledge of each other. By the time you complete all of the exercises in this chapter, you'll know there's truth in that old song "To Know You Is to Love You."

Don't pass judgment on what your spouse tells you or try to give each other advice. Remember that you are simply on a fact-finding mission. Your goal is to listen and learn about your mate.

EXERCISE 1: THE LOVE MAP 20 QUESTIONS GAME

Play this game together in the spirit of laughter and gentle fun. The more you play, the more you'll learn about the love maps concept and how to apply it to your relationship.

STEP 1. Each of you should take a piece of paper and a pen or pencil. Together, randomly decide on twenty numbers between 1 and 60.

STEP 2. Below is a list of numbered questions. Beginning with the top of your column, match the numbers you chose with the corresponding question. Each of you should ask your partner this question. If your spouse answers correctly (you be the judge), he or she receives the number of points indicated for that question, and you receive one point. If your spouse answers incorrectly, neither of you receives any points. The same rules apply when you answer. The winner is the person with the higher score after you've both answered all twenty questions.

1. Name my two closest friends. (2)
2. What is my favorite musical group, composer, or instrument? (2)
3. What was I wearing when we first met? (2)
4. Name one of my hobbies. (3)
5. Where was I born? (1)
6. What stresses am I facing right now? (4)
7. Describe in detail what I did today, or yesterday. (4)
8. When is my birthday? (1)
9. What is the date of our anniversary? (1)
10. Who is my favorite relative? (2)
11. What is my fondest unrealized dream? (5)
12. What is my favorite website? (2)

13. What is one of my greatest fears or disaster scenarios? (3)
14. What is my favorite time of day for lovemaking? (3)
15. What makes me feel most competent? (4)
16. What turns me on sexually? (3)
17. What is my favorite meal? (2)
18. What is my favorite way to spend an evening? (2)
19. What is my favorite color? (1)
20. What personal improvements do I want to make in my life? (4)
21. What kind of present would I like best? (2)
22. What was one of my best childhood experiences? (2)
23. What was my favorite vacation? (2)
24. What is one of my favorite ways to relax? (4)
25. Who is my greatest source of support (other than you)? (3)
26. What is my favorite sport? (2)
27. What do I most like to do with time off? (2)
28. What is one of my favorite weekend activities? (2)
29. What is my dream getaway place? (3)
30. What is my favorite movie? (2)
31. What are some of the important events coming up in my life? How do I feel about them? (4)
32. What are some of my favorite ways to work out? (2)
33. Who was my best friend in childhood? (3)
34. What is one of my favorite magazines? (2)
35. Name one of my major rivals or "enemies." (3)
36. What would I consider my ideal job? (4)
37. What do I fear the most? (4)
38. Who is my least favorite relative? (3)
39. What is my favorite holiday? (2)
40. What kinds of books do I most like to read? (3)
41. What is my favorite TV show? (2)
42. Which side of the bed do I prefer? (2)
43. What am I most sad about? (4)
44. Name one of my concerns or worries. (4)
45. What medical problems do I worry about? (2)
46. What was my most embarrassing moment? (3)
47. What was my worst childhood experience? (3)

48. Name two of the people I most admire. (4)
49. Name my major rival or enemy. (3)
50. Of all the people we both know, who do I like the least? (3)
51. What is one of my favorite desserts? (2)
52. What is my social security number? (2)
53. Name one of my favorite novels. (2)
54. What is my favorite restaurant? (2)
55. What are two of my aspirations, hopes, wishes? (4)
56. Do I have a secret ambition? What is it? (4)
57. What foods do I hate? (2)
58. What is my favorite animal? (2)
59. What is my favorite song? (2)
60. Which sports team is my favorite? (2)

Play this game as frequently as you'd like. The more you play, the more you'll come to understand the concept of a love map and the kind of information yours should include about your spouse.

EXERCISE 2: ASKING OPEN-ENDED QUESTIONS

Updating your love map is as important as the map itself. The process entails asking open-ended questions, and then remembering the answers. An open-ended question is one that can't be answered with a quick "yes" or "no." Instead, it invites your partner to offer up his or her experiences, opinions, and emotions. Asking an open-ended question demonstrates genuine interest in your partner's life and inner world.

Instructions: Below is a long list of open-ended questions. Choose four to ask each other. Switch off being the speaker and the listener. After your partner answers your question, follow up with an open-ended question of your own. Then answer that original question you asked your partner. Now it's your partner's turn to ask you an open-ended question and so on. Of course, you don't have to limit yourselves to just four of these questions. Over time, you can go through all of them—it can be entertaining and enlightening.

1. How would you like your life to be different three years from now?

2. Do you see your work changing in the future? How?

3. What is your opinion of our physical home? Would you make changes if you could?

4. How do you think your life would have been different if you lived 100 years ago?

5. How would you compare yourself as a mother (father) to your own mother (father)?

6. What kind of person do you think our child(ren) will become? Any fears? Any hopes?

7. How are you feeling about your job these days?

8. If you could redo a five-year period of your life, which would you choose?

9. How are you feeling right now about being a parent?

10. If you could change one thing in your past, what would it be?

11. What is the most exciting thing happening in your life right now?

12. If you could instantly possess three new skills, which would you choose?

13. When it comes to the future, what do you worry about most?

14. Who do you consider your best friends or closest allies? Has that list changed recently?

15. What qualities do you value most highly in friends right now?

16. What were the best and worst things that happened to you when you were a teen?

17. If you could live during any other time in history, when would you choose and why?

18. If you could choose a different career or vocation, what would it be, and why?

19. What is the one thing you would most like to change about your personality? Why?

20. Do you feel like certain things are missing from your life? What are they?

21. Do you think you've changed in the last year? How so?

22. If you could design the perfect home for us, what would it be like?

23. If you could live another person's life, whose would you choose?

24. Have any of your life goals recently changed?

25. What are some of your life dreams now?
26. What are your goals for us as a family?
27. What goals do you have just for yourself right now?
28. If you could change one thing about yourself, what would it be?
29. What have been the highlights and low points of the past year for you?
30. What adventures would you like to have in your life right now?

The love map questions above are useful for creating a broad outline of your current lives. But love maps shouldn't just be broad—they should also be deep. The next exercise will ensure that yours are.

EXERCISE 3: WHO AM I?

The more you know about each other's inner world, the more profound and rewarding your relationship will be. This questionnaire is designed both to guide you through some self-exploration and to help you share this exploration with your partner. Work on this exercise even if you and your spouse consider yourselves open books. There's always more to know about each other. Life changes us, so neither of you may be the same person who spoke those wedding vows five, ten, or thirty years ago.

Many of the questions in this exercise are powerful. Please make sure you have enough time and privacy to do them justice. In fact, it may be best to reserve this exercise for an uninterrupted stretch when you do not have work to do, deadlines to meet, e-mails to send, or children (or anybody else) to look after. Most likely, you won't be able to complete this questionnaire in one sitting, nor should you try. Instead, break it up by section and proceed slowly and together.

Answer the questions in each section as candidly as you can. You don't have to answer every aspect of each question—just respond to the parts that are relevant to your life. Write your answers in a private journal or notebook. If writing so much is hard, you can do it in outline form—but the process of writing this down is important to the success of the exercise. When you're ready, exchange notebooks and share with each other what you have written. Discuss each other's entries and what this added knowledge implies for your marriage and the deepening of your friendship.

My Triumphs and Strivings

1. What has happened in your life that you are particularly proud of? Write about your psychological triumphs, experiences that exceeded your expectations, periods when you came through trials and tribulations even better off.

2. How have these successes shaped your life? How have they affected the way you think of yourself and your capabilities? How have they influenced your goals and the things you strive for?

3. What role has pride (that is, feeling proud, being praised, expressing praise for others) played in your life? Did your parents show you that they were proud of you when you were a child? How? How have other people responded to your accomplishments?

4. Did your parents show that they loved you? How? Was affection readily expressed in your family? If not, what are the effects and implications of this for your marriage?

5. What role does pride in your accomplishments play in your marriage? What role do your own strivings have in your marriage? What do you want your partner to know and understand about these aspects of yourself, your past, present, and plans for the future? How do you show pride in each other?

Injuries and Healing

1. What difficult events or periods have you gone through? Write about any significant psychological insults and injuries you have sustained, your losses, disappointments, trials, and tribulations. Include periods of stress and duress, as well as any quieter periods of despair, hopelessness, and loneliness.

    Also include any deep traumas you have undergone as a child or adult. For example, harmful relationships, humiliating events, even molestation, abuse, rape, or torture.

2. How have you survived these traumas? What are their lasting effects on you?

3. How did you strengthen and heal yourself? How did you redress your grievances? How did you revive and restore yourself?
4. How did you gird and protect yourself against this ever happening again?
5. How do these injuries and the ways you protect and heal yourself affect your marriage today? What do you want your partner to know and understand about these aspects of yourself?

My Emotional World

1. How did your family express the following when you were a child:

   - Anger
   - Sadness
   - Fear
   - Affection
   - Interest in one another
   - Pride in one another

2. During your childhood, did your family have to cope with a particular emotional problem, such as aggression between parents, a depressed parent or a somewhat emotionally wounded one? What implications does this have for your marriage and your other close relationships (friendships, relationships with your parents, siblings, children)?
3. What is your own philosophy about expressing feelings, particularly sadness, anger, fear, pride, and love? Are any of these difficult for you to express or to hear your spouse express? What is the basis of your perspective on this?
4. What differences exist between you and your spouse in the area of expressing emotion? What is behind these differences? What are the implications of these differences for you?

My Mission and Legacy

1. Imagine that you are standing in a graveyard looking at your own tombstone. Now write the epitaph you would like to see there. Begin with the words: "Here lies . . ."
2. Write your own obituary. (It does not have to be brief.) How do you want people to think of your life, to remember you?
3. Now you're ready to write a mission statement for your own life. What is the purpose of your life? What is its meaning? What are you trying to accomplish? What is your larger struggle?
4. What legacy would you like to leave when you die?
5. What significant goals have you yet to realize? This can be creating something or having a particular experience. Minor examples are learning to play the banjo, climbing a mountain, and so on.

Who I Want to Become

Take a moment now to reflect on what you have just written. We are all involved in becoming the person we most want to be. In that struggle, we all have demons to fight and overcome.

1. Describe the person you want to become.
2. How can you best help yourself become that person?
3. What struggles have you already faced in trying to become that person?
4. What demons in yourself have you had to fight? Or still have to fight?
5. What would you most like to change about yourself?
6. What dreams have you denied yourself or failed to develop?
7. What do you want your life to be like in five years?
8. What is the story of the kind of person you would like to be?

The Next Step

All of the above exercises and questions will help you develop greater personal insight and a more detailed map of each other's life and world. Getting to know your spouse better and sharing your inner self with your partner is an ongoing process. In fact, it's a lifelong process. So expect to return to these pages from time to time to update your knowledge about yourselves and each other. Think about questions to ask your partner. One therapist I know has taken to wearing a Bugs Bunny pin and advising couples that the key to sustaining a happy marriage is to ask periodically, "What's up, doc?"

For all of their power, love maps are only a first step. Happily married couples don't "just" know each other. They build on and enhance this knowledge in many important ways. For starters, they use their love maps to express not only their understanding of each other but their fondness and admiration as well—my second principle.

5

Principle 2:
Nurture Your Fondness
and Admiration

*L*et's turn again to Dr. Rory, the husband whose love map was the size of a postage stamp and who couldn't even remember the name of the family dog. For years, his wife, Lisa, put up with his workaholism. But a turning point in their relationship occurred one year on Christmas Day, when Rory was, of course, working. Lisa decided to pack a Christmas picnic and, kids in tow, surprise her husband at the hospital.

As they ate together in the waiting room, Rory turned on Lisa, his face like an angry mask. He told her he resented being surprised with a picnic. "Why did you do this? It is really embarrassing." Just then, a resident called and as Rory answered his phone, his face softened and his voice became helpful, warm, and friendly. When he hung up, he turned back to Lisa, his face again full of anger. Something snapped inside Lisa. Clearly her husband was capable of kindness—just not toward her. She packed up the picnic and took the kids home.

Soon afterward she began going out in the evenings without him. After a while Rory asked her for a divorce. But in a last-ditch effort to work out their differences, they decided to try marital counseling. At first they got nowhere. When Lisa tried to be conciliatory toward Rory during their first session with a marital therapist, he was unable to respond in kind to her repair attempts.

But their marriage's hidden hope was discovered when the couple agreed to be taped in my lab for a segment of a TV news show. The interviewer asked Rory and Lisa about their early years together. As Rory began to describe their first date, his face lit up. Here's a little of what they recalled:

RORY: I think she was very nervous, and I had some background about why she was nervous, some cultural things that she was trying to live with. And because of this, I knew this was going to take a long, long time. So I wasn't nervous at all. I figured this was stage one of a five-year marathon. . . .
LISA: You mean you had a five-year plan on our first date?
RORY: Maybe that's exaggerating, but I knew it would take more than one lunch.
LISA: Wow.

Rory and Lisa actually held hands while they discussed this. Lisa was beaming—he had never before recounted his campaign to win her heart. This little vignette may not sound very dramatic (in fact, the TV show edited Rory and Lisa down to a snippet of airtime), but to a trained observer there was much in this couple's interaction that offered hope for their marriage. Rory and Lisa's fond memories of their early days were evidence that underneath the antagonism there were still glimmerings of what I call a fondness and admiration system. This means that they each retained some fundamental sense that the other was worthy of being respected and even liked.

If a couple still have a functioning fondness and admiration system, their marriage is salvageable. I'm not suggesting that the road to reviving a marriage as troubled as Rory and Lisa's is easy. But it can be done. In two years, everything changed for this couple. With the help of their therapist, Lois Abrams, Rory and Lisa used techniques like those you'll find in the pages ahead to unearth more of their positive feelings and put them to work to save their marriage. Rory revised his work schedule. He trained a resident to take over much of the hospital work that he had been doing single-handedly. He began to eat dinner every night with Lisa and the children. He and Lisa also went out together in the evenings, especially to folk dance. Despite the agony they had put each other through, Rory and Lisa saved their marriage.

Fondness and admiration are two of the most crucial elements in a rewarding and long-lasting romance. Although happily married couples may feel driven to distraction at times by their partner's personality flaws, they still feel that the person they married is worthy of honor and respect. They cherish each other, which is critical to keeping their Sound Relationship House intact and preventing betrayal. If fondness and admiration are completely missing, reviving the relationship is impossible.

Learning from History

As with Rory and Lisa, the best test of whether a couple still have a functioning fondness and admiration system is usually how they view their past. If a marriage is troubled, asking the couple about the current state of affairs is not likely to elicit much mutual praise. But query them about the past and you can often detect embers of positive feelings.

Of course, some marriages do come up empty. In these relationships, the antagonism has metastasized like a virulent cancer, actually spreading backward in time and destroying the couple's positive memories. We see that sad result in the marriage of Peter and Cynthia. They can remember very little about the beginning of their relationship. Asked what they used to do when they were dating, they give each other a brief "help me out here" glance and then sit silently, racking their brains. Peter can't remember a single quality he admired about Cynthia back then. Their marriage could not be resuscitated.

---

94 percent of the time, couples who put a positive spin on their marriage's history and their partner's character are likely to have a happy future as well. When happy memories are distorted, it's a sign that the marriage needs help.

In contrast, when another couple in my newlywed study, Michael and Justine, are asked about their history, they glow. Their wedding was "perfect," the honeymoon was "fabulous." What is telling isn't just their positive feelings about their early years, but how vivid those memories are. Justine recalls that they had gone to the same high school, he a few years ahead of her. He was a big sports hero. She had such a crush on him that she had clipped his picture from the newspaper and kept it in a scrapbook. (She confessed and showed him the scrapbook on their fourth date.) They met formally a few years later, when she tagged along with his foster sister (a friend of hers), who was going to visit him at college for the weekend.

Michael sensed right away that Justine was the one, but he worried that she wouldn't like him. She recounts with a giggle discovering the letter admitting his feelings that he slipped under her purse at the end of that weekend. "I was never very aggressive about chasing women," he says. "She was the first girl I ever actually pursued. That's how I knew something was different about this one."

They recall the long walks and talks they had, the letters they wrote every day while he was at school. The only bad part of those days, says Michael, was "being away from Justine. Just missing her a lot." You can hear Justine's fondness and admiration for Michael when she says, "I thought, 'God, if I don't marry this guy, someone else will. I'd better get him while I can.'" Michael says, "I would look at other girls, and I didn't want to be with them. I just wanted to be with her. I wanted to become a legal couple and let everybody know how special she is to me." Justine recalls the unity they felt in dealing with one of his buddies who resented that Justine was taking so much of Michael's time. "He didn't get it that I was *giving* her my time," Michael says.

It won't come as much of a surprise to hear that Michael and Justine continue to be happily married. Having a fundamentally positive view of your spouse and your marriage is a powerful buffer when bad times hit. Because they have this reserve of good feeling, Justine and Michael do not have cataclysmic thoughts about separation and divorce each time they have an argument.

The Antidote to Contempt

At first, this may all seem obvious to the point of being ridiculous: People who are happily married like each other. If they didn't, they wouldn't be happily married. But fondness and admiration can be fragile unless you remain aware of how crucial they are to the friendship that is at the core of any good marriage. By simply reminding yourself of your spouse's positive qualities—even as you grapple with each other's flaws—you can prevent a happy marriage from deteriorating. The simple reason is that fondness and admiration are antidotes for contempt. If you maintain a sense of respect for your spouse, you are less likely to act disgusted with him or her when you disagree. So fondness and admiration prevent you from being trounced by the four horsemen.

If your mutual fondness and admiration have been completely extinguished, your marriage is in dire trouble. Without the fundamental belief that your spouse is worthy of honor and respect, where is the basis for any kind of rewarding relationship? Yet it is possible for your fondness and admiration to recede to barely detectable levels and still be revivable. In such a case, the key to reinvigorating fondness and admiration is to get in the habit of scanning for qualities and actions that you can appreciate. And then, let your partner know what you've observed and are grateful for. These everyday thank-yous don't have to be about momentous acts on your spouse's part. Search for the small, everyday moments. Catch your partner doing some little thing right and then offer a genuine appreciation like "I love the way you handled the teacher conference yesterday" or "Thanks for making my sister feel welcome here" or even "You look so hot in that outfit, I'm having all kinds of bad thoughts."

Sometimes couples resist searching for and expressing gratitude for their spouse's positive behavior because, they tell me, doing so feels "phony" to them. But developing a positive habit doesn't "sugarcoat" a relationship. Instead it resets it to a *more realistic* perspective. Just knowing this can make all the difference for couples who are feeling pessimistic about their partner and marriage. Research by Elizabeth Robinson and Gail Price brings home this happy truth. They had objective, trained observers count how many positive acts they witnessed between a couple during the course of an evening. They then asked the spouses themselves to tally their positive interactions. When the researchers compared the scores the couple gave themselves with those of the objective observers, they discovered that couples who described themselves as unhappily married only noticed *half* of the positive interactions that actually occurred. Because they were so used to tuning in to their partner's mistakes, they each missed a full 50 percent of their partner's positive actions.

FONDNESS AND ADMIRATION QUESTIONNAIRE

To assess the current state of your fondness and admiration system, answer the following.

Read each statement and circle T for "true" or F for "false."

1. I can easily list the three things I most admire about my partner. **T F**
2. When we are apart, I often think fondly of my partner. **T F**
3. I will often find some way to tell my partner "I love you." **T F**
4. I often touch or kiss my partner affectionately. **T F**
5. My partner really respects me. **T F**
6. I feel loved and cared for in this relationship. **T F**

7. I feel accepted and liked by my partner. **T F**
8. My partner finds me sexy and attractive. **T F**
9. My partner turns me on sexually. **T F**
10. There is fire and passion in this relationship. **T F**
11. Romance is definitely still a part of our relationship. **T F**
12. I am really proud of my partner. **T F**
13. My partner really enjoys my achievements and accomplishments.
    T F
14. I can easily tell you why I married my partner. **T F**
15. If I had it all to do over again, I would marry the same person. **T F**
16. We rarely go to sleep without some show of love or affection. **T F**
17. When I come into a room, my partner is glad to see me. **T F**
18. My partner appreciates the things I do in this marriage. **T F**
19. My spouse generally likes my personality. **T F**
20. Our sex life is generally satisfying. **T F**

Scoring: Give yourself 1 point for each "true" answer.

10 or higher: This is an area of strength for your relationship. Because you value each other highly, you have a shield that can protect you from becoming overwhelmed by any negativity that also exists between you. Although it might seem obvious to you that people who are in love have a high regard for each other, it's common for spouses to lose sight of some of their fondness and admiration over time. Remember that this fondness and admiration is a gift worth protecting. Completing the exercises in this chapter from time to time will help you to reaffirm your positive feelings for each other.

Below 10: Your marriage could stand some improvement in this area. Don't be discouraged by a low score. There are many couples in whom the fondness and admiration system has not died but is buried under layers of negativity, hurt feelings, and betrayal. By reviving the positive feelings that still lie deep below, you can vastly improve your marriage.

If your fondness and admiration are being chipped away, the route to bringing them back always begins with realizing how valuable they are. Remember that they are crucial to the long-term happiness of a relationship because they prevent contempt—one of the marriage-killing four horsemen—from becoming an over-whelming presence in your life. Contempt is a corrosive that, over time, breaks down the bond between husband and wife. The better in touch you are with your deep-seated positive feelings for each other, the less likely that you will act with contempt toward your spouse when you have a difference of opinion.

Fanning the Flames

There's nothing complicated about reviving or enhancing your fondness and admiration. Even long-buried positive feelings can be exhumed simply by thinking and talking about them. You can do this by meditating a bit on your partner and what makes you treasure him or her. If you're feeling out of practice or have too much stress or anger to do this "free form," the following exercises will guide you. As simple as these exercises may seem to be, they have enormous power. When you acknowledge and openly discuss positive aspects of your partner and your marriage, your bond is strengthened. This makes it much easier to address the problem areas in your marriage and initiate positive changes. Feel free to work through these exercises as often as you wish. They are not intended only for troubled relationships. If your marriage is stable and happy, these exercises are an excellent way to heighten the romance.

EXERCISE 1: "I APPRECIATE . . ."

From the list below, select five appreciations you would like to express toward your partner in your own words, adding an example of when your partner demonstrated each action or displayed the positive qualities you are appreciating. In my workshops, I can see the benefit of this exercise immediately. Couples who began the session sitting stiffly and awkwardly suddenly relax. The room fills with laughter. Watching these couples while they engage in this exercise, I can tell that they are rediscovering something they had misplaced.

Thanks for making dinner. It was delicious.

Thanks for taking care of the kids.

Thanks for being such a great dad.

Thanks for cleaning up the kitchen.

Thanks for doing the laundry.

Thanks for supporting me when I talked about my stress.

Thanks for doing the dishes.

Thanks for listening to how my day went.

Thanks for being understanding when I talked about that rude person I met.

I enjoyed making love to you.

I really appreciated you being so affectionate lately.

I really enjoyed the conversation at dinner.

Thanks for being such a great mom.

Taking a walk together was really nice.

I really appreciated your giving me a hug.

That is a fantastic color on you.

Thanks for spending time with me.

Thank you for caring about what I need.

Thanks for bringing me flowers.

Thank you for desiring me.

It matters to me a lot when you are so great with the kids.

The way you treat my family means a lot to me.

Thanks for making me feel like I come first in your life.

Thanks for putting on music that I love.

Thanks for all the driving you are doing.

Thanks for working so hard for our family.

Thank you for taking me out to dinner. That was great.

Thanks for taking a bath with me.

You taste delicious.

Thank you for listening to me.

Thanks for calling the plumber (electrician, handyman, carpenter, gardener, etc.).

Thank you for just being there when I felt sad.

Thank you for being empathetic with me.

Thank you for being on my side.

Thanks for taking the kids to the pediatrician.

Thank you for comforting me.

Thank you for being gentle with me.

I had fun at the party. Thank you for being with me.

You are a great kisser.

Thank you for holding me.

Thanks for spending time with the kids.

Thanks for saving money for us.

Thank you for laughing.

Thank you for telling me what you need.

Thanks for driving me.

Thanks for giving me some time to myself.

I can hardly keep my hands off you.

Thank you for greeting me so warmly when I come home.

I really appreciate that drive we took.

Thanks for taking over the chores.

I loved the picnic we had.

You look great tonight.

Thanks for taking care of me when I was sick.

Thank you for telling me how you feel.

I love touching you here.

I appreciate what a loyal partner you are.

You smell so good.

Thank you for loving me.

Thanks for making our home so beautiful.

Thanks for spending time with my family.

Thanks for making coffee for me.

Those pastries were delicious. Thanks for getting them.

Thanks for calling the doctor when I needed an appointment.

Thanks for the way you are paying the bills.

Thanks for sticking up for me when I got criticized.

EXERCISE 2: THE HISTORY AND PHILOSOPHY OF YOUR RELATIONSHIP

Below is a version of the questionnaire that led Rory and Lisa to reconnect with their fondness and admiration for each other. Completing this questionnaire together will bring you face-to-face with the early years of your relationship, and help you remember how and why you became a couple. You will need a few hours of uninterrupted time to complete this exercise. There are no right or wrong answers to these questions—they are merely meant to guide you in recalling the love and perspective on marriage that led you to join your lives in the first place. Be sure to direct your thoughts toward positive memories—you definitely don't want to turn this exercise into a gripe session!

Part One: Your History

1. Discuss how the two of you met and got together. What were your first impressions of each other? What made your spouse stand out?

2. What do you remember most about beginning to date? What types of activities did you do together? What were some of the highlights?

3. How long did you know each other before you married? Talk about how you made the decision to marry. Was it easy or difficult? Were you in love? Of all the people in the world, what led you to decide that this was the person?

4. Share memories of your wedding and your honeymoon if you had one. What do you each remember most?

5. Recall your first year of marriage. Were there any adjustments you needed to make?

6. What about the transition to becoming parents? What was this period like for each of you?

7. Looking back over the years, what moments stand out as really happy times in your marriage? What is a good time for you as a couple? Has this changed over the years?

8. Many relationships go through periods of ups and downs. Would

you say that this is true of yours? Can you describe some of these periods?

9. Looking back over the years, what moments stand out as the really hard times? Why do you think you stayed together? How did you get through these difficult times?

10. Have you stopped doing things together that once gave you pleasure? Explore these with each other.

Part Two: Your Philosophy of Marriage

11. Why do you think some marriages work while others don't? Discuss two couples you know who you agree have a particularly good or bad relationship. What is the difference between these two marriages? How does yours compare to each of them?

12. Talk about your parents' marriages. Would you say they were very similar to or different from your own marriage?

13. Draw a chart or timeline of your marriage, noting its major turning points, ups, and downs. What were the happiest times for you? For your partner? How has your marriage changed over the years?

Most couples find that recalling their history recharges their relationship. Answering these questions often reminds couples of the love and great expectations that inspired their decision to marry in the first place. This can give couples who thought their marriage was over the glimmerings of hope that lead them to struggle on to save it. Just repeating the two exercises above from time to time may be enough to salvage and strengthen your fondness and admiration for each other.

Learning to Cherish Your Partner

How often do you think happily about your partner when you're *apart*? Do you reflect with pride on his or her many wonderful traits? Such thoughts comprise *cherishing*, which is a critical component of a couple's fondness-and-admiration system. Cherishing is a habit of mind in which, when you are separated during the course of the day, you maximize thoughts of your partner's positive qualities and minimize thoughts of negative ones. This active focusing on your partner's merits allows you to nurture gratefulness for what you have instead of resenting what is missing. Many couples do not realize they are neglecting to cherish each other. Fortunately, this is easily corrected. The following exercises can help you get into this crucial habit.

EXERCISE 3: CHERISHING YOUR PARTNER

Part One: From the list below, check ten qualities that you cherish in your partner. For each, note one recent occasion when your partner displayed it. Then say to yourself, "I am really lucky to be with my partner." Keep this list handy, and use it when you are alone to focus on your fond feelings toward your partner and trigger a sense of gratitude.

Part Two: Write your partner a love note expressing how much you cherish him or her for these qualities. Read it aloud to your partner during a romantic date.

WHAT I REALLY CHERISH ABOUT MY PARTNER IS THAT SHE OR HE IS SO:

Active	Caring	Determined
Adaptable	Cheerful	Devoted
Adventurous	Clever	Diligent
Ambitious	Commanding	Disciplined
Appreciative	Compassionate	Discriminating
Authentic	Confident	Dynamic
Aware	Conscientious	Eager
Balanced	Considerate	Easygoing
Bold	Courageous	Empathetic
Brave	Creative	Energetic
Bright	Curious	Enterprising
Calm	Daring	Ethical
Capable	Dedicated	Exuberant
Careful	Dependable	Fair

Fascinating	Loyal	Self-sufficient
Feisty	Mature	Sensitive
Flexible	Mellow	Sharp
Forgiving	Motivated	Sincere
Friendly	Natural	Skillful
Fun	Neat	Smart
Funny	Nurturing	Sociable
Generous	Observant	Spiritual
Gentle	Open-minded	Spontaneous
Giving	Optimistic	Stable
Gutsy	Organized	Steady
Happy	Original	Strong
Hardworking	Outgoing	Studious
Healthy	Patient	Successful
Honest	Peaceful	Supportive
Honorable	Perceptive	Surprising
Humble	Persevering	Sympathetic
Humorous	Persistent	Talented
Idealistic	Pleasant	Thorough
Imaginative	Positive	Thoughtful
Independent	Practical	Tireless
Ingenious	Principled	Tolerant
Inquisitive	Private	Trusting
Insightful	Problem-solving	Trustworthy
Intelligent	Proud	Truthful
Interesting	Quick-witted	Understanding
Intuitive	Quiet	Unique
Inventive	Rational	Unselfish
Joyful	Reasonable	Upbeat
Kind	Reflective	Vigilant
Knowledgeable	Reliable	Warm
Laid-back	Resilient	Wise
Lighthearted	Resourceful	Witty
Likable	Respectful	Worthy
Lively	Responsible	Other _____
Lovable	Self-confident	
Loving	Self-sacrificing	

EXERCISE 4: A SEVEN-WEEK COURSE IN FONDNESS AND ADMIRATION

This exercise is designed to get you into the habit of cherishing your partner. If you are angry, stressed, or feeling distant from your spouse, you may tend to focus on his or her negative characteristics. This leads to distress-maintaining thoughts, which in turn leave you feeling ever more distant and isolated in your marriage. This exercise counteracts that tendency by training you to focus on your partner's positive characteristics, even if you aren't having such a great day together.

For each day below there is a positive statement, or thought, followed by a task. Think about each statement, and say it to yourself many times throughout the day while you and your spouse are apart. In some cases, the thought may not seem to apply to your spouse or your marriage, especially if your fondness and admiration have dimmed. Keep in mind that the statement does not have to describe the typical state of affairs between you at the present time. If you can think of a single instant or episode where the statement applied, focus on that memory. For example, if you're not feeling overly attracted to your spouse these days, focus on one area of his or her anatomy that does appeal to you. Also be sure to complete the simple task that follows each positive statement. Do the exercise each day, no matter how you happen to feel about your relationship or your spouse. Don't stop even if you just had a major blowup or are feeling very distant from each other.

Although this exercise might sound silly or hokey, it is based on a wide body of research into the power of rehearsing positive thoughts. This approach is one of the tenets of cognitive therapy, which has proven highly successful in helping people overcome depression. When people fall into a depression, their thinking may become disordered—they see everything in an extremely negative light, which just adds to their sense of hopelessness. But if, over time, they deliberately accustom their mind to a different, positive way of thinking, the sense of hopelessness can be lifted.

This exercise is an experiment in offering the same hope to marriage. What you're really doing is rehearsing a more positive way to think about your partner and your relationship. Like any rehearsal, if you do it often enough, the words (and more important, the thoughts) will become second nature.

Note: Since most couples spend time apart on Monday through Friday, those are the days that are specified in the schedule below. You can switch the actual days around to better fit your schedule (if, for example, you work on the weekends), as long as you do the exercise five days a week.

Week 1

MONDAY
> Thought: I am genuinely fond of my partner.
> Task: List one characteristic you find endearing or lovable.

TUESDAY
> Thought: I can easily speak of the good times in our marriage.
> Task: Pick one good time and write a sentence about it.

WEDNESDAY
> Thought: I can easily remember romantic, special times in our marriage.
> Task: Pick one such time and think about it.

THURSDAY
> Thought: I am physically attracted to my partner.
> Task: Think of one physical attribute you like.

FRIDAY
> Thought: My partner has specific qualities that make me proud.
> Task: Write down one characteristic that makes you proud.

Week 2

MONDAY
> Thought: I feel a genuine sense of "we" as opposed to "I" in this marriage.
> Task: Think of one thing that you both have in common.

TUESDAY
> Thought: We have the same general beliefs and values.
> Task: Describe one belief you share.

WEDNESDAY

Thought: We have common goals.

Task: List one such goal.

THURSDAY

Thought: My spouse is my best friend.

Task: Think about a secret you've shared with your partner.

FRIDAY

Thought: I get lots of support in this marriage.

Task: Think of a time when your spouse was very supportive of you.

Week 3

MONDAY

Thought: My home is a place to come to get support and reduce stress.

Task: List a time when your spouse helped you reduce stress.

TUESDAY

Thought: I can easily recall the time we first met.

Task: Describe that first meeting on paper.

WEDNESDAY

Thought: I remember many details about deciding to get married.

Task: Write a sentence describing what you remember.

THURSDAY

Thought: I can recall our wedding and honeymoon.

Task: Describe one thing about them you enjoyed.

FRIDAY

Thought: We divide up household chores in a fair way.

Task: Describe one way you do this on a regular basis. If your partner doesn't share chores, think of other ways he or she contributes. If you don't do your share, decide on a chore you will take on (such as doing the laundry).

Week 4

MONDAY

Thought: We are able to plan well and have a sense of control over our lives together.

Task: Describe one activity you planned together.

TUESDAY

Thought: I am proud of this marriage.

Task: List two things about your marriage that make you proud.

WEDNESDAY

Thought: I am proud of my family.

Task: Recall a specific time when you especially felt this pride.

THURSDAY

Thought: I don't like things about my partner, but I can live with them.

Task: What is one minor fault you have adapted to?

FRIDAY

Thought: This marriage is a lot better than most I have seen.

Task: Think of a marriage you know that's awful.

Week 5

MONDAY

Thought: I was really lucky to meet my spouse.

Task: List one benefit of being married to your spouse.

TUESDAY

Thought: Marriage is sometimes a struggle, but it's worth it.

Task: Think of one difficult time you successfully weathered together.

WEDNESDAY

Thought: There is a lot of affection between us.

Task: Plan a surprise gift for your mate for tonight.

THURSDAY

Thought: We are genuinely interested in each other.

Task: Think of something to do or talk about that would be interesting.

FRIDAY

Thought: We are good companions.

Task: Plan an outing together.

Week 6

MONDAY

Thought: There is lots of good loving in my marriage.

Task: Think of a special trip you took together.

TUESDAY

Thought: My partner is an interesting person.

Task: Plan something to ask your mate about that interests both of you.

WEDNESDAY

Thought: We respond well to each other.

Task: Write and share a love letter to your spouse.

THURSDAY

Thought: If I had it to do over again, I would marry the same person.

Task: Plan an anniversary (or other) getaway.

FRIDAY

Thought: There is lots of mutual respect in my marriage.

Task: Consider taking a class together (sailing, ballroom dancing, etc.). Or tell your spouse about a time recently when you admired something he or she did.

Week 7

MONDAY

Thought: Sex is usually (or can be) quite satisfying in this marriage.

Task: Plan an erotic evening for the two of you.

TUESDAY

Thought: We have come a long way together.

Task: Think of all you have accomplished as a team.

WEDNESDAY

Thought: I think we can weather any storm together.

Task: Reminisce about having made it through a hard time.

THURSDAY

Thought: We enjoy each other's sense of humor.

Task: Plan to watch a comedy together.

FRIDAY

Thought: My mate can be very cute.

Task: Get very dressed up for an elegant evening together. Or if you don't like that kind of thing, plan another kind of evening out you would enjoy.

By the end of the seven weeks, you're likely to find that your perspective on your partner and your marriage is far sunnier.

Singing each other's praises can only benefit your marriage. But in order to ensure that the gains continue, you need to put your respect and affection to work. In the next chapter you'll do just that, by using them as the foundation for revamping—or reviving—your marriage's sense of romance.

6

Principle 3:
Turn Toward Each Other
Instead of Away

*I*f the Love Lab's footage were ever aired in movie theaters, no one would be winning any Oscars. Our archives are filled with endlessly dull scenes in which, for example, the husband looks out the picture window and says, "Wow, look at that boat," and the wife peers over her magazine and says, "Yeah, it looks like that big schooner we saw last summer, remember?" and the husband grunts.

You might think I'd consider viewing hour after hour of such scenes unbearably boring. On the contrary, my favorite Love Lab tapes are the sort that any competent Hollywood film editor would readily delete. That's because I find deep drama in the little moments. Will they read or listen to the news together or silently alone? Will they chat while they eat lunch? I watch filled with suspense because I know: couples who engage in lots of such interaction tend to remain happy. What's really occurring in these brief exchanges is that the husband and wife are connecting— they are attuning by *turning toward* each other. Couples who do so are building mutual trust. Those who don't are likely to lose their way. I rarely see small moments of connection in the tapes of couples who later divorce or report their marriage has permanently soured. More often, the wife doesn't even look up from her magazine—and if she does, her husband doesn't acknowledge what she says.

Hollywood has distorted our notions of romance and what makes passion sizzle. Watching Humphrey Bogart gather teary-eyed Ingrid Bergman into his arms may make your heart pound, but real-life romance is fueled by far more humdrum scenes. It is kept alive each time you let your spouse know he or she is valued during the grind of everyday life. In marriage, couples are always making what I call "bids" for each other's attention, affection, humor, or support. Bids can be as minor as asking for a back-rub or as significant as seeking help in carrying the burden when an aging parent is ill. The partner responds to each bid either by turning toward the spouse or turning away. A tendency to turn toward your partner is the basis of trust, emotional connection, passion, and a satisfying sex life. Comical as it may sound, romance is strengthened in the supermarket aisle when your partner asks, "Are we out of butter?" and you answer, "I don't know. Let me go get some just in case," instead of shrugging apathetically. It grows when you know your spouse is having a bad day at work and you take a few seconds out of your schedule to send him an encouraging text. In all of these instances, partners are making a choice to turn toward each other rather than away.

Our research confirms the central role that bids play in a relationship. In our six-year follow-up of newlyweds, we found that couples who remained married had turned toward their partner's bids an average of 86 percent of the time in the Love Lab, while those who ended up divorced had averaged only 33 percent. It's telling that most of the arguments between couples in both groups were not about specific topics like money or sex, but resulted from those failed bids for connection. There's a reason that seemingly small events are fundamental to a relationship's future: Each time partners turn toward each other, they are funding what I've come to call their emotional bank account. They are building up savings that, like money in the bank, can serve as a cushion when times get rough, when they're faced with a major life stress or conflict. Because they have stored an abundance of goodwill, such couples

are less likely to teeter over into distrust and chronic neg
during hard times.

The first step in turning toward each other more is simply to
be aware of how crucial these mini-moments are, not only to your
marriage's trust level but to its ongoing sense of romance. For
many couples, just realizing that they shouldn't take their everyday
interactions for granted makes an enormous difference in their relationship. Remind yourself that being helpful to each other will
do far more for the strength and passion of your marriage than a
two-week Bahamas getaway.

Many people think that the secret to reconnecting with their
partner is a vacation by the sea. But a romantic outing only turns
up the heat if a couple has kept the pilot light burning by staying
in touch in the little ways. It's easy to imagine Justine and Michael,
the couple who recalled their wedding and courtship with such
delight, at a candlelit restaurant. But sit Peter and Cynthia at the
next table and their evening would most likely be a fiasco, filled
with accusations, recriminations, or awkward silences.

One virtue of turning toward each other is that it is so easy to
accomplish. It only takes a small gesture to lead to another and
then another. "Turning toward" operates under a law of positive
feedback—like a snowball rolling downhill, it can start small yet
generate enormous results. In other words, you don't have to turn
toward your partner in a very dramatic way to see the benefit.
Just get started, and things will improve by themselves. Here's an
example from my own life: One day I overheard Julie grumbling
softly as she unloaded the dryer. I could easily have pretended not
to notice. But that grumble was a bid, a quiet one, but definitely a
bid. So I asked her what the matter was, and she said, "I don't mind
doing laundry, but I hate folding it." Well, I happen to like mindless
tasks like folding shirts! They give me a sense of accomplishment,
sort of like going over streams of numbers in the lab. So I turned
toward my wife by taking over the folding. I piled the laundry on
the bed, turned on music featuring jazz composer Bill Evans and
his magical piano, and I was in heaven. (Like many people, whenever possible, I try to do chores in a very self-indulgent, enjoyable

way.) Eventually Julie drifted into the room. I knew she expected me to ask her for help, even though she hates folding laundry. Instead, we both relaxed and enjoyed the music while I continued to fold. Julie pointed out that it had been a long time since we'd been to our favorite local jazz club. So we ended up heading there for dinner. In the end, my turning toward that pile of laundry turned out to be very romantic for us.

IS YOUR MARRIAGE PRIMED FOR ROMANCE?

To get a good sense of how your relationship is faring (or is likely to fare in the future), answer the following questions.

Read each statement and circle T for "true" or F for "false."

1. We enjoy doing small activities together, like washing the dishes or watching TV. **T F**
2. I look forward to spending my free time with my partner. **T F**
3. At the end of the day, my partner is glad to see me. **T F**
4. My partner is usually interested in hearing my views. **T F**
5. I really enjoy discussing things with my partner. **T F**
6. My partner is one of my best friends. **T F**
7. We are spiritually very compatible. **T F**
8. We just love talking to each other. **T F**
9. When we go out together, the time goes very quickly. **T F**
10. We always have a lot to say to each other. **T F**
11. We have a lot of fun together. **T F**
12. My partner tells me when he or she has had a bad day. **T F**
13. I think my partner would consider me a very close friend. **T F**
14. We tend to share the same basic values. **T F**
15. We like to spend time together in similar ways. **T F**
16. We really have a lot of common interests. **T F**
17. We have many of the same dreams and goals. **T F**
18. We like to do a lot of the same things. **T F**
19. Even though our interests are somewhat different, I enjoy my partner's interests. **T F**
20. Whatever we do together, we tend to have a good time. **T F**

Scoring: Give yourself 1 point for each "true" answer.

12 or higher: Congratulations! Turning toward is an area of strength in your marriage. Because you are so often "there" for each other during the minor events in your lives, you have built up a hefty emotional bank account that should support you over any rough patches in your marriage (and keep many at bay). It's those little moments that you rarely think about—when you forward a joke that's making the social-media rounds, set the table together, or have a quickie catch-up call while you're both still at work—that make up the heart and soul of a marriage. Having a surplus in your emotional bank account is what makes romance last and gets you through hard times, bad moods, and major life changes.

Below 12: Your relationship could stand some improvement in this area. By learning to turn toward each other more during the minor moments in your day, you will make your marriage not only more stable but more romantic. Every time you make the effort to listen and respond to what your spouse says, to help him or her, you make your marriage a little better.

Two Obstacles to Turning Toward

In my work with couples, I've noticed that two situations in particular tend to interfere with partners' turning toward each other and building up their sense of trust. Here's how you can prevent these roadblocks in your relationship.

1. "Missing" a bid because it's wrapped in anger or other negative emotion.
Sometimes, and especially if a relationship is going through a rocky period, a spouse may not recognize when the partner is making a bid for connection because it comes out sounding negative. The partner then reacts to the negativity and misses the hidden plea. For example, Lena says to her husband, Carl, in exasperation, "It would never occur to you to clear the table, would it?" Carl doesn't hear Lena's bid ("Please clear the table tonight"). Instead, he hears criticism, the first horseman. So it's no surprise that he responds

with defensiveness: "Well, when do *you* ever fill the gas tank?" From there, the argument escalates.

What if, instead, Carl responded by saying, "Oh, you're right. Sorry," and then cleared the table? He'd score enormous points and probably earn a sheepish smile from his wife, who might then realize that her harsh start-up was uncalled-for. Similarly, say Carl wants Lena to come to bed but she is returning e-mails. His bid is, "Please come to bed with me." But it comes out as, "You're dealing with your e-mails *now*? You had all night!" If Lena focuses on his plea and not his tone, she has the opportunity to respond positively: "Good point. I'll be right there."

So before you reply defensively to your partner, pause for a moment and search for a bid underneath your partner's harsh words. Then, focus on the bid, not the delivery. If you find it difficult not to react defensively, first take five really deep breaths, counting slowly from one to six as you inhale and then slowly from seven to fifteen as you exhale. Then say to your partner, "I want to respond to you positively, so can you please tell me what you need right now from me? I really want to know." If wrapping bids in criticism is a habit in your relationship and negativity is scrambling the signals between you, work on softening your start-up (see page 162).

2. Being distracted by the wired world.

In my work with couples, I've noticed that the Internet and digital devices pose a growing challenge to turning toward. Instant access and interaction with the outside world certainly offer enormous social benefits. It has become far easier to connect, and reconnect, with friends and kin and for isolated, lonely people to reach out for support and understanding from like-minded others. However, there are downsides to all this connection. The ease with which other people can contact us at all hours of the day and night can take a toll on the intimate communication that fuels both romantic love and family life. Of course, it doesn't help that many workplaces expect employees to be available via e-mail or social media during off hours.

In some cases, constantly checking e-mails, postings, tweets, and text messages can lead to a sort of addiction in which distraction itself becomes a habit. In his book *The Shallows: What the Internet Is Doing to Our Brains*, Nicholas Carr documents research that indicates self-distraction has become a permanent, unconscious habit for many people. All of those electronic devices have gotten us used to having our concentration and focus interrupted. This culture of distraction doesn't benefit intimate relationships, which require the opposite: the habit of being aware and paying attention. Often both partners will complain that the other is preoccupied and unavailable. The old cliché of the husband who hides behind the newspaper has been replaced by the spouse of either gender who is tapping out texts, scanning social media, or engrossed in one of those irresistible cell-phone games.

I want to tell you a little story that underlines just how important it is to be present with your partner. As part of a research study, my colleague Alyson Shapiro and I carefully analyzed videos of parents interacting with their three-month-olds. We found that the infants were totally focused on the present, and that nothing riveted them more than their parent's face and voice. But the parents didn't always realize when their babies wanted to play because young infants operate on a much slower time scale. For example, if a father stuck out his tongue at his newborn, the baby might imitate him—but not until a minute or two later because this feat takes great effort for a young baby. Only the parents who continued to focus and play patiently with their newborn had the pleasure of witnessing their child's amazing imitation, which was really a form of communication. Watching those videos really brought home to me how important it is to be truly present and not split your attention into a million pieces when engaging with someone you love—of any age.

Sometimes couples unconsciously use devices as self-distraction during marital conflict. For example, a spouse who is anxious about communication or ready to stonewall may use these diversions to shut down interaction. Instead of leaving the room or changing the subject when a delicate marital issue arises, he or she may just shift attention to the ever-present cell phone or tablet.

In such cases, the device is enabling turning away. Usually, though, I don't think high-tech distraction and the resulting inattention is deliberate or caused by a marital problem. We just don't realize how habit-forming these devices can become.

The best solution to this growing problem is for both partners to acknowledge if it *is* a concern between them and to establish rules of etiquette that work for both of them. (You'll find more about this on page 196.)

**Couples often ignore each other's emotional
needs out of mindlessness, not malice.**

If you feel that you or your partner could still benefit from help in turning toward each other, the following exercises are for you. They will make the third principle an easier, more natural part of your lives together.

EXERCISE 1: THE EMOTIONAL BANK ACCOUNT

Keeping an account in your head of how much your partner has been connecting with you in little ways can greatly benefit your marriage. But for some couples, the concept works best if they make their emotional bank account "real." You can do this by drawing a simple ledger and giving your partner one point each time he or she has turned toward you during the course of the day. You probably wouldn't want to document every encouraging nod you receive during a conversation. But you would include entries for such events as "Called me at work to see how my meeting went" and "Took our van to the car wash."

Share your ledgers with each other, but be careful not to turn this into a competition or a *quid pro quo* where you track each other's account "balance" and keep tabs on who has done what for whom. That approach defeats the purpose of this exercise. **The goal is to make small improvements by noticing how your partner has been turning toward and giving.** If you've gotten out of the habit of thanking your partner for turning toward you, it may take some time to see the benefits of this exercise. The big challenge is to notice when your partner *does* turn toward you. Remember: unhappy couples tend to *under*estimate how often this occurs.

Below is a long list of activities that some couples do together—everything from walking the dog to going bowling. Choose the three that you most appreciate your partner having done in the past. You can also circle an item if you and your spouse have done it jointly. Then simply thank your partner for having turned toward you in these ways.

1. Reunite at the end of the day and talk about how it went.
2. Shop for groceries. Make up the shopping list.
3. Cook dinner, bake.
4. Clean house, do laundry.
5. Shop together for gifts or clothes (for self, kids, or friends).
6. Go out (no kids) for brunch or dinner, or to your favorite haunt or bar.
7. Watch or read the news together.
8. Help each other with a self-improvement plan (e.g., a new class, weight loss, exercise, a new career).
9. Plan and host a dinner party.
10. Call and/or think about each other during the workday.
11. Stay overnight at a romantic hideaway.
12. Eat breakfast together during the workweek.
13. Go to a church, mosque, or synagogue together.
14. Do yard work, shovel the walk, do home repairs, do car maintenance and washing.
15. Perform committee work in the community (e.g., volunteering).
16. Exercise together.
17. Go on weekend outings (e.g., picnics, drives).
18. Stay in touch with/spend time with kin (parents, in-laws, siblings).
19. Watch TV or stream videos.
20. Order takeout.
21. Double-date with friends.
22. Talk or read together by an open fire.
23. Listen to music.
24. Go dancing or attend a concert, nightclub, jazz club, or theater.

25. Host your child's birthday party.
26. Take your child to lessons.
27. Attend your child's sporting event or performance (recital, play, etc.).
28. Pay bills.
29. Write letters or cards.
30. Work at home, but still be together in some way.
31. Go to a party.
32. Commute to work together.
33. Celebrate milestones in your children's lives (confirmation, graduation).
34. Celebrate other milestones in your lives (e.g., promotion, retirement).
35. Play computer games, surf the Internet.
36. Supervise your children's playdates.
37. Plan your future together. Dream.
38. Walk the dog.
39. Read out loud together.
40. Play a board game or a card game.
41. Put on plays or skits together.
42. Run errands together on a weekend.
43. Engage in hobbies (e.g., painting, sculpting, making music).
44. Talk over drinks (alcohol, coffee, or tea).
45. Find time to just talk without interruptions—find time for your spouse to really listen to you.
46. Gossip (talk about other people).
47. Attend a funeral.
48. Help out other people.
49. Hunt for a new house or apartment.
50. Test-drive new cars.
51. Other _____.

Now, share your top three choices with each other so that you both know which "turning toward" activities have scored you the most emotional points.

EXERCISE 2: THE STRESS-REDUCING CONVERSATION

Although you can earn points in your emotional bank account through just about any everyday activity listed above, we have found that the most effective one is the first: "Reunite at the end of the day and talk about how it went." This is because such discussions can be vital stress reducers that help you manage tensions outside your relationship. Learning to cope with these external pressures is crucial to a marriage's long-term health, according to research by Neil Jacobson.

Many couples automatically have this "How was your day, dear?" conversation, perhaps at the dinner table or after the kids fall asleep. But too often their discussion does not help either of them relax. Instead, it increases their stress levels because they end up feeling frustrated with each other for not really listening. If that's the case between you and your partner, changing your approach to these catch-up conversations can ensure that they do indeed help you both unwind.

For starters, think about the timing of the chat. Some people want to unburden themselves when they're barely through the door. But others need to decompress on their own for a while before they're ready to interact. Be aware of the ideal timing for each of you so that you are both in the mood to talk.

On a typical day, spend twenty to thirty minutes on this conversation. The cardinal rule is that you talk about whatever is on your mind outside your marriage. This is not the time to discuss any conflicts between you. Instead, it's an opportunity to support each other emotionally concerning other areas in your lives. This exercise is really a form of active listening, in which you respond to each other's venting with empathy and without judgment. Since the griping isn't about each other or your marriage, it's much easier to express support and understanding.

Sometimes your end-of-the-day discussion will be about celebrating good news—like a mini-victory in parenting or at work. In such cases, active listening means sharing and relishing the moment with your partner. Often, however, these conversations are opportunities to unload about minor (or sometimes major) irritants or problems. If

lining to your partner's sadness, fear, or anger, it is that
to it you strengthen the trust between you. Experiences
nerate the most negative emotions also have the capacity to
uild the strongest bonds.

In some cases, one or both partners find it uncomfortable to discuss each other's feelings. Often this uneasiness is rooted in childhood prohibitions against expressing negative emotions. If this is the case in your marriage, see "Coping with Your Partner's Sadness, Fear, and Anger" on page 103.

Here are detailed instructions for using active listening during the "Stress-Reducing Conversation."

1. **Take turns.** Each partner gets to be the complainer for fifteen minutes.
2. **Show genuine interest.** Don't let your mind or eyes wander. Stay focused on your partner. Ask questions. Make eye contact. Nod, say "Uh-huh," and so on.
3. **Don't give unsolicited advice.** When someone you love expresses pain, it is natural to want to fix the problem or make the person feel better. But oftentimes your spouse isn't asking you to come up with a solution at all—just to be a good listener or offer a ready shoulder to cry on. So unless your partner has specifically asked for help, don't try to fix the problem, change how your partner feels, or rescue him or her. Instead, your motto should be "Don't *do* something, just be there!"

   I see the fallout from unsolicited advice all the time in my work with couples. For example, Carrie was unhappy that her husband, Jeff, never shared his inner world with her. To find out what was happening between them, I had them carry out a stress-reducing conversation in my presence. Jeff began to complain about a difficult person he had to contend with at his volunteer work. Carrie immediately said, "I told you to resign from that job. It's too much stress for you." Jeff stopped talking, and Carrie turned to me, "You see how he clams up! What did I tell you?" I suggested they have the conversation again, but I instructed Carrie not to offer any advice this time. Instead she simply asked Jeff to tell her what made this person so insufferable. Eventually Jeff opened up, and they had a conversation that was satisfying to both of them.

Although this has changed somewhat over the years, I still find that in heterosexual couples it tends to be the husband who gets caught up in trying to solve his partner's problems. These men are often relieved when I tell them that it is not their responsibility to rescue their partner. In fact, such attempts to "save" her tend to backfire. When a wife shares her troubles, she usually reacts very negatively if her husband tries to give her advice right away. Instead, she wants to hear that he understands and feels compassion.

I'm not suggesting that it is never appropriate to problem-solve when your partner is upset. But to paraphrase psychologist Haim Ginott, the cardinal rule is "Understanding must precede advice." You have to let your partner know that you fully understand and empathize with the dilemma. Only then will he or she be receptive to suggestions.

4. **Communicate your understanding.** Let your spouse know that you empathize. If you tend to be on the quiet side or aren't in the habit of sharing emotions, you might be uncertain about what to say to show understanding. So here's a list of suggested phrases—use any that feel comfortable to you.

What a bummer.
I'd be stressed out, too.
I can see why you feel that way.
You're making total sense.
I get it.
You're in a tough spot here.
I wish you didn't have to go through that.
I'm on your side.
I wish I could have been there with you.
Oh, wow, that sounds terrible.
I totally agree with you.
No wonder you're upset.

It would be great to be free of this.

That must have annoyed you.

That sounds infuriating/frustrating.

I would have been disappointed, too.

That would have hurt my feelings, too.

That would make me feel sad/hurt/insecure/mad, too.

I would have trouble coping with that.

That sounds scary.

5. **Take your partner's side.** This means expressing support even if you think his or her perspective is unreasonable. Don't back the opposition—this will make your spouse resentful or dejected. If your wife's boss chewed her out for being five minutes late, don't say, "Oh, well, maybe Bud was just having a bad day." And certainly don't say, "Well, you shouldn't have been late." Instead, say, "That's so unfair!" The point isn't to be dishonest. It's just that timing is everything. When your partner comes to you for emotional support (rather than for advice), your job is not to cast moral judgment or to tell him or her what to do. It is to express empathy. In other words, your job is to say, "Poor baby!"

6. **Express a "we against others" attitude.** If your mate is feeling all alone in facing some difficulty, express solidarity. Let him or her know that the two of you are in this together.

7. **Show affection.** Hold your mate, put an arm on his or her shoulder, say, "I love you."

8. **Validate emotions.** Let your partner know that his or her feelings make sense to you. Phrases that communicate this include "Yeah, that is really so sad," "That would have me worried, too," and "I can see why you'd be annoyed about that."

Here are two brief examples of a stress-reducing conversation to give you an idea of what to do—and what not to.

DON'T:

HANK: I had another terrible meeting with Ethel today. She keeps challenging my knowledge, and she has been going to the boss telling him that she doubts my competence. I hate her.

WANDA: I think this is another example of you flying off the handle and overreacting. (*criticizing*) I have seen her be very constructive and reasonable. Maybe you are just not being sensitive to her concerns. (*siding with the enemy*)

HANK: The woman is out to get me.

WANDA: That's your paranoid streak coming out. You've got to try to control that. (*criticizing*)

HANK: Oh, forget it.

DO:

HANK: I had another terrible meeting with Ethel today. She keeps challenging my knowledge, and she has been going to the boss telling him that she doubts my competence. I hate her.

WANDA: I can't believe that woman! She is the meanest fighter and a terrible gossip. (*us against others*) What did you say? (*showing genuine interest*)

HANK: I told her she is just out to get me. And that she's not going to succeed.

WANDA: She can make anyone become paranoid. I'm sorry she's putting you through this. (*expressing affection*) I'd like to get even with her. (*us against others*)

HANK: So would I, but I think it'd be better to just forget it. Just ignore her.

WANDA: Your boss knows what she's like. Everyone does.

HANK: That's true. He doesn't like that she goes around saying everyone is incompetent but her.

WANDA: That's bound to backfire.

HANK: I hope so, or she'll give me an ulcer.

Below are some sample scenarios to help you practice being supportive during your spouse's whining session.

1. Your wife's brother yelled at her for not yet repaying money he loaned her two months ago. Your wife is feeling outraged and hurt by her brother's attitude. (She does owe him money.)

You say:

2. Your husband got a speeding ticket on his way home. "It was a speed trap!" he yells. "Everyone was going 80 mph. Why do I have to be the one who gets pulled over?"

   You say:

3. Your wife was late getting to a big job interview. Now she's worried she won't get the job. "I can't believe how stupid I was," she moans.

   You say:

4. Your husband asked his boss for a raise and was turned down. He got angry and stormed out of his boss's office. Now he's worried that his boss will hold this against him.

   You say:

Sample Answers

1. "I'm sorry he made you feel really hurt and angry." (Or "Poor baby.")
2. "How outrageous! That's so unfair!" (Or "Poor baby.")
3. "You weren't stupid. That could happen to anybody." (Or "Poor baby.")
4. "I understand how you feel." (Or "Poor baby.")

One last note: No one knows you better than your spouse. Sometimes advice may be just what you're looking for. The best strategy is to talk about what you'd each like from the other when you're feeling stressed. If your spouse is ranting about the promotion he didn't get, you can say something like, "You're obviously really upset about this. How can I help you? Do you need me just to listen, or do you want me to help you brainstorm what to do next?"

If you have this sort of conversation every day, it can't help but benefit your marriage. You'll come away with the conviction that your partner is on your side, and that's one of the foundations of a long-lasting friendship.

Coping with Your Partner's Sadness, Fear, and Anger

I have worked with couples who find that the de-stressing exercise above actually *adds* to their stress because one or both of them feel very uncomfortable listening to the other express negative emotions, even when they aren't the target. This is a form of turning away. I can't emphasize enough how beneficial it will be to your relationship to give your partner the gift of being there when he or she is upset. After years of studying couples in the lab and working with them directly, it has become clear to me that happy couples live by the credo **"When you are in pain, the world stops and I listen."** Of course, when your partner's negativity is directed at you, it's especially hard to listen. You'll find advice on handling that in chapter 9. But here, we are talking about those times in your day-to-day interactions when one of you shuts out the other's appeal for emotional support.

Usually this very common tendency to turn away from negative emotions is rooted in childhood. Clients will tell me that as children they knew their parents loved them but they didn't *show* it very often. They were raised in families that frowned on negativity and offered little or no comforting. Feeling or expressing fear or sadness meant you were a "wimp." A child's expression of anger was seen as a moral failing, a sign of disrespect, or even an indication of mental illness. Growing up in such an environment can teach you to compartmentalize your emotions so you become a self-reliant problem-solver who avoids "feelings." Because life presents us with plenty of hurdles, having a talent for problem-solving is certainly an asset. But in order to achieve real intimacy, you also need to be there for your partner, to see the world from his or her perspective and to empathize with negative feelings. If either of you finds it challenging to cope with the other's expression of emotional pain, the following tips will help.

1. **Acknowledge the difficulty.** Admitting to your partner that confronting and responding to negative emotions is tough for you is a great first step. Just making it known that you are willing to work on the issue can go a long way toward improving the situation.

2. **Self-soothe.** If you feel overwhelmed by your partner's emotions, use the self-soothing techniques recommended on page 181.

3. **Remember: the goal is understanding.** Don't try to problem-solve or minimize your partner's feelings. Just *tune in* to what he or she is expressing.

4. **Use exploratory statements and open-ended questions.** You want your partner to talk, so frame your reactions to what you're hearing as either exploratory statements or open-ended questions. These approaches both express support and encourage a response. (For more on open-ended questions, see page 60—Love Maps exercise.)

EXAMPLES OF EXPLORATORY STATEMENTS

Tell me the story of that.

I want to know everything you're feeling.

Nothing is more important to me right now than listening to you.

We have lots of time to talk.

Tell me your major concerns here.

I think you're being very clear. Go on.

Tell me all of your feelings here.

Tell me more about how you are seeing this situation.

Tell me the history of this situation.

EXAMPLES OF OPEN-ENDED QUESTIONS

What are your concerns? (This is my favorite question.)

Can you tell me more about what you're feeling?

What do you need from me right now?

What mixed feelings do you have?

What is your worst-case scenario?

What makes this situation so difficult or stressful?

Help me understand this situation from your point of view.
What are the most important points for you?
What are you most concerned about?
If you could change the attitude of one key person in this situation, who would it be?
Is there anything you want to add?

5. **Don't ask "Why?"** Here is a major exception to the suggestion that you ask open-ended questions: Avoid queries that start with "Why?" People who come from a problem-solving orientation tend to love this word. But in a discussion about what your partner is feeling, "Why?" will almost always sound like criticism. When you ask, "Why do you think that?" the other person is likely to hear, "Stop thinking that, you're wrong!" A more successful approach would be, "What leads you to think that?" or, "Help me understand how you decided that."

6. **Bear witness.** When someone is upset, they want to know that their experience matters to you, so they don't feel alone. You can give your partner this gift by *witnessing* his or her distress. This means making it clear that you are there for your partner, understanding and respecting the experience. A powerful way to do this is to repeat back what your partner says, in your own words. For example:

Your partner says: "I can't take my job anymore. It's too much. My boss is incompetent, and I have to do all the work."
You say: *It sounds like you're really stressed out because your boss is incompetent and you end up having to do not only your work but hers, too. Did I get it right?*

Part of witnessing your partner's distress is to acknowledge that his or her feelings make sense to you. For example:

Your partner says: "You should have heard how my brother talked to me on the phone. He is such a nasty piece of work, always putting me down."
You say: *So you're saying that your brother can be hostile and*

mean, right? I totally understand why you're upset. He's treated me that way, too!

7. **Use your partner's metaphors.** Sometimes people speak in metaphors, sort of like poetry. If you pick up on this when your partner is upset, and reflect it back as part of your response, you convey that you are fully aware of what he or she is experiencing. For example:

Your partner says: "This apartment is starting to feel like a prison."
You say: *Wow, sounds like you really feel trapped. Is that right? Am I getting it?*

Your partner says: "In my life, it feels like the train has left and I'm still standing on the platform."
You say: *So you feel like the world is passing you by and your own life is at a standstill. Is that right? I'm sure that does feel crappy.*

EXTRA TIPS FOR LISTENING TO SADNESS AND CRYING

Ask what's missing. When someone is sad, usually it's because they feel that they have lost someone or something. At times, what's missing will be obvious, such as when a parent dies. But on many occasions, it may not be so clear why your partner is feeling "at a loss." Asking can help him or her open up about the sadness. For example, Amber was moping around the house after her sister called to say she couldn't come over for lunch. Mario's first instinct was to say to his wife, "What's the big deal? You'll see her another day." But instead, he acknowledged Amber's sadness and asked where it was coming from. "You seem so sad about Ellen canceling. What's going on? Do you feel like you've lost something?" This question got Amber to acknowledge that Ellen seemed less interested in spending time with her since she'd become a mother. She missed feeling close to her sister.

Don't try to cheer up your partner. When someone is sad, it's a common response to attempt to make them smile, laugh, or otherwise erase their blues. But unless your partner asks for assistance in shaking the mood, it's usually more helpful to listen to sadness rather than trying to relieve it. Imagine that you're a traveler visiting the landscape of sadness. Your partner is the tour guide. This sort of "being there" when your partner is blue will bring you closer than the standard, "Don't cry!"

EXTRA TIPS FOR LISTENING TO ANGER

Don't take it personally. Your partner's anger is not about you. And even if it were, becoming defensive wouldn't help.

Don't ever tell your partner to "calm down." Your partner is likely to interpret this advice as a sign that you don't feel the anger is justified, or that expressing anger for whatever reason is not acceptable to you. Your goal here is not to change (or censor) your partner's emotions but to communicate that you understand and accept them.

Search out the goal and obstacle. Behind most anger is the feeling of being blocked from reaching a goal. For example, if your partner's ambition is to be promoted, the frustrating obstacle might be a supervisor who doesn't offer growth opportunities. If the goal is to feel special on his or her birthday, the obstacle might be a friend or relative who keeps forgetting it. Anger is not always rational, and you may not agree with your partner's perspective or his or her level of upset. But that doesn't change your job, which is to ask questions without judgment and express understanding and empathy.

EXTRA TIP FOR LISTENING TO FEAR AND STRESS

Don't minimize it. A common pitfall while listening to your partner express fear or worry is to minimize it as a way of reassuring. Phrases like "Don't be silly" and "There's nothing at all to be afraid of" may be well-intentioned, but they can come across as ridicule. In his book *The Gift of Fear*, security expert Gavin de Becker shows that our best guide for staying safe is to develop an intuitive sense of when we are confronting a dangerous situation or person. De Becker counsels that when we get such a gut feeling, we trust that fear *instead of dismissing it*. Even small worries or discomforts indicate that the person feels his everyday world is not a safe place.

Once your marriage gets set at a more positive level, it will be harder to knock it off course.

What to Do When Your Spouse Doesn't Turn Toward You

Considering how beneficial it is to turn toward each other, it's no wonder it can feel hurtful and rejecting when your spouse does the opposite. What steps should you take when this occurs? Very often couples turn away from each other not out of malice but out of mindlessness. They become distracted and start taking each other for granted. In such cases, realizing the importance of the little moments and paying more attention to them is usually sufficient to solve the problem. Sometimes there are deeper reasons why couples keep missing each other. For example, when one partner rebuffs the other, it could be a sign of hostility over some festering conflict. More commonly, I have found that when one spouse feels the other doesn't connect enough, the cause is a disparity in their respective needs for intimacy and independence.

Marriage is something of a dance. There are times when you feel drawn to your loved one and times when you feel the need to pull back and replenish your sense of autonomy. There's a wide spectrum of "normal" needs in this area—some people have a greater and more frequent desire for connection, others for independence. A marriage can work even if people fall on opposite ends of this spectrum—as long as they are able to understand the reasons for their feelings and respect their differences. If they don't, however, hurt feelings are likely to develop.

If you feel like your spouse gives you the cold shoulder in little ways throughout the day, or if your spouse's concept of closeness feels more like suffocation to you, the best thing you can do for your marriage is to talk it out. Reviewing these moments together will give you greater insight into each other and help you learn to give each other what you need. The following exercise can help.

EXERCISE 3: TALKING IT OUT

If one of you is feeling rebuffed by the other lately, or overwhelmed by your spouse's need for closeness, fill out the form below and then share your answers. There is no answer key for these questions; they are merely a point of departure for discussions with your spouse. The bottom line of this approach is that there isn't one reality when a couple misses each other in little ways. There are two equally legitimate perspectives. Once you understand and acknowledge this, you'll find that reconnecting just comes naturally.

DURING THIS EPISODE I FELT:

1. Defensive.	A great deal	Definitely	A little	Not at all
2. Hurt.	A great deal	Definitely	A little	Not at all
3. Angry.	A great deal	Definitely	A little	Not at all
4. Sad.	A great deal	Definitely	A little	Not at all
5. Misunderstood.	A great deal	Definitely	A little	Not at all
6. Criticized.	A great deal	Definitely	A little	Not at all
7. Worried.	A great deal	Definitely	A little	Not at all
8. Righteously indignant.	A great deal	Definitely	A little	Not at all
9. Unappreciated.	A great deal	Definitely	A little	Not at all
10. Unattractive.	A great deal	Definitely	A little	Not at all
11. Disgusted.	A great deal	Definitely	A little	Not at all
12. Disapproving.	A great deal	Definitely	A little	Not at all
13. Like leaving.	A great deal	Definitely	A little	Not at all

14. Like my opinions didn't matter.	A great deal	Definitely	A little	Not at all
15. I had no idea what I was feeling.	A great deal	Definitely	A little	Not at all
16. Lonely.	A great deal	Definitely	A little	Not at all

WHAT TRIGGERED THESE FEELINGS?

1. I felt excluded.	A great deal	Definitely	A little	Not at all
2. I was not important to my spouse.	A great deal	Definitely	A little	Not at all
3. I felt cold toward my spouse.	A great deal	Definitely	A little	Not at all
4. I definitely felt rejected.	A great deal	Definitely	A little	Not at all
5. I felt overwhelmed by demands.	A great deal	Definitely	A little	Not at all
6. I felt no affection toward my partner.	A great deal	Definitely	A little	Not at all
7. I felt that my partner was not attracted to me.	A great deal	Definitely	A little	Not at all
8. My sense of dignity was being compromised.	A great deal	Definitely	A little	Not at all
9. My partner was being domineering.	A great deal	Definitely	A little	Not at all
10. I could not get my partner's attention.	A great deal	Definitely	A little	Not at all

Now that you've identified your emotional reaction, it's time to see whether your response is rooted in your past. Look over your answers to the "Who Am I?" exercise on page 62. See if you can find connections there between earlier traumas or behavior and your current reaction. Use the following checklist to facilitate this search for links between the past and present.

**WHEN MY PARTNER (OR I) TURNED AWAY
IT REMINDED ME OF:**

(*check all that apply*)

___ The way I was treated in my family growing up.

___ A previous relationship.

___ Past injuries, hard times, or traumas I've suffered.

___ My basic fears and insecurities.

___ Things and events I have not yet resolved or put aside.

___ Unrealized hopes I have.

___ Ways other people treated me in the past.

___ Things I have always thought about myself.

___ Old "nightmares" or "catastrophes" I have worried about.

After you've read each other's answers, write out a short description of your point of view and then your partner's perspective. I hope you will come to see that your respective views of what happened and why are really not matters of "fact." We are all complicated creatures whose actions and reactions are governed by a wide array of perceptions, thoughts, feelings, and memories. In other words, reality is subjective, which is why your partner's take may be different from yours without either of you being right or wrong.

It's natural to make the fundamental error of assuming that the distance and loneliness are all your partner's fault. In truth, they're nobody's fault. In order to break the pattern, you both need to admit playing some role (however slight at first). To do that, read the following list and circle all that apply to you and that may have contributed to the turning away or the feelings of being swamped and smothered recently. (Do not try to do this if you are still upset. Follow the steps for self-soothing on page 181, including letting go of thoughts that maintain the distress, such as thoughts of righteous indignation or innocent victimhood.)

1. I have been very stressed and irritable.	Yes, definitely	Maybe a little
2. I have not expressed much appreciation toward my spouse.	Yes, definitely	Maybe a little

3. I have been overly sensitive.	Yes, definitely	Maybe a little
4. I have been overly critical.	Yes, definitely	Maybe a little
5. I have not shared very much of my inner world.	Yes, definitely	Maybe a little
6. I have been depressed.	Yes, definitely	Maybe a little
7. I would say that I have a chip on my shoulder.	Yes, definitely	Maybe a little
8. I have not been very affectionate.	Yes, definitely	Maybe a little
9. I have not been a very good listener.	Yes, definitely	Maybe a little
10. I have been feeling a bit like a martyr.	Yes, definitely	Maybe a little

OVERALL, MY CONTRIBUTION TO THIS MESS WAS:

_____
_____
_____
_____

HOW CAN I MAKE THIS BETTER IN THE FUTURE?

_____
_____
_____

WHAT ONE THING COULD MY PARTNER DO NEXT TIME TO AVOID THIS PROBLEM?

_____
_____
_____

As you work through the exercises above, you'll become more adept at turning toward each other regularly, and the bond with your spouse will deepen. This more profound friendship will be a powerful shield against conflict. It may not forestall every argument, but it can prevent your differences of opinion from overwhelming your relationship.

The Power of the First Three Principles

I hope that the information in these last three chapters has helped you bolster your marital friendship by updating your love maps, deepening your fondness and admiration, and increasing your tendency to turn toward each other. As we've seen, friendship is critical to a relationship's long-term health because it is the key to PSO, that powerful force that lets you maintain trust and offer each other the benefit of the doubt when conflicts arise. Once you've worked through these first three principles, I suggest you take a moment to fill out the following questionnaire before reading the rest of the book. It will help you assess your current level of PSO and determine whether it's been reinvigorated or could use some more attention and reinforcing.

POSITIVE SENTIMENT OVERRIDE QUESTIONNAIRE

Answer the following questions based on your recent interactions with your partner. Circle T for "true" or F for "false."

WHEN MY PARTNER IS IN A BAD MOOD I USUALLY:
 1. Feel like I am going to get blamed for some problem. **T F**
 2. Want to find out just what my partner is feeling. **T F**
 3. Fear a storm of negative emotion may be headed my way. **T F**
 4. Assume my partner may simply be a little stressed. **T F**
 5. Assume I am about to get personally attacked. **T F**
 6. Believe that I can probably help my partner feel better. **T F**
 7. Expect that my personality is about to get criticized. **T F**
 8. Want to comfort my partner, if I can. **T F**
 9. Just want my partner to be more positive. **T F**
10. Think to myself, "Something awful must just have happened." **T F**

Scoring: Count up the number of times you circled F for the odd-numbered items, and add to that total the number of times you circled

T for the even-numbered items. The result is your Positive Perspective Score. (Find out how your partner scored, if he or she is open to sharing.)

6 or higher: You and your partner have a strong friendship, which should greatly benefit your relationship.

Below 6: Your relationship needs work on at least one of the three principles: building love maps, nurturing fondness and admiration, and turning toward. Consider spending some more time on the exercises in chapters 4–6. I hope your current score motivates rather than frustrates you. Although it can take time to master these skills, remember: even small changes can improve a marriage dramatically. This means that every day offers you significant new opportunities to move your relationship forward.

One of the ways that a couple's underlying friendship creates PSO is by helping to balance the power between partners so that neither feels slighted. When you honor and respect each other, you're usually able to appreciate each other's point of view, even if you don't agree with it. When there's an imbalance of power, there's almost inevitably a great deal of marital distress. My next principle focuses on what can happen if one spouse is unwilling to share power with the other—and how to overcome this difficulty. Although power-mongering is more common in husbands, there are wives who have just as hard a time acceding to their spouse's wishes, so my fourth principle really applies to everybody.

7

Principle 4:
Let Your Partner
Influence You

*J*eremy was considering buying a used Honda coupe. The car seemed like a great deal since the seller, Phil, had only bought it a month ago and was offering a large discount because he was being transferred overseas. Jeremy loved the car's handling and power, not to mention the state-of-the-art sound system. But before doing a deal, he wanted a mechanic to check the car. "Why?" said Phil. "It's really brand-new. It only has three hundred miles, and you get the manufacturer's warranty."

"True," said Jeremy, "but I promised my wife I wouldn't buy a car without having it inspected first."

Phil gave Jeremy a withering look. "You let your *wife* tell you what to do about cars?" he asked.

"Sure," said Jeremy. "Don't you?"

"Well, no. I don't—didn't. I'm divorced," said Phil.

"Well," Jeremy chuckled. "Maybe that's why."

Jeremy had the car checked by his mechanic, and it turned out that the suspension system needed a costly repair, so he never bought Phil's car. But more important, he never bought Phil's attitude toward women. Jeremy has made his wife a partner in his decision making. He respects and honors his wife and her opinions and feelings. He understands that for his marriage to thrive, he has to share the driver's seat.

There was a time when Phil's macho attitude wasn't necessarily a liability for a husband. But our data suggest that this is no longer the case. In our long-term study of 130 newlywed couples, whom we followed for nine years, we found that, even in the first few months of marriage, men who allowed their wives to influence them had happier relationships and were less likely to eventually divorce than men who resisted their wives' influence. Statistically speaking, when a man is not willing to share power with his partner there is an 81 percent chance that his marriage will self-destruct.

Obviously, it takes two to make or break a marriage, so we're not singling out men here. The point of this chapter is not to scold, bash, or insult either gender. It's certainly just as important for wives to treat their husbands with honor and respect. But my data indicate that the vast majority of wives—even in unstable marriages—already do that. This doesn't mean that they don't get angry and even contemptuous of their husbands. It just means that they let their husbands influence their decision making by taking their opinions and feelings into account. But too often, men do not return the favor.

"Anything You Say, Dear"?

That was the sound bite that some members of the media used, erroneously, to sum up my study on accepting influence. It was parodied on *Saturday Night Live*, pilloried by radio talk show host Rush Limbaugh, and picked on by political pundit Bill Maher.

Our study didn't really find that men should give up all of their personal power and let their wives rule their lives. But we did find that the happiest, most stable marriages in the long run were those in which the husband did not resist sharing power and decision making with the wife. When the couple disagreed, these husbands actively searched for common ground rather than insisting on getting their way.

To arrive at these findings, we looked intently at what happened when these newlyweds discussed an area of conflict and also when they talked about the history of their romance. When we analyzed the data, we were struck by a significant gender difference. Although a wife would sometimes express anger or other negative emotion toward her husband, she rarely responded to him by *increasing* the negativity. Usually she either tried to tone it down or matched it. So if a husband said, "You're not listening to me!" the wife would usually say something like, "Sorry, I'm listening now" (a repair that ratchets down the negativity) or "I'm finding it hard to listen to you!" which matched her husband's anger but didn't go beyond it.

But 65 percent of the men did not take either of these approaches. Instead, their response escalated their wives' negativity. They did this in a very specific way: by trotting out one of the four horsemen. If the wife of one of these men said, "You're not listening to me!" the husband would either ignore her (stonewall), become defensive ("Yes, I am!"), criticize ("I don't listen because what you say never makes any sense"), or express contempt ("Why waste my time?"). Using one of the four horsemen to escalate a conflict is a telltale sign that a man is resisting his wife's influence.

Rather than acknowledging his wife's feelings, this kind of husband is using the four horsemen to drown her out, to obliterate her point of view. One way or another, this approach leads to instability in the marriage. Even if the husband doesn't react this way very often, there's still an 81 percent chance that he's damaging the relationship.

Although it is important for both husband and wife to try to keep the four horsemen from taking over in times of conflict, it is especially important that men be aware of the danger to their marriage when they escalate the negativity this way. For some reason, when a wife uses the four horsemen in the same manner, the marriage does not usually become more unstable. At this point, I believe this asymmetry may have sociological causes. An overly compliant wife who doesn't feel empowered to ever *reject* her spouse's influence would likely become depressed, which is detrimental to both her health and the relationship. So perhaps it is a lesser evil for a wife to escalate conflict somewhat rather than fully comply. This may explain why it doesn't harm the marriage when a wife occasionally harnesses one of the four horsemen (with the exception of contempt) to emphasize what she needs from her husband. Perhaps this show of strength balances the power between spouses, particularly if the husband is able to focus on his wife's expressed needs rather than her delivery.

Whatever the reason for the gender disparity, the data indicate that husbands are far more likely than their wives to use the four horsemen to escalate a marital disagreement. And when they do, they are also more likely to put their marriage at risk. So although it certainly makes sense for both partners to avoid intensifying conflicts in this way, the bottom line is that husbands need to be particularly vigilant about accepting their wives' influence.

Signs of Resistance

I've met enough angry husbands and sparred with enough irate radio talk show hosts to know that some men are quite up front in their refusal to share power with their wives. Even in these days of gender equity, there are still husbands who simply refuse to consider any opinions their wives air and never take their feelings or ideas into account when making decisions.

Some men claim that religious conviction requires them to be in control of their marriages and, by extension, their wives. But no religion I know of says that a man should be a bully. I am not advocating a particular spiritual belief system about the roles of men and women. Our research has included couples who believe the man should be the head of the family as well as couples who hold egalitarian viewpoints. In both kinds of marriages, emotionally intelligent husbands have figured out the one big thing: how to convey honor and respect. All spiritual views of life are consistent with loving and esteeming your spouse. And that's what accepting influence is all about. After all, do you really want to make decisions that leave your wife feeling disrespected? Is that really consistent with religious beliefs? It is not.

This was brought home to me by a colleague who follows a religious doctrine that exalts patriarchy. He believes that the husband should make all decisions for the family. But he and his wife have an emotionally intelligent marriage. He sees no conflict between his beliefs and accepting influence from his wife. He told me, "I wouldn't think about making a decision she disagreed with. That would be very disrespectful. We talk and talk about it till we both agree, and then I make the decision." This man intuitively realizes that a marriage can't work unless both partners honor and respect each other. That's true whatever your belief system.

In many cases, I suspect that men who resist letting their wives influence them are not even aware of this tendency. There are men who consider themselves feminists who interact with their wives in ways that belie that label. Case in point: a hardworking lab technician named Chad. If you asked him whether he believed in an egalitarian marriage, he'd nod his head vigorously. But that's not what was playing out in the new home he shared with his wife, Martha. One night he announced that he would have to work late the following Thursday. Martha reminded him that her mother was coming to visit Friday morning and that she was counting on him being available Thursday night to clean the house with her and get the guest room ready. "I'm really upset with you," Martha said bluntly. "Didn't you remember that my mother is coming? Why can't you change your shift?"

"Why didn't *you* remember I have this big project due? There's no way I can change my schedule. I have to work—maybe even the entire weekend," said Chad. His response upped the ante. First he was defensive—instead of responding to Martha's complaint, he volleyed back a complaint of his own: Why didn't she remember *his* schedule? Then he threatened her by suggesting that he would have to work even more than he had initially indicated. This was really a kind of belligerence.

Martha became furious. She called him a lot of unfortunate names and stormed out of the room. Chad felt mistreated. After all, he had to work! As usual, her fury seemed to have come out of nowhere. His heart started racing, and his head pounded. He became flooded, which made it difficult to think about the problem clearly or come up with a solution. All he wanted was to escape from his wife's unfair, irrational attitude. He certainly wasn't in the mood to find a compromise. So, feeling victimized, he poured himself a beer and turned on the TV. When Martha came back into the room wanting to talk, he simply ignored her. When she started to cry, he left the room and announced he was going to bed early.

The wives of men who accept their influence are far less likely to be harsh with their husbands when broaching a difficult marital topic. This increases the odds their marriage will thrive.

When a couple have an argument like this, there are so many accusations and counteraccusations that sometimes it can be hard to determine the underlying cause. In the case of Martha and Chad, though, there's a glaring clue that the fundamental problem is his unwillingness to accept her influence: When she becomes negative ("I'm really upset with you"—a straightforward complaint), he responds by *escalating* the conflict. He injects belligerence and the third horseman, defensiveness, into their conversation. Martha becomes furious and Chad becomes flooded, which leads him to stonewall—the fourth horseman. Their marriage has just taken a nasty tumble.

Accepting influence doesn't mean never expressing negative emotions toward your partner. Marriages can survive plenty of flashes of anger, complaints, even criticisms. Trying to suppress negative feelings in your spouse's presence wouldn't be good for your marriage or your blood pressure. The problem comes when even mild dissatisfaction on the wife's part is met by a barrage from her husband that, instead of toning down or at the most matching her degree of negativity (yelling back, complaining, etc.), goes beyond it.

What Husbands Can Learn from Wives

When a husband accepts his wife's influence, he also strengthens their friendship. This occurs not just because the absence of frequent power struggles makes the marriage more pleasurable, but because such a husband is open to learning from his wife. And there's no doubt that women have plenty to teach men about friendship. In his book *The Complete Book of Guys*, humorist Dave Barry writes about the huge gap between men and women in this regard. He recounts that every year he and his wife get together with some old friends. The wives immediately begin an intense catching-up conversation about their inner feelings. He and the other husband watch the playoffs. The men do get emotional at times—usually when deciding which kind of pizza to order. Later, when the couples have parted company, Barry's wife will say something like, "Isn't it amazing how well George has adjusted to having his leg amputated?" And Barry will pretend that of course he had noticed George was missing a leg. Barry is exaggerating, but the story is funny because it reveals a basic truth: women tend to be more oriented toward discussing and understanding feelings than are men.

I'm not suggesting that all women are savvier about emotions and have better "people skills" than all men. There are plenty of women who are tone deaf to social nuances and men who are deeply sensitive to others. But usually women are more emotionally intelligent than their husbands for one simple reason: they've had an enormous head start in acquiring these skills. Observe children at any playground and you'll see this head start in action. When young boys play (usually run-and-chase games), their priority tends to be the game itself—not their relationship with each other or their emotions. But for little girls, feelings are usually paramount. A cry of "I'm not your friend anymore" will stop a game cold. Whether it starts up again will depend on whether the girls make up.

Even when a boy and girl play with the same toy, the gender difference is often apparent. When four-year-old best friends

Naomi and Eric shared her baby doll, she wanted to pretend that the doll was their baby and they were going to show it off to their friends (relationship-based play). He went along with this for about ten minutes, and then the game roller-coastered into boy territory: "Hey, Naomi, this baby is dead!" he announced. "We have to get it to the hospital right away!" He climbed into an imaginary ambulance, and away he went, "Brrrrrrrr." Naomi urged him not to drive too fast. Suddenly they both became surgeons and saved the baby's life. (Eric wanted Naomi to be the nurse, but she objected that girls can be surgeons, too, so some things have changed!) After the baby's life was saved, they went back to playing Naomi's way—showing off the baby to friends. The play styles of Naomi and Eric are equally charming and delightful. But the plain truth is that "girlish" games offer far better preparation for marriage and family life because they focus on relationships. Boys don't often include games with relationship and domestic themes in their repertoire.

Where does this difference in play styles between boys and girls originate? Because it occurs in virtually every culture, I suspect that biology rather than socialization is the cause. But whether nature or nurture is at the heart of these differences, their effect is undeniable. Because their play emphasizes social interactions and feelings, girls undergo an extensive education in emotions by childhood's end. Boys learn how to pitch overhand. A boy's experience at playing cooperatively and quickly getting past conflict will be an asset later in the boardroom or on the construction site, but it will be a liability in marriage if it comes at the expense of understanding the emotions behind his wife's perspectives.

This disparity in training is heightened by the fact that as they get older, boys rarely play with girls, so they miss the chance to learn from them. In landmark research, Eleanor Maccoby at Stanford University found that while about 35 percent of preschool best friendships are between boys and girls, like Naomi and Eric, by age seven that percentage plummets to virtually zero. From then till puberty, the sexes will have little or nothing to do with each other. This is a worldwide phenomenon. Many explanations have been given for this voluntary segregation. Maccoby offers an intriguing theory that dovetails with my findings on accepting influence. She has found that even at very young ages (one and [?] years), boys will accept influence only from other boys when [?] play, whereas girls accept influence equally from girls or boys [?] around ages five to seven, girls become fed up with this state [?] affairs and stop wanting to play with boys. From that age until puberty, our culture (and virtually all others) offers no formal structure for ensuring that boys and girls continue to interact.

By the time Naomi and Eric are grown, the difference in their knowledge of homemaking will be apparent. Once a couple move in together or get engaged, the groom-to-be is suddenly immersed in what is probably an alien world. In the Broadway play *Defending the Caveman*, a man says that when he was first married, he saw his wife cleaning the bathroom and asked, "Are we moving?" In his bachelor days, that was the only time he and his roommates bothered to clean the bathroom. Many young husbands discover they have a lot to learn from their wives about maintaining a home. You can see the shell-shocked look on the face of the young fiancé in any home furnishings store. He neither knows nor cares about the difference between suede and microfiber. All of the dishes look remarkably alike to him. Most of all, he's thinking that this is taking an awfully long time, and if he turns around suddenly he will do about $10,000 worth of damage since all of the shelves are made of glass and placed about two feet apart, probably just to intimidate guys like him. How will he react? If pretty soon he hears himself saying, "Hey, that's a great pattern," another emotionally intelligent husband has been born.

Emotionally Intelligent Husbands

My data on newlywed couples indicate that more husbands are being transformed in this way. About 35 percent of the men we've studied are emotionally intelligent. Research from previous decades suggests the number used to be much lower. Because this type of husband honors and respects his wife, he will be open to learning more about emotions from her. He will come to understand her world and those of his children and friends. He may

...ne way that his wife does, but he will learn ... with her emotionally. As he does so, he'll ... he esteems her. When she needs to talk, ... etball game and listen. He will choose "us"

... the emotionally intelligent husband is the next step ... evolution. This doesn't mean that he is superior to other ...en in personality, upbringing, or moral fiber. He has simply figured out something very important about being married that the others haven't—yet. And that is how to honor his wife and convey his respect for her. It is really that elementary.

The new husband is likely to make his career less of a priority than his family life because he has revised his definition of success. Unlike husbands of earlier generations, he naturally incorporates the first three principles into his daily life. He makes a detailed map of his wife's world. He keeps in touch with his admiration and fondness for her. And he communicates it by turning toward her in his daily actions. This benefits not only his marriage but his children as well. Research shows that a husband who can accept influence from his wife also tends to be an outstanding father. He is familiar with his children's world, including their friends and their fears. Because he is not afraid of emotions, he teaches his children to respect their own feelings—and themselves. He turns off the basketball game for them, too, because he wants them to remember him as having had time for them.

One great trend among fathers is that more of them are passing on to their children an understanding and respect for one's own emotions and those of others. We call this approach to parenting "emotion coaching." Children benefit when mothers *and* fathers follow this parenting style.[1] This new type of husband and father leads a meaningful and rich life. Having a happy family base makes it possible for him to create and work effectively. Because he is so connected to his wife, she will come to him not only when she is troubled but also when she is delighted. When the city awakens

[1] Want to read more? See Gottman and DeClaire's *Raising an Emotionally Intelligent Child*, and the Gottmans' *And Baby Makes Three*. If you are expecting a baby, see www.gottman.com and look for Bringing Baby Home workshops in your area.

to a beautiful fresh snowstorm, his children will com̲ ̲
him to see it. The people who matter most to him will ca̲
him when he lives and lament his demise.

The other kind of husband and father is a very sad story. He responds to the loss of male entitlement with righteous indignation or a sense of victimization. He may become more authoritarian or withdraw into a lonely shell, protecting what little he has left. He does not give others very much honor and respect because he is engaged in a search for the honor and respect he thinks is his due. He will not accept his wife's influence because he fears any further loss of power. And because he will not accept influence, he will not *have* very much influence. The consequence is that no one will much care about him while he lives nor mourn him when he dies.

Learning to Yield

It's understandable that some men have problems with the shift in the husband's role. For centuries men were expected to be in charge of their families. That sense of responsibility and entitlement gets passed down from father to son in so many subtle ways that revising the husband's role can be a challenge for many men, even in these days when 60 percent of married women work outside the home and often derive both economic power and self-esteem from their jobs. A significant number of the core issues we see between couples today have to do with this change in gender roles. Often, wives complain that men still aren't doing their fair share of domestic chores and child care. This is not just an issue for young couples. We have observed the same pattern among partners in their forties and sixties. Men who are willing to accept influence are happily married. Those who are unwilling see their marriages become unstable.

Perhaps the fundamental difference between husbands who accept influence and those who don't is that the former have learned that often in life you need to yield in order to win. When you drive through any busy city, you encounter frustrating bottlenecks and unexpected barricades that block your rightful passage.

You can take one of two approaches to these impossible situations. One is to stop, become righteously indignant, and insist that the offending obstacle move. The other is to drive around it. The first approach will eventually earn you a heart attack. The second approach—which I call yielding to win—will get you home.

The classic example of a husband yielding to win concerns the ubiquitous toilet seat issue. It's common for a woman to get irritated when her husband always leaves the toilet seat up, even though it only takes her a millisecond to put it down herself. For many women, a raised toilet seat is symbolic of the male's sense of entitlement. So a man can score major points with his wife just by putting the seat down. The wise husband smiles at how smart he is as he drops the lid.

Accepting influence is an attitude, but it's also a skill that you can hone if you pay attention to how you relate to your spouse. In your day-to-day life, this means working on the first three principles by following the advice and exercises in chapters 4, 5, and 6. And when you have a conflict, the key is to be willing to compromise. You do this by searching through your partner's request for something you can agree to. For example, Chad might not be able to work fewer hours in deference to his mother-in-law's visit, but perhaps he could shift the timing. He could, for example, postpone the late night until Friday so that he could help Martha get the house ready for her mother's visit. Perhaps Martha, Grandma, and little brother could take the daughter to soccer practice on Saturday (traditionally his task) so that he could get some work done then.

If despite plenty of effort a man is still unable to accept influence from his wife on a particular issue, it's a sign that an unacknowledged, unsolvable problem is stymieing his attempts. In such a case, the key is to learn how to cope with the gridlock, using the advice in chapter 11. One couple we studied, Tim and Kara, faced this dilemma. They constantly argued about his unemployed childhood friend Buddy, who Kara thought was anything but a pal. He often fought with his live-in girlfriend and ended up boozing and then crashing on their living room sofa. Kara feared that Buddy would be a bad influence on Tim and saw his frequent presence in their home as an invasion and a threat. But whenever she tried to talk to Tim about it, he insisted that this was his home and that he could invite over anyone he wanted. When she disagreed with him, he would stonewall, which made her so angry she would start yelling. Then he would accuse her of being the one with the problem, not Buddy. Kara was infuriated by Tim's attitude. As she saw it, he refused to respect that this was her home, too, and that he had to share decisions about houseguests with her.

More than 80 percent of the time, it's the wife who brings up sticky marital issues, while the husband tries to avoid discussing them. This isn't a symptom of a troubled marriage—it's true in most happy marriages as well.

When I interviewed Tim and Kara, his unwillingness to accept her influence seemed to be the core of their problem—especially since he admitted that he saw no grounds for compromise on the issue. But when I asked him what his friendship with Buddy meant to him, it turned out there was more to the story. During high school, when his parents were going through a bitter divorce and his home life was coming apart, Tim spent countless nights on Buddy's couch. He believed it was now his responsibility to help out the friend who had so often rescued him. He resented what he perceived to be Kara's attempts to get him to abandon Buddy, which would go against his sense of honor. He wasn't concerned that Buddy would be a bad influence. He saw himself as a stable, married man and took pride in his ability to help his friend.

The more Tim talked about Buddy, the clearer it became that he and Kara were grappling with an ever-present problem in their relationship concerning their views of friendship and loyalty. By recognizing this difference and working on the problem together, they were able to transform the issue. Tim stopped thinking about it in the context of his "right" to do what he wanted in his own home. Kara acknowledged that it had been Tim's "piggish" attitude—not just Buddy's presence—that was making her so angry. She told him that she really admired his loyalty—it was one of the things she loved about him. She just worried that Buddy was taking advantage of him. He acknowledged that Buddy could be a "user." By identifying the issue for what it was—a perpetual problem—and agreeing to work on it with Kara, Tim had effectively accepted her influence. They each became better able to see the other's perspective. In the end, they agreed that Buddy could continue to use their living room as a crash pad, but less frequently than before.

It took getting to the heart of a perpetual problem before Tim was able to accept influence from his wife. But in most cases, the husband just needs to be open to sharing power and then to get plenty of practice doing so. A husband can start by taking the quiz below, which can assess the current influence level in a relationship. There's no reason why wives shouldn't take the quiz as well, since the more open to influence both partners are, the smoother a marriage. Couples can then work through the fun exercises that follow, which offer practice in power-sharing.

ACCEPTING INFLUENCE QUESTIONNAIRE

Read each statement and circle T for "true" or F for "false."

1. My partner is really interested in my opinions on our basic issues. **T F**
2. My partner usually learns a lot from me even when we disagree. **T F**
3. My partner wants me to feel that what I say really counts. **T F**
4. My partner wants me to be influential in this marriage. **T F**
5. My partner can listen to me, but only up to a point. **T F**
6. My partner thinks I have a lot of common sense. **T F**
7. My partner tries to communicate respect even when we disagree. **T F**
8. If my partner keeps trying to convince me, he or she eventually wins out. **T F**

9. My partner doesn't reject my opinions out of hand. **T F**
10. My partner doesn't think I am rational enough to take seriously when we discuss our issues. **T F**
11. My partner believes in lots of give and take in our discussions. **T F**
12. My partner is very persuasive and usually wins our arguments. **T F**
13. My partner wants me to have an important say when we make decisions. **T F**
14. My partner usually thinks I have good ideas. **T F**
15. My partner thinks I am basically a great help as a problem-solver. **T F**
16. My partner tries to listen respectfully even when we disagree. **T F**
17. My partner usually thinks his or her solutions are better than mine. **T F**
18. My partner can usually find something to agree with in my position. **T F**
19. My partner thinks I'm usually too emotional. **T F**
20. My partner thinks he or she needs to make the major decisions in our relationship. **T F**

Scoring: Give your partner 1 point for each "true" answer, except for questions 5, 8, 10, 12, 17, 19, and 20. Then subtract 1 point for each "true" answer to questions 5, 8, 10, 12, 17, 19, and 20.

6 or higher: This is an area of strength in your marriage. Your partner willingly cedes power to you, a hallmark of an emotionally intelligent marriage.

Below 6: Your marriage could stand some improvement in this area. Your partner is having some difficulty accepting influence from you, which can make a marriage dangerously unstable. Your partner should reread this chapter if he or she is still unclear about why power-sharing is essential. Then the following exercises will help you move forward.

EXERCISE 1: YIELD TO WIN

Below are some common situations faced by couples I've studied. Try to visualize these scenes as if you and your wife were the ones having this conflict. (Wives who are doing this exercise should flip the genders accordingly.) The more vividly you put yourself into each situation, the more effective the exercise will be. No matter how negative you envision your partner as sounding in these scenarios, try to view her attitude as a way of emphasizing how important this issue is—not as an attack on you. In other words, try to respond to the message, not to your partner's tone of voice. Assume that within that message is a reasonable request with which you could easily agree. (In some of these scenarios, the demand is implied rather than directly spoken.) Write down that request in a sentence. Then note what you could say to express your cooperation. There is no single right answer to each of these scenarios, but you'll find examples of effective responses on page 132.

EXAMPLE: Usually, when you come home from your sales job, you're tired from having to be "on" all day. All you want is to play video games. But your wife, whose job entails far more interaction with computers than people, craves connection. One night she gets very angry when she tries to talk to you, but you don't peel your eyes away from the screen. You tell her you're tired of chatting. She yells, "Well, what about me? I will go crazy if I can't talk about my day!"

Reasonable part of wife's request: To talk about her day.

You say: "I'm sorry. What if you give me a half hour to just chill out and then we can talk?"

1. You pride yourself on being an unsentimental person. Your wife, however, wants you to make a fuss over a multitude of events—her birthday, Valentine's Day, your anniversary, etc. On her birthday she expresses hurt that you didn't plan a party and says she was "forced" to make the plans herself. You say birthday celebrations are for children. She says, "Why can't you just give me what I want? Why is this such a big deal?"

Reasonable part of wife's request:

_____

You say:

_____

2. Your wife is upset that you didn't check with her before accepting a dinner invitation from your friends Matt and Sally. She can't stand eating at their place because she thinks Sally is overly focused on health foods and dietary supplements. "Tell them we can't come," your wife insists.

Reasonable part of wife's request:

_____

You say:

_____

3. Your wife wants to spend money on house repairs. You tell her it's just not affordable unless she cuts back her spending in other areas. She says your attitude is unfair and asks, "Why is there somehow always money to spend on the things that *you* think are important?"

Reasonable part of wife's request:

_____

You say:

_____

4. Sometimes you make a bit of a mess in the living room when you get home from work, but you usually clean it up after dinner when you have more energy. One night, when you haven't cleaned up, your wife says, "It really makes me mad the way you leave your stuff around. I'm tired, too, and I wish I didn't have to pick up after you. Why can't you clean up before dinner?"

Reasonable part of wife's request:

_____

You say:

_____

5. You've just come home from work feeling tired, and you still have to run to the hardware store. Your wife, a stay-at-home mom, says that she's had an exhausting day chasing after your two toddlers. She wants you to take them along so she can have some alone time.

Reasonable part of wife's request:

_____

You say:

_____

Sample Answers

1. Reasonable part of wife's request: She deserves to feel special some of the time.

   You say: I can see why you'd want these times to be special. Can we select two or three of them and make them big celebrations?

2. Reasonable part of wife's request: Sally *does* deliver sermons about food, and it can be hard to take.

   You say: I understand why you feel that way about Sally. But she was really generous to us when we first moved into the neighborhood, and I really like Matt. How about if I make sure it's not just Matt and me talking and you being left with Sally? And I promise to check with you before making any more plans for the four of us.

3. Reasonable part of wife's request: Your house does need some repairs.

   You say: "Okay, maybe you're right. What repairs do you think we need to do?"

4. Reasonable part of wife's request: For you to clean up before dinner.

   You say: "Sorry, okay, I'll clean up." Then follow through.

5. Reasonable part of wife's request: To get a break from the kids.

   You say: "Okay. Let's go for a ride, kids. Ice cream on the way for everybody!"

Now that you've worked through these examples, you should have a better sense of what it means to "give" in a relationship. The next step is to get used to giving to your spouse and sharing power more in your own marriage. The following fun exercise lets you work on making decisions together. Remember that the goal is for both of you to be influential *and* to accept each other's influence.

EXERCISE 2: THE GOTTMAN ISLAND SURVIVAL GAME

Imagine that your cruise ship just sank in the Caribbean, and you awaken to find yourselves on a deserted island. The cast members of *Lost* are nowhere in sight—the two of you are the only survivors. One of you is injured. You have no idea where you are. You think there's some chance that people know of the ship's distress, but you're not sure. A storm appears to be on the way. You decide that you need to prepare to survive on this island for some time and also to make sure you'll be spotted by a rescue party. There is a bunch of stuff from the ship on the beach that could help you, but you can only carry ten items.

Your Mission

STEP 1: Each of you writes down on a separate piece of paper what you consider the ten most important items to keep from the inventory list below, based on your survival plan. Then rank-order these items based on their importance to you. Give the most crucial item a 1, the next most crucial a 2, and so on. There are no right or wrong answers.

Ship's Inventory

1. Two changes of clothing
2. AM/FM and shortwave radio receiver
3. Ten gallons of water
4. Pots and pans
5. Matches
6. Shovel
7. Backpack
8. Toilet paper
9. Two tents
10. Two sleeping bags
11. Knife
12. Small life raft, with sail
13. Sunblock lotion

14. Cookstove and lantern
15. Long rope
16. Two walkie-talkie sender/receiver units
17. Freeze-dried food for seven days
18. One change of clothing
19. One fifth of whiskey
20. Flares
21. Compass
22. Regional aerial maps
23. Gun with six bullets
24. Fifty packages of condoms
25. First-aid kit with penicillin
26. Oxygen tanks

STEP 2: Share your list with your partner. Together come up with a consensus list of ten items. That means talking it over and working as a team to solve the problem. Both of you need to be influential in discussing the problem and in making the final decisions.

When you've finished, it's time to evaluate how the game went. You should both answer the questions below.

1. How effective do you think you were at influencing your spouse?
    a) Not at all effective
    b) Neither effective nor ineffective
    c) Somewhat effective
    d) Very effective

2. How effective was your spouse at influencing you?
    a) Not at all effective
    b) Neither effective nor ineffective
    c) Somewhat effective
    d) Very effective

3. Did either of you try to dominate the other, or were you competitive with each other?
    a) A lot
    b) Somewhat

    c) A little

    d) Not at all

4. Did you sulk or withdraw?

    a) A lot

    b) Somewhat

    c) A little

    d) Not at all

5. Did your partner sulk or withdraw?

    a) A lot

    b) Somewhat

    c) A little

    d) Not at all

6. Did you have fun?

    a) Not at all

    b) A little

    c) Somewhat

    d) A lot

7. Did you work well as a team?

    a) Not at all

    b) A little

    c) Somewhat

    d) A great deal

8. How much irritability or anger did you feel?

    a) A lot

    b) Some

    c) A little

    d) None

9. How much irritability or anger did your partner feel?

    a) A lot

    b) Some

    c) A little

    d) None

10. Did you both feel included?
    a) Not at all
    b) A little
    c) A reasonable amount
    d) A great deal

Scoring: Give yourself 1 point for each "a" answer, 2 points for each "b" answer, 3 points for each "c" answer, and 4 points for each "d" answer. Tally your score.

If your final number is over 24, you're doing a good job of accepting each other's influence and working together as a team. If you scored 24 or lower, your marriage needs further work in this area.

If you're having difficulty accepting influence, you will benefit your marriage enormously by acknowledging this tendency and talking about it with your spouse. Nobody can change old habits overnight. But if you're able to take responsibility for your difficulty with power-sharing, that will be a major leap forward. Your spouse is likely to feel a great sense of relief and renewed optimism about improving your marriage. The next step is to make your partner an ally in your crusade to overcome this problem. Ask her (or him) to gently point out to you instances where you are being unwittingly domineering, defensive, or disrespectful.

Because the Seven Principles are interrelated, you will find it easier to accept influence as you master the other tenets of this program. Likewise, the more skilled you become at accepting influence, the easier it will be to adhere to the other principles. A willingness to share power and to respect the other person's view is a prerequisite for compromising. For that reason, becoming more adept at accepting influence will especially help you better cope with marital conflict—the focus of Principles 5 and 6. As you'll see, there are two major categories of disagreements that virtually all couples experience. But the ability to accept influence is a cornerstone of success no matter which type of conflict you're facing.

8

The Two Kinds of Marital Conflict

*E*very marriage is a union of individuals who bring to it their own opinions, personality quirks, and values. So it's no wonder that even in very happy marriages spouses must cope with a profusion of marital issues. Some conflicts are just minor irritants, but others can seem overwhelmingly complex and intense. Too often couples feel mired in conflict or distance themselves from each other as a protective device.

Although you may feel your situation is unique, we have found that all marital conflicts, ranging from mundane annoyances to all-out wars, really fall into one of two categories: either they can be resolved, or they are perpetual, which means they will be a part of your lives forever in some form or another. Once you are able to identify and define your various disagreements, you'll be able to customize your coping strategies, depending on which of these two types of conflict you're having.

Perpetual Problems

Unfortunately, the majority of marital conflicts fall into this category—69 percent, to be exact. Time and again at four-year follow-ups we'd find couples still arguing about precisely the same issue. They'd altered their hairstyles, donned new clothes, and gained (or lost) a few pounds and wrinkles, but they were still having the same argument. It was as if four minutes had passed rather than four years. Here are some typical perpetual problems that the *happy* couples in our studies were living with:

1. Meg wants to have a baby, but Donald says he's not ready yet—and doesn't know if he ever will be.
2. Walter wants sex far more frequently than Dana.
3. Chris is lax about housework and rarely does his share of the chores until Susan nags him, which makes him angry.
4. Tony wants to raise their children as Catholics. Jessica is Jewish and wants their children to follow her faith.
5. Angie thinks Ron is too critical of their son. But Ron thinks he has the right approach: their son has to be taught the proper way to do things.

Despite their differences, these couples remain very satisfied with their marriages because they have hit upon a way to deal with their unmovable problems so that they don't become overwhelming. They've learned to keep them in their place and approach them with a sense of humor. For example, Melinda and Andy have an ongoing conflict over his reluctance to go on outings with her family. But when they talk to me about this problem, they don't get angry; they simply relate good-naturedly what happens. Andy starts to tell me what he always ends up saying. Melinda, who knows it all so well, jumps in and offers up his quote for him, mimicking his put-upon voice: "All right, I'll go." Then Andy adds that he also says, "Okay, sure, anything you say, dear."

"We still continue to do that," Melinda explains to me. Then Andy chuckles and adds, "We don't even disagree good, do we?"

Melinda and Andy haven't solved their problem, but they've learned to live with it and approach it with good humor.

Despite what many therapists will tell you, you don't have to resolve your major marital conflicts for your marriage to thrive.

Another happy couple, Carmen and Bill, have a perpetual problem over their disparate degrees of orderliness. Carmen has the discipline of a drill sergeant, while her husband is a classic absentminded professor. For Carmen's sake, Bill tries to think about where he's putting things. For his sake, she tries not to nag him when items go missing. When she finds, say, an old half-full coffee mug behind a pile of magazines, she'll make her point by holding her nose and gently teasing him—unless she's feeling excess stress that day, in which case she'll probably raise her voice, after which he'll give her a back rub as contrition, and they'll go on happily with their day. In other words, they are constantly working it out, for the most part good-naturedly. At times it gets better; on occasion it gets worse. But because they keep acknowledging the problem and talking about it, they prevent it from overwhelming their relationship.

These couples intuitively understand that some difficulties are inevitable, much the way chronic physical ailments are unavoidable as you get older. They are like a trick knee, a bad back, an irritable bowel, or tennis elbow. We may not enjoy having these problems, but we are able to cope by avoiding situations that worsen them, and by developing strategies and routines that help ease them. Psychologist Dan Wile said it best in his book *After the Honeymoon*: "When choosing a long-term partner . . . you will inevitably be choosing a particular set of unsolvable problems that you'll be grappling with for the next ten, twenty, or fifty years." Marriages are successful to the degree that the problems you choose are ones you can cope with. Wile writes: "Paul married Alice and Alice gets loud at parties and Paul, who is shy, hates that. But if Paul had married Susan, he and Susan would have gotten into a fight before they even got to the party. That's because Paul is always late and Susan hates to be kept waiting. She would feel taken for granted, which she is very sensitive about. Paul would see her complaining about this as her attempt to dominate him, which he is very sensitive about. If Paul had married Gail, they wouldn't have even gone to the party because they would still be upset about an argument they had the day before about Paul's not helping with the housework. To Gail, when Paul does not help, she feels abandoned, which she is sensitive about, and to Paul, Gail's complaining is an attempt at domination, which he is sensitive about." And so it goes.

In unstable marriages, perpetual problems like these eventually kill the relationship. Instead of coping with the problem effectively, the couple get *gridlocked* over it. They have the same conversation about it over and over again. They just spin their wheels, resolving nothing. Because they make no headway, they feel increasingly hurt, frustrated, and distrustful of each other. The four horsemen become ever more present when they argue, while humor and affection become less so. They grow all the more entrenched in their positions. Gradually they feel physiologically overwhelmed. When a couple face gridlock, they may attempt to improve the situation by slowly isolating or enclosing the problem area—for example, by tacitly agreeing not to notice or discuss it. They may say, "Let's just agree to disagree." They shove it under the rug, but it becomes, in the words of our great poet Robert Creeley, a place where "the rug bunches." As much as they try to remember to sidestep that place on the rug, they trip over it again and again.

Avoiding conflict over a perpetual problem leads to emotional disengagement. The couple's trust in each other and the relationship declines as they become increasingly trapped in the negativity—the Roach Motel for Lovers. As the gridlock worsens, they each come to feel that the other is just plain selfish and cares only about him- or herself. They may still live together but are on the course toward leading parallel lives and inevitable loneliness—the death knell for any marriage.

The Signs of Gridlock

If you're not sure whether you're gridlocked over a perpetual problem or are coping well with it, this checklist will help. The characteristics of a gridlocked problem are:

- The conflict makes you feel rejected by your partner.
- You keep talking about it but make no headway.
- You become entrenched in your positions and are unwilling to budge.
- When you discuss the subject, you end up feeling more frustrated and hurt.
- Your conversations about the problem are devoid of humor, amusement, or affection.
- You become even more "unbudgeable" over time, which leads you to vilify each other during these conversations.
- This vilification makes you all the more rooted in your positions and polarized, more extreme in your views, and all the less willing to compromise.
- Eventually you disengage from each other emotionally.

If this sounds painfully familiar, take comfort in knowing that there is a way out of gridlock, no matter how entrenched. As you'll see when we get to Principle 6, all you need is motivation and a willingness to explore the hidden issues that are really causing the gridlock. The key will be to uncover and share with each other the significant personal dreams you have for your life. I have found that unrequited dreams are at the core of every gridlocked conflict. In other words, the endless argument symbolizes some profound difference between the two of you that needs to be addressed before you can put the problem in its place.

Solvable Problems

These problems may sound relatively simple compared with unsolvable ones, but they can cause a great deal of pain. Simply because a problem is solvable doesn't mean it gets resolved. If a couple doesn't possess effective techniques for conquering a solvable problem, it can cause excessive tension. My fifth principle for making marriage work tackles solvable problems head-on. It offers an approach to conflict resolution based on my research into what goes right when emotionally intelligent couples handle a disagreement. In the next chapter, we'll show you how to (1) make sure your start-up is soft rather than harsh, (2) learn the effective use of repair attempts, (3) monitor your physiology during tense discussions for warning signs of flooding, (4) learn how to compromise, and (5) become more tolerant of each other's imperfections. Follow this advice and you're likely to find that solvable problems no longer interfere with your marital happiness.

Telling the Difference

If you and your spouse are entrenched in conflict, it may not be obvious which of the two types of disagreement you're having—gridlocked or solvable. One way to identify solvable problems is that they seem less painful, gut-wrenching, or intense than perpetual, gridlocked ones. That's because when you argue over a solvable problem, your focus is only on a particular dilemma or situation. There is no underlying conflict that's fueling your dispute.

For example, for years Eleanor has been arguing with her husband, Miguel, that he drives too fast. He always tells her the same thing, that he's never had an accident, he's an assertive driver not an aggressive one. She ends up yelling that he's selfish and doesn't care that his speeding scares her. He retorts that the real problem is her lack of trust in him. Each time they have this squabble, they feel all the more frustrated and hurt and entrenched in their positions. There's a lot of vilifying on both sides. For this couple, speeding constitutes a perpetual problem they will probably never fully resolve. They are really arguing about Big Issues like trust, security, selfishness. To keep their ongoing battles over driving from ruining their marriage, they'll need to understand the deeper meaning that this battle has for each of them.

But for Rachel and Jason, disagreements over driving speeds constitute a solvable problem. Every morning they commute together from their suburban home to downtown Pittsburgh. She thinks he drives too fast. He says he has to speed because she takes so long to get ready and he doesn't want to be late to work. Rachel says it takes her so long in the morning because he showers first and takes forever. Plus, he always leaves the breakfast dishes on the table. While she's busy washing them, he's honking the horn for her to hurry. By the time Jason drops Rachel off at her office, he's stonewalling and she's fighting back tears.

This couple's difficulty over driving is a solvable problem. For starters, it is situational—it occurs only when they are going to work, and it doesn't reverberate into other areas of their lives. Unlike Eleanor and Miguel, they don't vilify each other. Their arguments aren't about selfishness or trust—they're simply about driving and their morning routine. By learning a more effective way to talk with each other about the issue, they could readily find a compromise. Maybe they could set their alarm fifteen minutes earlier, or she could shower first, or he could just remember to deal with the dishes.

However, if Rachel and Jason don't find a way to compromise on this issue, it's likely that they will become increasingly resentful and entrenched in their positions. The conflict could deepen and take on more symbolic meaning. In other words, it could evolve into a gridlocked, perpetual problem.

Below I've described various scenarios of marital conflict. For each one, mark whether you think it's solvable or perpetual.

1. Cliff and Lynn agree that it's Cliff's job to take out the kitchen trash every evening after dinner. But lately he's been so distracted by a big deadline looming at work that he forgets. Either Lynn ends up throwing out the garbage herself or the trash just sits there. By

morning the apartment smells like a city dump, and Lynn is in a rage.

Solvable _____   **Perpetual** _____

2. Elise wants to spend less time with Joel and more time with her friends. Joel says this makes him feel abandoned. Elise says that she needs time away from him. He seems very needy to her, and she's feeling suffocated by him.

Solvable _____   **Perpetual** _____

3. Ingrid doesn't like it that Gary sulks when he's upset with her, rather than telling her what's bothering him. But when he does let her know all the reasons he's unhappy, she criticizes him for bringing up so many issues at once. He says that since it's so hard for him to discuss such things, he doesn't want Ingrid to criticize his style of communication when he does acknowledge he's upset with her. Instead, he wants a reward: namely, he wants Ingrid to say she's sorry.

Solvable _____   **Perpetual** _____

4. Helena gets together with her friends every Monday night. Jonathan wants her to take a ballroom dancing class together with him, but the class is only held on Monday nights. Helena doesn't want to give up her girls' night out.

Solvable _____   **Perpetual** _____

5. Penny complains that Roger expects her to do all the work taking care of their newborn son. Roger says he'd like to do more, but because he works during the day, he isn't as experienced as his wife at diapering, bathing, and the like. Whenever he does try to do something, like pick up the baby when he cries, Penny tells him he's doing it wrong. This makes him angry, and he ends up telling her to do it herself.

Solvable _____   **Perpetual** _____

6. Jim wants Thea to be more organized. He doesn't like it that the house rarely gets cleaned unless he attends to it and that the

kids often don't get to school on time. She thinks he acts smug and superior to her and gives her the sense that the disorganization in their house is due to a character flaw she has. She feels attacked and gets defensive whenever he raises the subject. She says their house is supposed to be a home, not an army barracks, and that he needs to relax about these issues because his demands are unreasonable. They have been arguing about this for four years.

Solvable ____   **Perpetual** ____

7. Whenever Brian and Allyssa have a disagreement, he quickly raises his voice. Allyssa feels intense stress when he yells and tells him to stop. Brian says he doesn't see anything wrong with yelling when he's upset. Allyssa starts to cry and tells him she can't take it. So they find themselves fighting over his yelling rather than whatever issue they disagreed about.

Solvable ____   **Perpetual** ____

8. Ever since Isabel decided to leave her job and stay home with the baby, Anthony has felt squeezed out of her life. It seems to him that she doesn't have time for him anymore. She tells Anthony she doesn't want their son, Brendan, to feel abandoned by her, as she did by her own mother. Her parents divorced when she was two, and she was shuffled between relatives' homes for years. But Anthony feels betrayed—he has always loved how nurturing and attentive Isabel was toward him. Now it seems that's all being directed at the baby, and he feels cheated.

Solvable ____   **Perpetual** ____

9. Oscar just inherited $2,000 from his great-aunt. He wants to use it to buy home exercise equipment. But Mary thinks they should save it for a down payment on a house. Oscar says the inheritance is really not enough to make a dent in a down payment, so why not use it for something they could enjoy right away? But Mary believes that every little bit adds up and that they have to save as much as they can all the time.

Solvable ____   **Perpetual** ____

10. Sarah thinks Ryan is stingy about tipping waiters, cabdrivers, and so on. This upsets her because part of her image of a strong, sexy man is someone who's generous. When she's disappointed with Ryan, she gets very contemptuous of him. Meanwhile, Ryan believes that Sarah is too loose with their money, which makes him nervous. To him, money represents security and a sense of control over his life, so it's hard to give any of it up.

Solvable ____   **Perpetual** ____

ANSWERS

1. Solvable. Cliff has stopped taking out the garbage only recently and for a specific reason that's not deeply related to relationship dynamics—he's under a lot of stress at work. This problem could be solved in any number of ways. For example, they could put a sign on the refrigerator door to remind him or reshuffle their domestic chores so that Lynn gets garbage detail until Cliff's work deadline passes.

2. Perpetual. This problem suggests a core difference between Elise and Joel in their personalities and what they need from each other to feel close and connected. This difference is unlikely to change—they'll need to adjust to it.

3. Perpetual. Ingrid and Gary are engaged in a metacommunication war. This means they're having difficulty communicating about how to communicate. This is not related to a specific situation but is present whenever they have a disagreement.

4. Solvable. Helena and Jonathan can resolve this issue in a number of ways. Perhaps they could switch off weekly between dancing class and Helena's girls' night out. Or maybe her friends would be willing to switch the night. Or Jonathan could find another dancing class on another night or on the weekend. Or one of them could simply agree to sacrifice one of these activities.

5. Solvable. Roger just needs to spend more time with his son so that he can get up to speed on his care. And Penny needs to back off and let Roger approach baby care his way. Because this issue isn't related to deep-seated needs either of them has, it can be readily solved through compromise.

6. Perpetual. This problem probably started out as a situational one about housecleaning and organization. Perhaps Jim and Thea have different tolerance levels for clutter, dirt, and how planned out one's life should be. But because they haven't found a compromise position, they have continued to argue about these differences. Thea has come to feel her husband doesn't value or respect her, while he feels that she's not holding up her end of the marriage by keeping the household well organized. The argument has become about their mutual resentment rather than about housekeeping.

7. Perpetual. Brian and Allyssa have different emotional styles. He tends to be volatile, meaning that he's very passionate and "out there" with his emotions. Allyssa prefers to discuss issues quietly and rationally. When Brian starts yelling at her, she feels overwhelmed and quickly becomes flooded. Since emotional style is part of one's personality, neither of them is likely to change. But by becoming aware of and respecting each other's emotional style, they can find an approach to conflict resolution they are both comfortable with.

8. Perpetual. Isabel and Anthony have different emotional needs. Their child's birth has highlighted this difference. Anthony should try to understand how important it is for Isabel to not fear she will repeat the tragedy of her own childhood with their child. He can join her in making sure that she is being a great mom. However, Anthony is experiencing a great loss in Isabel's turning away from him and becoming so baby-centered. Unless she can understand what that loss means to Anthony, he will drift away from her.

9. Solvable. Oscar and Mary may have different philosophies about savings, but their conflict over money doesn't appear to be symbolic. Instead, it's a straightforward difference of opinion about what to do with Oscar's inheritance. For that reason, they could probably find a straightforward compromise. Perhaps, for example, they could spend half of the amount on equipment and save the rest.

10. Perpetual. Money has very different meanings to Ryan and Sarah. Since the symbolic significance of money is usually rooted in childhood experiences, it's unlikely that Ryan will naturally transform into a big tipper or that Sarah will suddenly learn to love clipping coupons. But if they work together on this perpetual problem (and especially Sarah's contempt for her husband about this issue), it will cease to be a major sore spot in their relationship.

QUESTIONNAIRE: ASSESSING YOUR MARITAL CONFLICTS

Now that you have a greater understanding of the differences between solvable and perpetual problems, it's time to categorize your own marital issues in this way. By doing so, you'll know which strategies to use to cope with them. Below is a list of seventeen common causes of conflict in a marriage. For each, mark whether it is a perpetual problem in your marriage, a solvable problem for you, or not a problem right now. If it is either a solvable or a perpetual problem, check all of the specific subareas that you think are currently troublesome.

I. We are becoming emotionally distant.

Perpetual ____ **Solvable** ____ **Not a problem right now** ____

Check any of the specific items below that are problems within this general area:

___ We have difficulty just simply talking to each other.

___ We are less in touch with each other emotionally.

___ I feel taken for granted.

___ I feel my spouse doesn't know me right now.

___ My spouse is (or I am) emotionally disengaged.

___ We spend less time together.

Comments:

_____

_____

_____

2. There is spillover of nonmarital stresses (such as job tension) into our marriage.

Perpetual _____ **Solvable** _____ **Not a problem right now** _____

Check any of the specific items below that are problems within this general area:

___ We don't always help each other reduce daily stresses.

___ We don't talk about these stresses together.

___ We don't talk together about stress in a helpful manner.

___ My spouse doesn't listen with understanding about my stresses and worries.

___ My spouse takes job stress or other tensions out on me.

___ My spouse takes job stress or other tensions out on the children or others.

Comments:

_____

_____

_____

3. Our marriage is becoming nonromantic and passionless; the fire is dying.

Perpetual _____ **Solvable** _____ **Not a problem right now** _____

Check any of the specific items below that are problems within this general area:

___ My spouse has stopped being verbally affectionate.

___ My spouse expresses love or admiration less frequently.

___ We rarely touch each other.

___ My spouse or I have stopped feeling very romantic.
___ We rarely cuddle.
___ We have few tender or passionate moments.

Comments:

_____

_____

_____

4. We are having problems in our sex life.

Perpetual ____ **Solvable** ____   **Not a problem right now** ____

Check any of the specific items below that are problems within this general area:

___ Sex is less frequent.
___ At least one of us gets less satisfaction from sex.
___ We have problems talking about sexual problems.
___ Each of us wants different things sexually.
___ Desire is less than it once was.
___ Our lovemaking feels less loving.

Comments:

_____

_____

_____

5. Our marriage is not dealing well with an important change (such as the birth of a child, a job loss, a move, an illness, or the death of a loved one).

Perpetual ____ **Solvable** ____   **Not a problem right now** ____

Check any of the specific items below that are problems within this general area:

___ We have very different views on how to handle things.
___ This event has led my partner to be very distant.
___ This event has made us both irritable.
___ This event has led to a lot of fighting.
___ I'm worried about how this will all turn out.
___ We are now taking very different positions.

Comments:

_____

_____

_____

6. Our marriage is not handling well a major issue about children. (This category includes whether to have a child.)

Perpetual _____ **Solvable** _____   **Not a problem right now** _____

Check any of the specific items below that are problems within this general area:

___ We have very different goals for our children.

___ We differ on what to discipline children for.

___ We differ on how to discipline our children.

___ We have issues on how to be close to our kids.

___ We are not talking about these problems well.

___ There is much tension and anger about these differences.

Comments:

_____

_____

_____

7. Our marriage is not handling well a major issue or event concerning in-laws or another relative(s).

Perpetual _____ **Solvable** _____   **Not a problem right now** _____

Check any of the specific items below that are problems within this general area:

___ I feel unaccepted by my partner's family.

___ I sometimes wonder which family my spouse is in.

___ I feel unaccepted by my own family.

___ I feel my partner takes sides against me.

___ There is tension between us about what might happen.

___ This issue has generated a lot of irritability.

___ I worry about how this will turn out.

Comments:

_____

_____

_____

8. One of us is flirtatious outside the marriage, or may have had a recent affair, and/or there is jealousy.

Perpetual _____   Solvable _____   Not a problem right now _____

Check any of the specific items below that are problems within this general area:

___ This area is the source of a lot of hurt.

___ This is an area that creates insecurity.

___ I can't deal with the lies.

___ It is hard to reestablish trust.

___ There is a feeling of betrayal.

___ It's hard to know how to heal over this.

Comments:

_____

_____

_____

9. Unpleasant fights have occurred between us.

Perpetual _____   Solvable _____   Not a problem right now _____

Check any of the specific items below that are problems within this general area:

___ There are more fights now.

___ Fights seem to come out of nowhere.

___ Anger and irritability have crept into our marriage.

___ We get into muddles where we are hurting each other.

___ I don't feel very respected lately.

___ I feel criticized.

Comments:

_____

_____

_____

10. We have differences in our basic goals and values or desired lifestyle.

Perpetual ____   **Solvable** ____   **Not a problem right now** ____

Check any of the specific items below that are problems within this general area:

___ Differences have arisen in life goals.
___ Differences have arisen about important beliefs.
___ Differences have arisen on leisure-time interests.
___ We seem to want different things out of life.
___ We are growing in different directions.
___ I don't much like who I am with my partner.

Comments:

_____

_____

_____

11. Very disturbing events (for example, violence, drugs, an affair) have occurred within our marriage.

Perpetual ____   **Solvable** ____   **Not a problem right now** ____

Check any of the specific items below that are problems within this general area:

___ There has been physical violence between us.
___ There is a problem with alcohol or drugs.
___ This is turning into a marriage I hadn't bargained for.
___ Our marriage "contract" is changing.
___ I find some of what my partner wants upsetting or repulsive.
___ I am now feeling somewhat disappointed by this marriage.

Comments:

_____

_____

_____

12. We are not working well as a team.

Perpetual ____   **Solvable** ____   **Not a problem right now** ____

Check any of the specific items below that are problems within this general area:

___ We used to share more of the family's workload.
___ We seem to be pulling in opposite directions.
___ My spouse does not fairly share in housework or child care.
___ My spouse is not carrying his or her weight financially.
___ I feel alone managing this family.
___ My spouse is not being very considerate.

Comments:

_____

_____

_____

13. We are having trouble sharing power and influence.

Perpetual ____   Solvable ____   Not a problem right now ____

Check any of the specific items below that are problems within this general area:

___ I don't feel influential in decisions we make.
___ My spouse has become more domineering.
___ I have become more demanding.
___ My spouse has become passive.
___ My spouse is "spacey," not a strong force in our marriage.
___ I am starting to care a lot more about who is running things.

Comments:

_____

_____

_____

14. We are having trouble handling financial issues well.

Perpetual ____   Solvable ____   Not a problem right now ____

Check any of the specific items below that are problems within this general area:

___ One of us doesn't bring in enough money.
___ We have differences about spending or saving money.
___ We are stressed about finances.

___ My spouse is financially more interested in self than in us.

___ We are not united in managing our finances.

___ There is not enough financial planning.

Comments:

_____

_____

_____

15. We are not having much fun together these days.

Perpetual ___   **Solvable** ___   **Not a problem right now** ___

Check any of the specific items below that are problems within this general area:

___ We don't seem to have much time for fun.

___ We try but don't seem to enjoy our times together very much.

___ We are too stressed for fun.

___ Work takes up all our time these days.

___ Our interests are so different, there are no fun things we like to do together.

___ We plan fun things to do, but they never happen.

Comments:

_____

_____

_____

16. We are not feeling close about spiritual issues these days.

Perpetual ___   **Solvable** ___   **Not a problem right now** ___

Check any of the specific items below that are problems within this general area:

___ We do not share the same beliefs.

___ We do not agree about religious ideas and values.

___ We differ about the specific house of worship.

___ We do not communicate well about spiritual issues.

___ We have issues about spiritual growth and change.

___ We have spiritual issues involving family or children.

Comments:

_____

_____

_____

17. We are having conflict(s) about being a part of and building community together.

Perpetual ____   Solvable ____   Not a problem right now ____

Check any of the specific items below that are problems within this general area:

___ We feel differently about being involved with friends and other people or groups.

___ We don't care to the same degree about the institutions that build community.

___ We have different opinions about putting time into the institutions of community (political party, school, hospital, house of worship, agencies, and the like).

___ We disagree about doing projects or working for charity.

___ We disagree about doing good deeds for others.

___ We have different views about whether to take a leadership role in the service of our community.

Scoring: For each of the general areas that cause you problems, count up the number of specific bones of contention that you've checked. If you've marked more than two, then this is an area of significant conflict in your marriage. For solvable problems, you'll find advice in chapter 9. But if some of your problems are perpetual, follow the advice in chapter 11 as well. No doubt you'll discover that your marriage, like most, is coping with both types of problems.

The Keys to Managing Conflict

In the chapters ahead, you will find specific techniques for handling marital troubles, whether perpetual or solvable. But first, some overall advice:

Negative emotions are important. Although it is stressful to listen to your partner's negative feelings, remember that successful relationships live by the motto "When you are in pain, the world stops and I listen." This is true even when your partner's anger, sadness, disappointment, or fear is directed at *you*. Negative emotions hold important information about how to love each other better. It takes a lot of understanding and proficiency in attunement to be able to really hear what your partner is saying when he or she is upset. One of the goals of this book is to guide partners toward expressing their negative emotions in ways that allow each other to listen without feeling attacked so that the message gets through in a manner that encourages healing rather than more hurt. These sorts of discussions can be tough for both parties. It will help if you can both acknowledge this and remember to be gentle with each other.

No one is right. There is no absolute reality in marital conflict, only two subjective ones. This is true whether the disagreement is solvable or perpetual. As my friend Dan Siegel says, "There is no immaculate perception." It will help you resolve your differences if you remember this basic truth.

Acceptance is crucial. It is virtually impossible for people to heed advice unless they believe the other person understands, respects, and accepts them for who they are. When people feel criticized, disliked, or unappreciated, they are unable to change. Instead, they feel under siege, and they dig in. Therefore, the basis for coping effectively with relationship issues, whether solvable or perpetual, is to communicate basic acceptance of your partner's personality. Before you ask your spouse to change the way he or she drives, eats, vacuums, or makes love, you must make sure your partner feels known and respected rather than criticized or demeaned. There's a big difference between "Sheesh, you're a lousy driver! Slow down before you kill us!" and "I know you enjoy driving fast, but I get really nervous. Could you please slow down?" Maybe that second approach takes a bit longer. But that extra time is worth it since it is the only method that works!

Adults could learn something in this regard from research into child development. Children thrive when we express understanding and respect for their emotions ("That doggie scared you," "You're crying because you're sad right now," "You sound very angry; let's talk about it") rather than belittle or punish them for their feelings ("It's silly to be afraid of such a little dog," "Big boys don't cry," "Go to your room till you calm down"). When you let children know that all their emotions, including the negative ones, are okay to have, you are also communicating that they themselves are acceptable even when sad, crabby or scared. This helps children feel positive about themselves, which makes growth and change possible. The same is true for adults. In order to improve our relationship, we need to express acceptance of our partner.

Focus on fondness and admiration. If you or your spouse finds it hard to accept each other's perspective, it may help if you work more on the exercises in chapter 5 ("Nurture Your Fondness and Admiration"). I have found that a robust fondness-and-admiration system is central to remaining happily married—foibles and all. Many of the older couples I studied with colleagues Bob Levenson and Laura Carstensen in the San Francisco Bay area were masters at this. They had been married for a very long time—some for more than forty years. Through the course of their marriage, they had learned to view their partner's shortcomings and oddities as amusing parts of the whole package.

One wife, for example, accepted with a chuckle that her husband would never stop being a Dagwood—always running late and frantic. She found ways around it. Whenever they had to get to the airport, she'd tell him their plane left thirty minutes sooner than the actual takeoff time. He knew she was deceiving him, and they laughed about it. Then there was the husband who looked upon his wife's weekly shopping sprees with as much amusement as dread, even though her shopping style made bill-paying very confusing—she almost always returned about half of her purchases.

Somehow couples such as these have learned to mellow about their partner's faults. So although they communicate to each other every emotion in the spectrum, including anger, irritability, disappointment, and hurt, they also communicate their fundamental fondness and respect. Whatever issue they are discussing, they

give each other the message that they are l⟨
"warts and all."

When couples are not able to do this, som⟨
is that they are unable to forgive each other for p⟨
It's all too easy to hold a grudge. For a marriage to g⟨
happily, you need to pardon each other and give up on past
sentments. This can be hard to do, but it is well worth it. When
you forgive your spouse, you both benefit. Bitterness is a heavy
burden. As Shakespeare wrote in *The Merchant of Venice*, mercy is
"twice blessed. It blesses him that gives and him that takes."

9

Principle 5:
Solve Your Solvable Problems

*I*t stands to reason that when a husband and wife respect each other and are open to each other's point of view, they have a good basis for resolving any differences that arise. And yet too often couples lose their way when trying to persuade each other or settle disagreements. A conversation that could have been productive instead ends in a screaming match or angry silence. If this sounds like you, and you're certain the problem you want to tackle is indeed solvable, then the key to resolving this difficulty is to learn a new approach to settling conflict. (The advice offered here will also be somewhat helpful in coping with gridlocked problems, but it won't be enough. To break the stranglehold a perpetual problem has on your marriage, be sure to read about Principle 6, overcoming gridlock, in chapter 11.)

The popular approach to conflict resolution, advocated by many marital therapists, is to attempt to put yourself in your partner's shoes while listening intently to what he or she says, and then to communicate, with empathy, that you see the dilemma from his or her perspective. It's not a bad method—if you can do it. But, as I've said, many couples can't—including many very happily married couples. Plenty of the people we studied who had enviable, loving relationships did not follow the experts' rules of communi-cation when they argued. But they were still able to resolve their conflicts.

By studying intently what these couples did do, I have come up with a new model for resolving conflict in a loving relationship. My fifth principle entails the following steps:

1. Soften your start-up.
2. Learn to make and receive repair attempts.
3. Soothe yourself and each other.
4. Compromise.
5. Process any grievances so that they don't linger.

Most of these steps take very little training because we all pretty much have these skills already; we just get out of the habit of using them in our most intimate relationship. To a certain degree, my fifth principle comes down to having good manners. It means treating your spouse with the same respect you offer to company. If a guest leaves an umbrella, we say, "Here. You forgot your um-brella." We would never think of saying, "What's wrong with you? You are constantly forgetting things. Be a little more thoughtful, for God's sake! What am I, your slave to go picking up after you?" We are sensitive to the guest's feelings, even if things don't go so well. When a guest spills wine, we say, "No problem. Would you like another glass?" not, "You just ruined my best tablecloth. I can't depend on you to do anything right. I will never invite you to my home again."

I'm reminded again of the case of Dr. Rory who was so nasty to his wife yet was able to quickly turn on the charm when a resident phoned. This is not an infrequent phenomenon. In the midst of a bitter dispute, the husband or wife answers a call and is suddenly all smiles: "Oh, hi. Yes, it would be great to have lunch. Tuesday would be fine. Oh, I am so sorry to hear that you didn't get the job. You must feel so disappointed," and so on. Suddenly the angry, rigid spouse has been transformed into a flexible, rational, under-standing, and compassionate being—until the phone call is over.

Then he or she morphs right back into someone scowling and immovable all for the partner's benefit. It just doesn't have to be this way! Keep in mind, as you work your way through these steps, that what's really being requested of you is no more than would be asked if you were dealing with an acquaintance, much less the person who has vowed to share his or her life with you.

Step 1: Soften Your Start-Up

If there's one similarity between happy and unhappy heterosexual marriages, it's that the wife is far more likely than the husband to bring up a touchy issue and to push to resolve it. Husbands are more likely to try to distance themselves from hard-to-face concerns. Again, there are physiological reasons for this gender gap. Men tend to experience flooding much more easily because their bodies are more reactive to emotional stress than their wives'. So they are more inclined to avoid confrontation.

But there can be dramatic differences in *how* a wife initiates touchy discussions with her husband. Remember Dara, who lit into her husband, Oliver, as soon as they began discussing housework? Within a minute she was being sarcastic and batting down every suggestion he made: "Do you think you really work well with lists?" and "I think you do a pretty good job of coming home and lying around and disappearing into the bathroom."

Compare Dara's harsh approach with that of Justine, who is happily married to Michael but has the same problem: he doesn't do his share around the house. What bugs her most is that she always ends up folding the laundry, which (like my wife) she hates. Here's what she says in the Love Lab, when she broaches the topic with Michael.

JUSTINE: Okay. (*deep breath*) Housework.
MICHAEL: Yeah. Well, I mean, I definitely clean off the counters in the kitchen and the table whenever we do stuff. (*defensive*)
JUSTINE: Hm-hmm. You do. (*repair attempt*)

MICHAEL: Hm-hmm. (*He yawns, relaxed; Justine's repair attempt was successful.*)

JUSTINE: I think it's just, like, sometimes when things are just kind of left, or the laundry just piles up . . . (*softened start-up*)

MICHAEL: Yeah. I haven't even been thinking about laundry. (*laughs*) I mean, I just haven't been thinking about it at all. (*not defensive*)

JUSTINE (*laughs*): That's kind of cute. Who do you think's doing it? You keep having clothes to wear.

MICHAEL: Yeah, I guess.

JUSTINE: And maybe that's okay. But it just gets to me after a while.

MICHAEL: Well, it hasn't even crossed my mind that, like, we have to do the laundry. (*chuckles*)

JUSTINE: Actually, Tim's been folding them. [A neighbor in their apartment complex—the washer and dryer are in a communal laundry room.] I left a load in, and then when I passed by, the sheets were folded.

MICHAEL: Maybe we should put our hamper in his room?

JUSTINE (*laughs*): (*Shared humor de-escalates tension and lowers heart rates.*)

MICHAEL: So, okay, like maybe every other day or something when I first get back home from work . . .

JUSTINE: Yeah, you could fold what makes sense, especially towels and underwear and the sheets . . .

MICHAEL: Yeah, I'll just look in the basket. (*He is accepting her influence.*)

JUSTINE: Okay.

Perhaps the most important quality of this exchange is the virtual absence of the four horsemen. There is no criticism, contempt, defensiveness, or stonewalling. The reason these harbingers of doom don't make an appearance is that Justine's start-up is soft. In contrast, a harsh start-up usually begins the cycle of the four horsemen, which leads to flooding and, in turn, increased emotional distance and loneliness that lets the marriage wither. Only 40 percent of the time do couples divorce because they are having frequent, devastating fights. More often marriages end because, to avoid constant skirmishes, husband and wife distance themselves so much that their friendship and sense of connection are lost.

That's why it's so important that when Michael admits that he doesn't even think about the laundry, Justine doesn't get critical or contemptuous. She laughs and says she thinks that's "cute." Because Justine is gentle with Michael, their conversation actually produces a result: they come up with a plan to resolve the conflict. Since they are able to do this, their discussion leaves them feeling positive about themselves and their marriage. That feeling is "money in the bank" for any couple—it inspires an optimistic attitude that will help them resolve the next conflict that comes along.

In another happy marriage, the big issue is that Andrea wants Dave to become more involved with the church. But she hardly bangs him over the head with a Bible. Instead she says, "Going to church is not something I need every day. But it's a comfort." Then she tells him, "I don't like you going just because of me." By the time she tells him directly, "I want a little bit more involvement from you than just Easter, Christmas, and Mother's Day," he is ready to compromise. "Okay, I'll go to church on big, important days and . . . maybe some Sundays."

A seven-year study of repair conducted by my former students Jani Driver and Amber Tabares found that taking some responsibility for the problem is a very important part of softened start-up. So if a wife is upset that her husband forgot to pick up the kids from school, it helps if she starts the conversation with, "I realize that I didn't remind you of the schedule this morning. Still I want to talk about your forgetting that it was your turn to pick up the kids." If you aren't comfortable claiming some specific share of the responsibility, then try a simple statement like "I know this isn't all your fault. I know I play a role in this issue as well." Taking responsibility is a critical component of a softened start-up no matter whom you're addressing. But I have found that it is especially important for wives to incorporate this into their delivery. For many men, hearing their wife acknowledge a shared responsibility is like manna from heaven and prevents tensions from escalating.

The best soft start-up has four parts: (1) "I share some respo sibility for this . . ." (2) Here's how I feel . . . (3) about a specific situation and . . . (4) here's what I need . . . (positive need, not what you *don't* need). Instead of pointing your finger at your partner, you are pointing your finger at yourself. To convert a negative need to a positive one, focus on your negative emotions and look for the longing behind those feelings. If you could wave a magic wand, what would you wish for? What is your recipe for your partner to be successful with you right now?

In order to be effective, a soft start-up doesn't have to be very diplomatic. But it must be devoid of criticism or contempt. In a healthy but volatile marriage, which can be very confrontational, the wife may say something like, "Hey, I know I can be a slob sometimes myself, but I'm really angry that you walked by the laundry basket last night without stopping to fold any sheets. I didn't like having to fold them all myself." Or: "I feel really strongly that we need to go to church together more often. This is very important to me." These are soft start-ups because they are direct complaints rather than criticisms or contemptuous accusations.

HARSH START-UP QUESTIONNAIRE

To get a sense of whether harsh start-up is a problem in your marriage, answer the following questions.

Read each statement and circle T for "true" or F for "false."

WHEN WE BEGIN TO DISCUSS OUR MARITAL ISSUES:

1. My partner is often very critical of me. **T F**
2. I hate the way my partner raises an issue. **T F**
3. Arguments often seem to come out of nowhere. **T F**
4. Before I know it, we are in a fight. **T F**
5. When my partner complains, I feel picked on. **T F**
6. I seem to always get blamed for issues. **T F**
7. My partner is negative all out of proportion. **T F**
8. I feel I have to ward off personal attacks. **T F**
9. I often have to deny charges leveled against me. **T F**

r's feelings are too easily hurt. **T F**

wrong is often not my responsibility. **T F**

criticizes my personality. **T F**

issues get raised in an insulting manner. **T F**

14. My partner will at times complain in a smug or superior way. **T F**
15. I have just about had it with all this negativity between us. **T F**
16. I feel basically disrespected when my partner complains. **T F**
17. I just want to leave the scene when complaints arise. **T F**
18. Our calm is suddenly shattered. **T F**
19. I find my partner's negativity unnerving and unsettling. **T F**
20. I think my partner can be totally irrational. **T F**

Scoring: Give yourself 1 point for each "true" answer.

Below 5: This is an area of strength in your marriage. You and your spouse initiate difficult discussions with each other gently—without being critical or contemptuous. Because you avoid being harsh, your chances of resolving your conflict or learning to manage it successfully together are dramatically increased.

5 or higher: Your marriage could stand some improvement in this area. Your score suggests that when you address areas of disagreement with your spouse, one of you tends to be harsh. That means you immediately trot out at least one of the four horsemen, which automatically prevents the issue from being resolved.

Although the wife is usually responsible for a harsh start-up, the secret to avoiding it is for both partners to work together on the first four principles. Do this, and the wife's start-up softens as a matter of course. So if your spouse tends to raise issues harshly, the best advice I can give is to make sure she (or he) is feeling known, respected, and loved by you, and that you accept your partner's influence. Harsh start-up is often a reaction that sets in when a wife feels her husband doesn't respond to her low-level complaints or irritability. So if you comply with a minor request like "It's your turn to take out the garbage, please," you avoid having the situation escalate into "What the hell is wrong with you? Are you deaf? Take out the damn garbage!"

If you are the one more responsible for harsh start-ups in your relationship, I can't emphasize enough how important it is to the fate of your marriage to soften up. Remember: If you go straight for the jugular, you're going to draw plenty of blood. The result will be war or retreat on your partner's part rather than any meaningful, productive discussion. If you're angry with your spouse, it's worth taking a deep breath and thinking through how to broach the subject. Softening your start-up will be easier if you constantly remind yourself that it is the optimum strategy for resolving the conflict. If you feel too angry to discuss the matter gently, your best option is not to discuss it at all until you've calmed down. Follow the steps for self-soothing on page 181 before talking it out with your spouse.

Here are some suggestions to ensure that your start-up is soft:

Complain but don't blame. Remember: "I feel . . ."; about what? . . . ; and "I need . . ." Let's assume that you're angry because your spouse insisted on adopting a dog despite your reservations. He swore up and down that he'd clean up after the dog, but now you're finding poop all over the yard. It's certainly okay to complain. You could say something like, "Hey, there's poop all over the backyard. We agreed you'd clean up after Banjo. I'm really upset about this. Would you please clean it up?" While this is confrontational, it's not an attack. You're simply complaining about a particular situation, not your partner's personality or character.

What's not okay is to say something like, "Hey, there's poop all over the backyard. This is all your fault. I just knew you'd be irresponsible about that dog. I should never have trusted you about it in the first place." However justified you may feel in blaming your spouse, the bottom line is that this approach is not productive. Even if it does lead your partner to clean up the yard, it also leads to increased tension, resentment, defensiveness, and so on.

Make statements that start with "I" instead of "You." "I statements" have been a staple of interpersonal psychology ever since the mid-1960s when Thomas Gordon noted that phrases starting with "I" were usually less likely to be critical and to make the listener defensive than statements starting with "You." Here's the difference:

"You are not listening to me" versus "I would like it if you'd listen to me."

"You are careless with money" versus "I want us to save more."

"You just don't care about me" versus "I'm feeling neglected."

Clearly, the "I" statements above are gentler than their "You" counterparts. Of course, it's possible to twist this general rule and come up with accusatory "I" statements like "I think you are selfish" that are hardly gentle. So the point is not to start talking to your spouse in some stilted psychobabble. Just keep in mind that if your words focus on how *you* feel rather than on accusing your spouse, your discussion will be far more successful.

Describe what is happening. Don't evaluate or judge. Instead of accusing or blaming, just communicate what you see. Instead of, "You never watch the baby," say, "I seem to be the only one chasing after Charlie today." Again, this will help prevent your spouse from feeling attacked and waging a defense rather than really considering your point.

Be clear about your positive need. Don't expect your partner to be a mind reader. Instead of, "You left the kitchen a total mess," say, "I'd appreciate it if you would clean your stuff off the kitchen table." Instead of, "Would you take care of the baby for once?" say, "Please change Emmy's diaper and give her a bottle."

Be polite. Add phrases such as "Please" and "I would appreciate it if . . ."

Be appreciative. If your partner has handled this situation better in the past, then couch your request within an appreciation of what your partner did back then and how much you miss that now. Instead of, "You never have time for me anymore," say, "Remember how we used to go out every Saturday night? I loved spending so much time alone with you. And it felt so good knowing that you wanted to be with me, too. Let's start doing that again."

Don't store things up. It's hard to be gentle when you're ready to burst with recriminations. So don't wait too long before bringing up an issue—otherwise it will just escalate in your mind. As the Bible says (Ephesians 4:26), "Let not the sun go down upon your wrath."

To see how all of these steps combine to create a softened start-up, compare what Iris says in the following two dialogues:

Harsh Start-Up

IRIS: Another Saturday, and once again I'm spending my free time picking up after you. The trouble with you, Richard, is that . . . (*criticism, blame*)

RICHARD: Yep, here we go again. "The trouble with you, Richard, the trouble with you, Richard." There's nothing wrong with me!

IRIS: Then why do I always have to tell you what to do? Never mind, I've finished cleaning up your stuff anyway, or were you too busy texting friends to notice? (*contempt*)

RICHARD: Look, I hate cleaning up. I know you do, too. I've been thinking about what we should do. (*repair attempt*)

IRIS: This I've got to hear. (*more contempt*)

RICHARD: Well, actually I was thinking that we could use a vacation. Wouldn't it be nice for you to be waited on hand and foot? (*second repair attempt*)

IRIS: Come on, we can't afford a cleaning lady, much less a vacation like that.

Softened Start-Up

IRIS: This house is an incredible mess, and we're having company tonight. (*describing*) I'm really upset that I'm doing all this cleaning, alone, on a Saturday. (*"I" statement*) Perhaps I should have asked sooner (*accepting responsibility*) but could you please help me. Maybe you could do the vacuuming? (*being clear*)

RICHARD: All right. I hate cleaning up, but I guess vacuuming is the best of the worst. I'll do the bathrooms, too.

IRIS: That'd be a big help. (*appreciation*) Thank you. (*politeness*)

RICHARD: When we're done, we deserve a reward—let's go out for lunch.

IRIS: Yes!

Here are some other examples that illustrate the difference between a harsh start-up and a softened alternative:

Harsh start-up: You never touch me.
Softened alternative: I loved it when you kissed me in the kitchen the other day. You are a natural-born kisser. Let's do that some more.
Harsh start-up: I see you dented the car again. When are you going to stop being so reckless?
Softened alternative: I saw that new dent. What happened? I am really getting worried about your driving, and I want you to be safe. Can we talk about this?
Harsh start-up: You never have time for me!
Softened alternative: I have been missing you lately, and I'm getting a little lonely.

EXERCISE 1: SOFTENED START-UP

Now test your own ability to soften a harsh start-up. For each item below, supply a softened alternative. (Sample answers follow, but try not to peek.)

1. When your mother-in-law visits tonight, you plan to tell her how much it hurts you when she criticizes your parenting skills. You want your partner, who is very defensive when it comes to Mom, to back you up.

   Harsh start-up: I can't stand it when your mother comes over.
   Your softened alternative:

2. You wish that your partner would cook dinner or take you out.

   Harsh start-up: You never take me anywhere. I'm sick of doing all the cooking.
   Your softened alternative:

3. When you go to parties together, you think that your partner spends too much time with other people instead of you.

> *Harsh start-up*: I just know that tonight you're gonna be flirting shamelessly again at the party.
> *Your softened alternative*:

4. You're upset that you have not made love in some time. You're feeling unsure that your partner finds you attractive. You wish that the two of you could make love tonight.

> *Harsh start-up*: You're always so cold to me!
> *Your softened alternative*:

5. You want your partner to ask for a raise.

> *Harsh start-up*: You're too wimpy to get a raise for your own family.
> *Your softened alternative*:

6. You want to do more fun things together on the weekends.

> *Harsh start-up*: You have no idea how to have a good time. You're a workaholic.
> *Your softened alternative*:

7. You wish that the two of you could save more money.

> *Harsh start-up*: You don't have a clue about how to manage money.
> *Your softened alternative*:

8. You wish your partner would spend more money buying you surprise presents.

> *Harsh start-up*: When was the last time you bought me anything?
> *Your softened alternative*:

Sample Answers

1. I'm worried that your mom is going to be critical of me tonight and that you won't back me up.
2. I'm tired of cooking. It'd be real nice if you cooked or we went out.
3. I'm feeling very shy tonight. Please spend time with me and make it easier for me to talk to other people. You're so good at that.
4. I'm really missing you lately, you know how much you turn me on.
5. It would be great if you could ask for a raise soon. Could we talk about some strategies for doing that?
6. I really want to spend some fun time with you this weekend. How about not working and let's do something fun together? There's a great movie I'd like to see.
7. I'm feeling anxious about our savings. Let's come up with a savings plan, okay?
8. I'm feeling very deprived lately, and I would love it if we surprised each other with a present out of the blue this week. What do you think?

Don't expect your partner to automatically react with great sweetness and cooperation once you begin to soften your start-ups. He or she may still be anticipating the arrival of criticism and contempt and therefore won't respond positively to your new, softer style. Don't fall into the trap of giving up and escalating the conflict. Continue to broach topics gently, and eventually you will see a change in how your spouse responds, especially if you are working together on all Seven Principles.

Step 2: Learn to Make and Receive Repair Attempts

When you take driving lessons, the first thing you're taught is how to stop the car. Putting on the brakes is an important skill in a marriage, too. You can prevent plenty of disasters by terminating discussions that get off on the wrong foot and by shutting down those seemingly endless cycles of recriminations. How do you do this? By using repair attempts.

When Michael gets defensive and says, "I definitely clean off the counters in the kitchen and the table whenever we do stuff," Justine doesn't immediately discount his point. "Hm-hmm, you do," she says. This is a repair attempt. It de-escalates the tension so that Michael is more receptive to finding a compromise. What separates stable, emotionally intelligent marriages from others is not that their repair attempts are necessarily more skillful or better thought out but that repair attempts get through to the spouse. This is because the air between them hasn't been clouded by a lot of negativity.

REPAIR ATTEMPTS QUESTIONNAIRE

To assess the effectiveness of repair attempts in your own relationship, answer the following.

Read each statement and circle T for "true" or F for "false."

DURING OUR ATTEMPTS TO RESOLVE CONFLICT:

1. We are good at taking breaks when we need them. **T F**
2. My partner usually accepts my apologies. **T F**
3. I can say that I am wrong. **T F**
4. I am pretty good at calming myself down. **T F**
5. We can maintain a sense of humor. **T F**
6. When my partner says we should talk to each other in a different way, it usually makes a lot of sense. **T F**
7. My attempts to repair our discussions when they get negative are usually effective. **T F**
8. We are pretty good listeners even when we have different positions on things. **T F**
9. If things get heated, we can usually pull out of it and change things. **T F**
10. My spouse is good at soothing me when I get upset. **T F**
11. I feel confident that we can resolve most issues between us. **T F**

12. When I comment on how we could communicate better, my spouse listens to me. **T F**
13. Even if things get hard at times, I know we can get past our differences. **T F**
14. We can be affectionate even when we are disagreeing. **T F**
15. Teasing and humor usually work to get my spouse over negativity. **T F**
16. We can start all over again and improve our discussion when we need to. **T F**
17. When emotions run hot, expressing how upset I feel makes a real difference. **T F**
18. We can discuss even big differences between us. **T F**
19. My partner expresses appreciation for nice things I do. **T F**
20. If I keep trying to communicate, it will eventually work. **T F**

Scoring: Give yourself 1 point for each "true" answer.

13 or higher: This is an area of strength in your marriage. When marital discussions are at risk of getting out of hand, you are able to put on the brakes and effectively calm each other down.

Below 13: Your marriage could stand some improvement in this area. By learning how to repair your interactions, you can dramatically improve the effectiveness of your problem solving and develop a more positive perspective on each other and your marriage.

Getting the Message Through

Remember that the key factor in whether a repair attempt is effective is the state of the relationship. In happy marriages, couples send and receive repair attempts with ease. In unhappy ones, even the most eloquent repair attempt can fall on deaf ears. But now that you know this, you can "buck the system." You don't have to wait for your marriage to improve before you start hearing each other's repair attempts. Start now by focusing intently on these brakes and training each other to recognize when one is sent your way. Do this, and you can pull yourselves out of a negative cycle.

Your future together can be bright even if your disagreements tend to be very negative. The secret is learning the right kind of damage control.

One reason couples miss each other's repair attempts is that these messages don't always arrive sugarcoated. If your spouse yells, "You're getting off the topic!" or grumbles, "Can we take a break?" that's a repair attempt despite the negative delivery. If you listen to his or her tone rather than the words, you could miss the real message, which is "Stop! This is getting out of hand."

Because repair attempts can be difficult to hear if your relationship is engulfed in negativity, the best strategy under such circumstances is to make your attempts obviously formal in order to emphasize them. Below you'll find a long list of scripted phrases. These are specific words you can say to your spouse to de-escalate the tension. By using them when arguments get too negative, you'll be able to keep your discussions from spiraling out of control. Some couples even copy this list and stick it on their refrigerator for handy reference. Formalizing repair attempts by using these scripted phrases can help you defuse arguments in two ways. First, the formality of a script ensures that you will use the type of words that work well for putting on the brakes. Second, these phrases are like megaphones—they help ensure that you pay attention to a repair attempt when you're on the receiving end.

Many, if not all, of these phrases will probably sound phony and unnatural to you. That's because they offer a very different way of speaking with your spouse when you're upset. But their phoniness is not a reason to reject them. If you learned a better and more effective way to hold your tennis racket, it would feel "wrong" and "unnatural" initially, simply because you weren't used to it yet. The same goes for these repair attempts. Over time they'll come easily to you, and you'll modify them to more closely suit your style of speech and personality.

I Feel

1. I'm getting scared.
2. Please say that more gently.
3. Did I do something wrong?
4. That hurt my feelings.
5. That felt like an insult.
6. I'm feeling sad.
7. I feel blamed. Can you rephrase that?
8. I'm feeling unappreciated.
9. I feel defensive. Can you rephrase that?
10. Please don't lecture me.
11. I don't feel like you understand me right now.
12. I am starting to feel flooded.
13. I feel criticized. Can you rephrase that?
14. I'm getting worried.

I Need to Calm Down

1. Can you make things safer for me?
2. I need things to be calmer right now.
3. I need your support right now.
4. Just listen to me right now and try to understand.
5. Tell me you love me.
6. Can I have a kiss?
7. Can I take that back?
8. Please be gentler with me.
9. Please help me calm down.
10. Please be quiet and listen to me.
11. This is important to me. Please listen.
12. I need to finish what I was saying.
13. I am starting to feel flooded.
14. I feel criticized. Can you rephrase that?
15. Can we take a break?

Sorry

1. My reactions were too extreme. Sorry.
2. I really blew that one.
3. Let me try again.

4. I want to be gentler toward you right now, and I don't know how.
5. Tell me what you hear me saying.
6. I can see my part in all this.
7. How can I make things better?
8. Let's try that over again.
9. What you are saying is . . .
10. Let me start again in a softer way.
11. I'm sorry. Please forgive me.

Get to Yes

1. You're starting to convince me.
2. I agree with part of what you're saying.
3. Let's compromise here.
4. Let's find our common ground.
5. I never thought of things that way.
6. This problem is not very serious in the big picture.
7. I think your point of view makes sense.
8. Let's agree to include both our views in a solution.
9. I am thankful for . . .
10. One thing I admire about you is . . .
11. I see what you're talking about.

Stop Action!

1. I might be wrong here.
2. Please, let's stop for a while.
3. Let's take a break.
4. Give me a moment. I'll be back.
5. I'm feeling flooded.
6. Please stop.
7. Let's agree to disagree here.
8. Let's start all over again.
9. Hang in there. Don't withdraw.
10. I want to change the topic.
11. We are getting off track.

I Appreciate

1. I know this isn't your fault.
2. My part of this problem is . . .
3. I see your point.
4. Thank you for . . .
5. That's a good point.
6. We are both saying . . .
7. I understand.
8. I love you.
9. I am thankful for . . .
10. One thing I admire about you is . . .
11. This is not your problem, it's our problem.

Now it's time to use the above list to help you resolve an issue in your marriage. Choose a low-intensity conflict to discuss. Each of you gets to talk for fifteen minutes. Make sure you both use at least one phrase from the list during the discussion. Announce to your partner beforehand that you're about to make a repair attempt. You can even refer to the attempt by number, as in, "I'm making repair attempt number six under I Feel: 'I'm feeling sad.'"

When your partner announces a repair attempt, your job is simply to try to accept it. View the interruption as a bid to make things better. Accept the attempt in the spirit in which it was intended. This entails accepting your partner's influence. For example, if he or she says, "I need to finish what I'm saying," acknowledge that need and then encourage your partner to keep talking to you. As you continue to use the list in your conversations, eventually you might consider replacing it with some other ritual, like raising your hand and announcing point-blank, "This is a repair attempt!" Or you may come up with other effective repairs that better fit your personality and relationship. For example, a couple we know say "clip clop" to each other if one of them introduces one of the four horsemen into a discussion. The humor in this repair helps defuse the negativity all the more.

Step 3: Soothe Yourself and Each Other

While Justine is in the middle of discussing laundry with Michael, he does something that seems incidental but really has great significance for their chances of a happy future: he yawns. Cleaning house is not the most fascinating subject, but Michael doesn't yawn because Justine is boring him. He yawns because he is relaxed. When you're feeling angry or anxious, yawning is just about the least likely physiological reaction you're going to have. Michael's yawn is like an announcement that he's feeling soothed by Justine, even though she's discussing an area of conflict. Because no alarms are going off in his body (or mind), he is able to discuss housework and reach a compromise with Justine easily.

It is harder for a man's body to calm down after an argument than a woman's.

In less stable marriages, however, conflict discussions can lead to the opposite reaction—they can trigger flooding. When this occurs, you feel overwhelmed both emotionally and physically. Most likely you think thoughts of righteous indignation ("I don't have to take this anymore") or innocent victimhood ("Why is she always picking on me?"). Meanwhile, your body is in distress. Usually your heart is pounding, you're sweating, you're holding your breath.

I have found that in the vast majority of cases, when one spouse does not "get" the other's repair attempt, it's because the listener is flooded and therefore can't really hear what the spouse is saying. When you're in this condition, the most thoughtful repair attempt in the world won't benefit your marriage.

FLOODING QUESTIONNAIRE

To determine whether flooding is a significant problem in your relationship, answer the following questions.

Read each statement and circle T for "true" or F for "false."

1. Our discussions get too heated. **T F**
2. I have a hard time calming down. **T F**
3. One of us is going to say something we will regret. **T F**
4. My partner gets too upset. **T F**
5. After a fight, I want to keep my distance. **T F**
6. My partner yells unnecessarily. **T F**
7. I feel overwhelmed by our arguments. **T F**
8. I can't think straight when my partner gets hostile. **T F**
9. Why can't we talk more logically? **T F**
10. My partner's negativity often comes out of nowhere. **T F**
11. There's often no stopping my partner's temper. **T F**
12. I feel like running away during our fights. **T F**
13. Small issues suddenly become big ones. **T F**
14. I can't calm down very easily during an argument. **T F**
15. My partner has a long list of unreasonable demands. **T F**

Scoring: Give yourself 1 point for each "true" answer.

Below 6: Flooding is not a significant problem in your marriage. You are able to confront differences of opinion with your spouse without feeling overwhelmed. This means that you are not feeling victimized or hostile toward your spouse during disagreements. That's good news since it indicates that you are able to communicate with each other without negativity getting out of hand. As a result, you're better able to resolve conflicts (and avoid gridlock over issues that are unresolvable).

6 or higher: Your score suggests that you tend to get flooded during arguments with your spouse. Flooding almost guarantees that your discussion won't end the conflict. You are feeling too agitated to really hear what your spouse is saying or to learn any helpful conflict-resolution skills. Read on to find out how to cope with this problem.

EXERCISE 2: SELF-SOOTHING

The first step in dealing with flooding is to end the discussion. *Now*. If you keep going, you'll find yourself exploding at your partner or imploding (stonewalling), neither of which will get you anywhere. Don't think, "We'll take a break as soon as I've made my point," because you'll end up never taking a break at all. Just. Stop. Let your spouse know that you're feeling flooded. The break should last at least twenty minutes, since it will take that long for your body to calm down. It's crucial that during this time you avoid thoughts of righteous indignation and innocent victimhood. Spend your time doing something soothing and distracting, like listening to music, taking a walk, or reading. Exercising is also a good choice as long as you enjoy it and don't spend your workout time nursing your anger or sadness or rehearsing the verbal arrows you will launch after the break.

Many people find that the best approach to self-soothing is to focus on calming the body through a meditative technique. Here's a simple one:

1. Sit in a comfortable chair, or lie on your back on the floor.
2. Focus on controlling your breathing. Usually when you get flooded, you either hold your breath a lot or breathe shallowly. So close your eyes, and focus on taking deep, regular breaths.
3. Relax your muscles. One at a time, tightly squeeze the muscle groups that seem tense (usually, your forehead and jaw, neck, shoulders, arms, and back). Hold for two seconds, and then release.
4. Let the tension flow out of each muscle group, and get that muscle group to feel heavy by imagining that it is weighed down.
5. Now get each heavy muscle group to feel warm. One popular method is to keep your eyes closed and concentrate on a calming vision or idea. Many people find it effective to think of a place they associate with tranquillity, like a forest, lake, or beach. For example, I think of a place I know on Orcas Island in Washington State, where the loudest sound is the wind rustling the trees as young eagles that reside in a nearby rookery soar by. Conjuring

that image relaxes me and automatically triggers all of the other steps of self-soothing. Imagine your soothing place as vividly as you can. Keep focused on this peaceful image for about thirty seconds.

Taking a break of this sort is so critical that I schedule it into the conflict-resolution section of every workshop we run. Invariably, participants at first moan and groan about this "forced" relaxation. Many are quite skeptical that closing their eyes and thinking about a lake can help cure their marital woes. Yet once they engage in the exercise, they realize how powerful and helpful it really is. Suddenly everybody in the room loosens up. You can see the difference in how couples relate to each other. Their voices grow softer; there is more chuckling. Relaxing makes them better able to work on their conflicts as a team rather than as adversaries.

If you need more evidence of the benefit of these exercises, consider one experiment we conducted in the Love Lab. We had couples spend fifteen minutes discussing a marital issue, and then we told them we needed to "adjust the equipment." Over the next thirty minutes, while we "fixed" the apparatus, we asked them to avoid the topic and just read magazines. When we restarted the experiment, their heart rates were significantly lower than beforehand and their interactions more productive.

EXERCISE 3: SOOTHING EACH OTHER

Once you're feeling calmer, you can benefit your marriage enormously if you then take some time to soothe your partner. Obviously, doing so is quite difficult if you're feeling very angry or hurt, but the results can be so impressive that it's worth trying. Remember: only attempt this after you've already spent twenty minutes calming yourself.

Soothing your partner is of enormous benefit to a marriage because it's really a form of reverse conditioning. In other words, if you frequently have the experience of being calmed by your spouse, you come to associate him or her with feelings of relaxation rather than of stress. This automatically increases the positivity in your relationship.

To comfort each other, you first need to talk earnestly about flooding. Ask yourself and each other these questions:

- What makes each of us feel flooded?
- How do we each typically bring up issues, feelings of irritability, or complaints?
- Do either of us store things up?
- Is there anything I can do that soothes you?
- Is there anything you can do that soothes me?
- What signals can we develop for letting the other know when we feel flooded? Can we take breaks?

If your heart rate exceeds 100 beats per minute (80 if you're an athlete), you won't be able to hear what your spouse is trying to tell you no matter how hard you try. Take a twenty-minute break before continuing.

There are many different ways to calm your spouse. What matters most is that your partner determines the method and enjoys it. Some couples find massage the perfect antidote to a stressful discussion. Another helpful technique is to take turns guiding each other through a meditation like the one described on page 181. Think of it as a verbal massage. You can even write an elaborate script in which you have your spouse tighten and relax different muscle groups and then visualize a calm, beautiful scene that brings him or her pleasure. Consider taping your rendition for future use—perhaps give it to your spouse as a special gift. You don't need to wait for a tense situation to use this exercise. Soothing each other regularly is a wonderful way to prevent future flooding and enrich your marriage.

Another strategy to counter flooding is for each of you to try a pulse oximeter—an inexpensive device that fits on your index finger and assesses your heart rate and other measures of stress. Choose a model that is FDA-approved and can be programmed to alert you if your heart rate climbs above a certain level (100 beats a minute or 80 if you're in great physical shape). If the alarm sounds you both take at least a thirty-minute break. Then try to have the discussion again. Couples in our studies have also had excellent results using a small bio-feedback device called the emWave (made by HeartMath) that helps train the body and mind to self-soothe.

Step 4: Compromise

Like it or not, compromise is the only way to solve marital problems. In an intimate, loving relationship, it just doesn't work for either of you to get things all your way, even if you're convinced that you're right. This approach would create such inequity and unfairness that the marriage would suffer.

Often when couples don't succeed at compromising, it isn't through lack of trying but because they've gone about it the wrong way. Negotiation is possible only after you've followed the steps above—softening start-up, repairing your discussion, and keeping calm. Together, these will create a positive atmosphere. Remember: Compromise is not about just one person changing. It's about negotiating and finding ways to accommodate each other. You will not be able to compromise successfully if you don't accept your partner's flaws and foibles. Instead, you will be on a relentless campaign to alter your spouse. Too often a marriage gets bogged down in "if only." *If only* your spouse were taller, richer, smarter, neater, or sexier, all of your problems would vanish. Unlike cherishing, which nurtures gratitude for what you have, "if only" nurtures resentment for what you don't have. As long as this attitude prevails, conflicts will be very difficult to resolve.

Before you try to resolve a conflict, remember that *the cornerstone of any compromise is the fourth principle of marriage— accepting influence*. This means that for a compromise to work, you can't have a closed mind to your spouse's opinions and desires. You don't have to agree with everything your spouse says or believes, but you have to be open to *considering* his or her position. That's what accepting influence is really all about. If you find yourself sitting with your arms folded and shaking your head no (or just thinking it) when your spouse is trying to talk out a problem, your discussion will never get anywhere.

As I've said, men tend to have a harder time accepting influence from their wives than vice versa. But whatever your gender, an inability to be open-minded is a real liability when it comes to conflict resolution. So if you haven't already, work through the exercises in chapter 7 on accepting influence. Realize that it may take time and continued self-awareness to break out of this tendency. Your partner can assist you in seeing things from his or her perspective. Ask questions to help you understand his or her point of view. Remember to search for the part of your spouse's perspective that an objective bystander would consider reasonable.

Once you're really ready to negotiate, there's nothing magical about finding a solution you both can live with. Often compromise is just a matter of talking out your differences and preferences in a systematic way. This is not difficult to do as long as you continue to follow the steps above to prevent your discussion from becoming overwhelmingly negative.

EXERCISE 4: FINDING COMMON GROUND

Decide together which solvable problem you want to tackle. Start by sitting separately and thinking about the problem. On a piece of paper, draw two circles—a smaller one inside a larger one. In the inner circle, make a list of the aspects of the problem you can't give in on. In the outer circle, list all of the aspects of the problem you *can* compromise over. Remember the aikido principle of yielding to win—the more able you are to make concessions, the better able you'll be to persuade your spouse. So try hard to keep your outer circle as large as possible and your inner circle as small as possible.

Here are the inner and outer circles of a couple named Raymond and Carol, who were both dissatisfied with their sex life.

Carol

INNER CIRCLE:

1. I want to feel like we're making love when we're having sex.
2. I want you to hold me and stroke me a lot. I want a lot of foreplay.

OUTER CIRCLE:

1. I prefer to have sex at night because I love falling asleep in your arms afterward, but sex in the morning would be okay, too.
2. Talking to me a lot while we make love is nice, but I can compromise on this, too.

Raymond

INNER CIRCLE:

1. I want sex to be more erotic.
2. I want there to be fantasy play with you wearing very sexy lingerie.

OUTER CIRCLE:

1. I can compromise on whether to have sex in the morning or at night even when I'm tired.
2. I can talk more during sex.

Once you've filled in your circles (your lists may be much longer than Raymond and Carol's), come back and share them with each other. Look for bases of agreement. Remember to make use of all the problem-solving strategies outlined in this chapter—namely, softened start-up and soothing yourself or each other if flooding occurs.

In the case of Carol and Raymond, their inner circles are very different, but they are not incompatible. Once they accept and respect their sexual differences, they can create lovemaking sessions that incorporate his desire for erotic fantasy with her longing for intimacy and lots of touching. And although their outer circles are in opposition as well, they are willing to give in these areas, so compromise should be

easy. Maybe they'll decide to switch off with morni
depending on how tired Raymond is. And they can v
they speak during sex as well.

The goal of this circle exercise is to try to develop a comm
of thinking about the issue so that you work together to constru
real plan that you can both live with. As you share your circles, ask
yourselves the following questions:

1. What do we agree about?
2. What are our common feelings or the most important feelings here?
3. What common goals can we have?
4. How can we understand this situation or issue?
5. How do we think we should accomplish these goals?

Most likely if you're grappling with a solvable problem, following these steps will lead you to find a reasonable compromise. Once you do, try out the solution for an agreed-upon time before revisiting it and deciding if it's working. If it's not, begin the process again, and work together to resolve it.

Step 5: Dealing with Emotional Injuries

When you are able to compromise on a solvable problem in a way that leaves you both satisfied, you prevent the issue from turning into a damaging, gridlocked conflict. But these arguments can still leave scars, even if you get past the issues that triggered them. I call this residual damage an "emotional injury." William Faulkner said it best in *Requiem for a Nun*: "The past is never dead. In fact, it's not even past." We can revisit the past because it still lives in our bodies in the present. If emotional injuries aren't addressed, they tend to become constant irritants—like a stone in your shoe that you keep walking on. People tend to ruminate about these incidents, and emotional distance can build up over time. It is perfectly normal to have past emotional injuries that need talking about, or "processing."

If this has happened to you when you disagreed or hurt each

ner, the culprit is not *what* you were fighting about but *how* you were fighting. The following in-depth exercise gets to the bottom of this by examining what tends to go on between you during a disagreement. Analyzing this together will afford you a deeper understanding of how you are each experiencing your arguments. This knowledge will help make your future conflicts less emotionally bruising.

EXERCISE 5: PROCESSING A PREVIOUS EMOTIONAL INJURY

As you work through this exercise, remember that all experience is subjective. There is no God-camera that has recorded the ultimate Truth of what happened between you. Each of your perceptions is equally valid. So your aim isn't to persuade or to debate whose perceptions were more accurate. Instead, your goal is to gain greater understanding of each other's subjective reality and of how the issue was handled. That's how you process past emotional injuries. (Note: You'll see that parts of this exercise are similar to the briefer "Talking It Out" exercise in chapter 6. That's because the processes for working through minor and major conflicts share much in common.)

STEP 1: Choose a specific incident to work through. Select a conflict that you both feel you can now discuss with some emotional distance. For the purpose of this exercise, imagine that you are sitting in the balcony of a theater during the intermission, discussing what happened during Act One—except that Act One was the unfortunate incident and you were the actors on stage.

STEP 2: Decide who will speak first. For this exercise, you will take turns being speaker and listener. Don't switch roles until the speaker is finished talking. When you're the listener, sit back and take in what your partner has to say *without interrupting*.

STEP 3: Say out loud what you were feeling then. When you are the speaker, list aloud all of the feelings you had to any degree during the argument or regrettable incident. (See the list below for help.) *Do not discuss why you had these emotions.* When you are the listener, don't comment on your partner's emotions.

DURING THAT ARGUMENT I FELT:
 1. Abandoned
 2. Afraid
 3. Alienated
 4. Angry
 5. Ashamed
 6. Both of us were partly right
 7. Criticized
 8. Depressed
 9. Defensive
10. Disapproving
11. Disgusted
12. Disloyal
13. Exhausted
14. Flooded
15. Foolish
16. Frustrated
17. Guilty
18. Hopeless
19. Hungry
20. Hurt
21. I had no idea what I was feeling
22. I had no influence
23. I was right and you were wrong
24. Like an innocent victim
25. Like leaving
26. Like my opinions didn't matter
27. Like you didn't even like me
28. Lonely
29. Misunderstood
30. Morally justified
31. Out of control
32. Overwhelmed with emotion

33. Powerless
34. Remorseful
35. Righteously indignant
36. Sad
37. Shocked
38. Stubborn
39. Stupid
40. Taken for granted
41. Tense
42. Tired
43. Ugly
44. Unappreciated
45. Unloved
46. Unsafe
47. Worried
48. Other (write down any additional emotions you had)

STEP 4: Share your subjective reality and what you needed.
Now let your partner know why you think you had those feelings at the time. In talking about your reality, be like a reporter. Avoid attack, blame, or criticism. Don't in any way attribute intentions or motivations to your partner. Only discuss yourself. Use "I statements" ("I heard you say . . .") not "You statements" ("You said . . ."). Also, tell your partner what you think you might have needed at the time of the incident. For example, if in Step 1 you said you felt that your opinions didn't matter, perhaps, in retrospect, what you needed was to hear your partner say your opinions *were* valued. Or, if you felt sad, perhaps you needed to feel comforted.

Here are some examples of common needs people might express during this exercise:

IN RETROSPECT . . .
1. I needed to feel like you were listening.
2. I needed to feel like you were being patient with me.
3. I needed to feel like you wouldn't overreact.
4. I needed you to tell me you loved me.
5. I needed a break from talking.

6. I needed to feel like you validated my point of view, even a little bit.
7. I needed to feel like you respected me.
8. I needed to feel I had your support and empathy.

STEP 5: Identify and explore your triggers. So often our negative reactions during an argument are rooted in those "enduring vulnerabilities"—issues or responses that we are, perhaps, overly sensitive to. As you rewind the videotape of your own memories, stop at a place when you felt some of the same emotions as you did during the argument you're now processing. It might be a time in your childhood or in a past relationship. For example, some people are particularly anxious about being abandoned by a loved one because as a child their parents were unreliable. By becoming more aware of your triggers, and your partner's, you can better avoid unduly upsetting each other when you're having a disagreement. It's important to tell your partner the story of these enduring vulnerabilities so that he or she understands why you have particular triggers.

Separately, both of you should circle your response(s) to the following.

DURING THAT ARGUMENT I FELT:
1. Excluded.
2. Like I was not important.
3. Cold (very unemotional) toward you.
4. Strongly rejected.
5. I was being criticized.
6. Like I had no affection toward you.
7. Like you weren't attracted to me.
8. My sense of dignity was being compromised.
9. Like I was being bullied.
10. I could not persuade you at all.
11. Other (write down any additional feelings you had).

After you've told your partner the history of these triggers, do some more self-exploration. Look over your answers to the "Who Am I?" exercise on page 62. See if you can find connections there between earlier traumas or behavior and this argument you had with your partner. Use the checklist below to facilitate this search for links.

MY REACTIONS WERE ROOTED IN:

(*check all that apply*)

___ The way I was treated in my family growing up.

___ A previous relationship.

___ Past injuries, hard times, or traumas I've suffered.

___ My basic fears and insecurities.

___ Things and events I have not yet resolved or put aside.

___ Unrealized hopes I have.

___ Ways other people treated me in the past.

___ Things I have always thought about myself.

___ Old "nightmares" or "catastrophes" I have worried about.

MY SPECIFIC TRIGGERS DURING THIS INCIDENT MIGHT HAVE BEEN:

___ I felt judged. I'm very sensitive to that.

___ I felt excluded. I'm very sensitive to that.

___ I felt criticized. I'm very sensitive to that.

___ I felt flooded. I'm very sensitive to that.

___ I felt ashamed. I'm very sensitive to that.

___ I felt lonely. I'm very sensitive to that.

___ I felt belittled. I'm very sensitive to that.

___ I felt disrespected. I'm very sensitive to that.

___ I felt powerless. I'm very sensitive to that.

___ I felt out of control. I'm very sensitive to that.

___ I felt hopeless. I'm very sensitive to that.

When you are the listener, respond to your partner with understanding and empathy. Summarize what you heard in a sentence, such as: "I can see why that's a big trigger for you. Hearing the story of that trigger helps me understand you better. And I get why these are enduring vulnerabilities for you."

STEP 6: Acknowledge your role in what happened. After you've discussed each other's answers in the steps above, I hope you've come to see that we are all complicated creatures whose actions and reactions are governed by a wide array of perceptions, thoughts, feelings, and memories. It's natural to believe that your partner was solely responsible for the fight, but that is erroneous thinking. To break this pattern, you both need to admit some role (however slight at first) in creating the conflict.

The first (and easiest) step is to describe what your state of mind may have been like at the time of the regrettable incident—that is, what may have set you up for the reaction you had. Try to recall which of the following were true for you and circle all that apply.

1. I had been very stressed and irritable.
2. I hadn't expressed much appreciation toward you.
3. I had been overly sensitive.
4. I had been overly critical.
5. I hadn't shared very much of my inner world.
6. I was depressed.
7. I wasn't being a very good listener.
8. I was feeling a bit like a martyr.
9. I had needed to be alone.
10. I had been preoccupied.
11. I had not wanted to take care of anybody.
12. I had not had much confidence in myself.
13. I had been running on empty.
14. I had felt taken for granted.
15. I had not been emotionally available.
16. I had taken you for granted.
17. I had not made time for good things between us.
18. Other _____.

Next, tell your partner what you want to apologize for. Begin by telling your partner what your specific regrets are and what you see as your contributions to the event. Then clearly apologize to your partner. Saying you're sorry is magical in a relationship. Examples:

I WANT TO APOLOGIZE AND I AM SORRY THAT:

1. I overreacted.
2. I was really grumpy.
3. I was defensive.
4. I was so negative.
5. I attacked you.
6. I didn't listen to you.
7. I wasn't respectful.
8. I was unreasonable.
9. Other _____.

Finally, the partner accepts the apology. (The speaker can then respond with "Thank you.") If the partner finds it hard to fully accept the apology, this indicates more work needs to be done on the exercise.

STEP 7: Looking Ahead: Constructive Plans. Take turns each answering these two questions:

1. What's one thing I can do to avoid having this kind of regrettable incident or argument again?
2. What's one thing my partner can do to avoid having this kind of regrettable incident or argument again? (Be as agreeable as possible to the plans suggested by your partner.)

When you have mastered the general problem-solving skills outlined in this chapter, you'll discover that many of your problems find their own solutions. Once you get past the barriers that have prevented clear communication, difficulties are much easier to resolve. In fact, the next chapter offers some creative and simple solutions to some of the most common conflicts couples face— money, sex, housework, kids, work stress. But remember: These remedies work only for problems that can be solved. If compromise still seems like a distant goal to you, then the problem you are grappling with may not be solvable after all. That means it's time to turn to the advice on coping with perpetual problems in chapter 11.

10

Coping with Typical Solvable Problems

ork stress, in-laws, money, sex, housework, Internet-fueled distractions, a new baby: these are the most typical areas of marital conflict, so there's a good chance at least some of them are hot buttons in your relationship. Even in very happy and stable marriages, these issues are perennials. Although every relationship is different, there's a reason why these particular conflicts are so common: they touch upon some of the marriage's most important tasks.

Many people readily agree with the notion that a good marriage takes "work." But what specifically does this mean? Every marriage is faced with certain emotional tasks that spouses need to accomplish together for the marriage to grow and deepen. These missions come down to attaining a rich understanding between partners that will allow both of them to feel safe and secure in the relationship. When these tasks are not accomplished, the marriage doesn't feel like a port in the storm of life. It feels like just another storm.

When there's conflict in one of these seven common areas, usually it's because you have different ideas about these tasks, their importance, or how they should be accomplished. If the conflict is perpetual, no amount of problem-solving savvy will fix it.

The tension will de-escalate only when you both feel comfortable living with your ongoing difference. But when the issue is solvable, the challenge is to find the right strategy for conquering it. (If you're not sure whether your conflict is solvable or perpetual, see page 142.) Here we've listed these seven hot spots, the task they each represent for a marriage, and specific advice for addressing the solvable disagreements they often trigger.

"Unplugging" from Distractions

The task: Maintaining connection and intimacy amid the distractions of the Internet Age.

How much time do you think most couples spend (or should spend) talking with each other? In a recent study of young professional couples, researchers in Los Angeles calculated (after monitoring them 24/7) that the average amount of time they actually engaged in conversation was thirty-five minutes. A week! What's more, much of their conversation was really what I would call errand-talk, such as who was going to take out the garbage or walk the kids to the school bus. I find this very sad. While there are many causes for this lack of communication, one culprit is the seemingly endless interruption that electronic gadgetry and the Internet impose on us. For many people, the instant access to information and entertainment that websites, e-mails, texts, Twitter, and video games provide transforms self-distraction into an entrenched habit that can get in the way of real connection.

The solution: If your partner is complaining that you seem more focused on your social-media profile than your marital status, that's an issue you need to take seriously, even if you disagree. I recommend that all couples establish rules of etiquette that work for them. At the very least, such rules ought to include a ban on texting, checking e-mail, or other "cyber crimes" during mealtime, date night, or when either of you needs to talk. After all, most of us readily turn off our devices at houses of worship or theaters. We need to extend that same respect and courtesy to our spouses.

Some couples may also want to make ironclad rules about privacy to avoid disagreements over what information or images are appropriate to post online. Again, it's important to establish policies that feel fair to you both—and then to respect them.

To get a sense of whether the issue of high-tech distractions is a significant one in your relationship and requires some extra attention, answer the following.

QUIZ: ELECTRONIC DISTRACTIONS

	Rarely	At Times	Usually	Often
1. I worry that my partner spends too much time attending to e-mail or other online tasks.	(0)	(1)	(2)	(3)
2. Often when I want to talk to my partner, he or she is busy texting or on the web.	(0)	(1)	(2)	(3)
3. Because of digital distractions, I find it hard to feel like I come first to my partner.	(0)	(1)	(2)	(3)
4. I feel that my partner wants to zone out far too much with TV or digital media.	(0)	(1)	(2)	(3)
5. It hurts me when I come into a room and my partner hardly notices me because he or she is immersed in social media.	(0)	(1)	(2)	(3)
6. I feel that because of electronic media my partner isn't really fully available to me.	(0)	(1)	(2)	(3)
7. Digital media seem to burn up whatever time there is for the two of us.	(0)	(1)	(2)	(3)
8. My partner is too distracted by all of the electronic options and social media to be able to be fully present with me.	(0)	(1)	(2)	(3)

9. **Attention to social media or other** such distractions is a real issue between us.	Rarely (0)	At Times (I)	Usually (2)	Often (3)
10. **Sometimes I would like to come** first in my partner's attention rather than tech.	Rarely (0)	At Times (I)	Usually (2)	Often (3)

Scoring. Add up the points (indicated in each column).

0 to 10. Being too "plugged in" is not a serious issue for the two of you.

11 to 20. Your score suggests that your relationship might benefit from some extra problem solving in this area. Apply the negotiating advice in the preceding chapter (on solvable problems) to the activities that are causing the most conflict (such as setting limits for when and where to text, answer cell phones, respond to e-mails, play video games, etc.). Being up front and loving as you discuss your needs can keep these issues from overwhelming your relationship.

21 to 30. Your score suggests that excessive attention to social media and related distractions may be interfering with your relationship. See if you can agree on a specific daily time limit for engaging in these activities. Stick to this schedule for a week, say, and then reevaluate your feelings about the issue. Sometimes couples use diversions as a way to avoid communication and connection. If you need extra help in this area, begin by reading or rereading chapter 6, "Turn Toward Each Other Instead of Away." Be sure to work through the exercises in that chapter. If differences in this area remain unsolvable, follow the advice in chapter 11, "Overcome Gridlock."

THE PROBLEM WITH PORN

No discussion of high-tech distractions would be complete without mentioning the immense popularity of pornography. There are an estimated 500 million pages of sexually explicit porn on the Internet, and they cater to every conceivable turn-on. A report by the American Association for Marriage and Family Therapy estimates that between 20 and 33 percent of Internet users in the

United States go online for sexual purposes—either to view por-nographic images or to engage in some sort of sexual interaction. Most of these people are married men. I believe that porn is inher-ently anti-romantic because it is impersonal—almost any "object" will do. In addition, many porn sites are degrading to women, or combine violence toward women with sexual release.

It's little surprise to me, therefore, that research indicates habit-ual porn use hurts the nature and quality of sex in relationships—particularly when (as is usually the case) a partner is viewing porn alone and not as part of a couple's mutual sexual enjoyment. The impact of habitually masturbating to porn includes:

Less frequent sex. In general, when one partner is a habitual porn user, the couple will have sex *less often*. This is not so when masturbation is used without porn; in that case, couples are likely to have sex *more often*.

Less sexual communication. Because it doesn't require in-teraction with a partner or any awareness or discussion of another person's desires, porn use obviously does not entail two-way com-munication. This tendency leads to minimizing communication with one's partner during sex.

Less mutually satisfying sex. If you are frequently having orgasms in response to a specific image and fantasy, a condition-ing takes place that leads you to seek out that same stimulation in real life. In part, this conditioning comes courtesy of oxytocin and dopamine, the "bonding and pleasure hormones" that the body releases during orgasm. As a result, the porn user may become so transfixed by particular masturbatory fantasies that sex becomes unsatisfying unless the partner is willing to engage in them. But the partner may not share the turn-on or feel comfortable re-creating it. Result: nobody is happy in bed.

Increased risk of betrayal. Porn can be "step one" in a tra-jectory that ends in a sexual affair. Sometimes porn usage becomes a gateway to online chatting and, eventually, to actual encounters with others who share the preferred fantasy.

Despite the potential dangers of porn, there is no denying its popularity and allure. So it would be wise for couples to discuss porn usage and whether either of them perceives any adverse effects on their relationship. Without explicit agreement, the use of porn is really a form of relationship betrayal.

Sometimes porn usage becomes so central to an individual's life that it really constitutes a compulsion or addiction. If your relationship is grappling with such a problem, the addicted partner needs to seek help from a qualified mental health expert. Like other forms of addiction (alcoholism, substance abuse), porn dependency places an enormous burden on a relationship and requires specialized assistance.

Stress and More Stress

The task: Making your marriage a place of peace.

Most days, Stephanie and Todd get home from work within a few minutes of each other. Too often, instead of a loving reunion, they find themselves in a shouting match. Todd, who has been kowtowing to a difficult boss all day, gets annoyed when he can't find the mail because Stephanie moved it off the table for the umpteenth time. Stephanie, who has a deadline at work and knows she'll be up late working, feels her anger surge when she opens the refrigerator and discovers nothing but Strawberry Snapple. "There's no food!" she yells. "I can't believe you didn't go to the supermarket like you promised. What's wrong with you?"

The real question is, What's going wrong between Todd and Stephanie? The answer is that they are bringing their work stress home, and it is sabotaging their marriage.

Scheduling formal griping sessions can prevent the spillover of everyday stress into your marriage.

There's no doubt that work stress has become an increasing factor in marital dissatisfaction. Today's couples work an average of one thousand hours more each year than people did thirty years ago. There is less time for talking, relaxing, eating, and even sleeping. No wonder the days of the cheerful "Honey, I'm home!" are history for so many families. Most likely "Honey" is working, too, and has come home with an in-box full of e-mails she has to contend with. Or maybe she has been waiting tables all day, and the last thing she wants to do is wait on her partner.

The solution: Acknowledge that at the end of a long, stressful day you may need time to yourselves to decompress before interacting with each other. If you are feeling suddenly outraged by something your spouse did, realize that the incident may be overblown in your mind because you're feeling so tense. Likewise, if your spouse comes home with a cloud over his or her head and your "What's wrong?" gets answered with a snarl, try not to take it personally. He or she probably just had a bad day. Rather than making the situation worse by lashing out, let it go.

Build time to unwind into your daily schedule. Make it a ritual, whether it entails lying on your bed and watching silly videos, going for a jog, or meditating. Of course, some couples find that the easiest way to relax is to enlist each other's help. If so, try the soothing techniques described on page 182.

Once you're both feeling relatively composed, it's time to come together and talk about each other's day. Consider this a sanctioned whining session during which each person gets to complain about any catastrophes that occurred, while the other is understanding and supportive.

Relations with In-Laws

The task: Establishing a sense of "we-ness," or solidarity.

Although mother-in-law jokes told by men are a traditional staple of comedy routines, the real family tension is more frequently between the wife and her mother-in-law. Invariably, the differences between the two women's opinions, personalities, and life views become evident the more time they spend together. A decision to go out to dinner can create dissension over such minutiae as where to eat, when to eat, what to eat, how much to spend, who gets the check, and so on. Then, of course, there are the deeper issues of values, jobs, where to live, how to live, how to pray, and whom to vote for.

Although such conflicts usually surface quite early in a marriage, in-law difficulties can be triggered or revived at many other times, such as when children are born or pass major milestones in their development, and again as the parents age and become increasingly dependent on the couple.

At the core of the tension is a turf battle between the two women for the husband's love. The wife is watching to see whether her husband backs her or his mother. She is wondering, "Which family are you really in?" Often the mother is asking the same question. The man, for his part, just wishes the two women could get along better. He loves them both and does not want to have to choose. The whole idea is ridiculous to him. After all, he has loyalties to each, and he must honor and respect both. Unfortunately, this attitude often throws him into the role of peacemaker or mediator, which invariably makes the situation worse.

The solution: The only way out of this dilemma is for the husband to side with his wife against his mother. Although this may sound harsh, remember that one of the basic tasks of a marriage is to establish a sense of "we-ness" between husband and wife. So the husband must let his mother know that his wife does indeed come first. He is a husband, then a son. This is not a pleasant position to take. His mother's feelings may be hurt. But eventually she will probably adjust to the reality that her son's family unit, where he is the husband, takes precedence to him over all others. It is absolutely critical for the marriage that the husband be firm about this, even if he feels unfairly put upon and even if his mother cannot accept the new reality.

This is not to suggest that a man do anything that he feels demeans and dishonors his parents or goes against his basic values. He should not compromise who he is. But he has to stand with his wife and not in the middle. He and his wife need to establish their own family rituals, values, and lifestyle and insist that his mother (and father) respect them.

For this reason, creating or renewing your sense of solidarity with your spouse may involve some rending and tearing away from your primary families. That's the challenge David faced when his parents came for a weekend visit to his new home, an event that led to what he and his wife, Janie, now call the Great Osso Buco Crisis. Janie always dreaded her in-laws' visits because she felt her mother-in-law acted as if Janie, who worked full-time, was sweet but incompetent, while she was the great savior who would set their household right. Though Janie was always polite to her mother-in-law, privately she would give David an earful about what a control freak his mother was and how disdainful she was of Janie's dedication to her job. David always insisted Janie was imagining or exaggerating slights, which just made her angrier.

For this visit, Janie had made dinner reservations at her favorite Italian eatery. She was very excited about showing off the restaurant to her Italian in-laws, who were very knowledgeable about cuisine. But when she and David arrived home from running errands that afternoon, they were greeted by the savory aroma of garlic and veal. The older woman had gone to the butcher and was preparing David's favorite dish for dinner—osso buco. She said she thought her son would appreciate a home-cooked meal "for a change."

Janie was furious and David was faced with a dilemma. The veal looked delicious, and he knew how hurt his mother would be if he didn't eat it. He really wanted to tell Janie to cancel the reservations. Although this hardly sounds like a major crisis, it led to a turning point in David and Janie's marriage. Janie held her breath as she watched David survey the feast his mother had prepared. He cleared his throat, put his arm around his mother, and thanked her for cooking such a wonderful meal. Then he insisted it would keep for another day in the refrigerator. He explained that it was important to him and Janie to share with her and his dad how they liked to spend Saturday night together as a couple at their favorite restaurant.

His mother was highly offended. She got teary-eyed and made a bit of a scene. (David let his father deal with that.) But it was worth it to David to see Janie look so happy and triumphant. In the end, David's message was loud and clear: She comes first, Mom. Get used to it. "That's when our real marriage began," Janie recalls. "When he let his mother know that I was now first in his heart."

An important part of putting your spouse first and building this sense of solidarity is to not tolerate any contempt toward your spouse from your parents. Noel and Evelyn's marriage was heading for disaster until Evelyn learned this lesson. After their daughter was born, they decided that Noel would be the baby's primary caretaker, since Evelyn had the more demanding, higher-paying, and more personally rewarding career. But this decision didn't sit well with Evelyn's parents, who didn't trust Noel's child-raising skills. Every other weekend, Evelyn gave Noel a break by bringing the baby for a visit with her parents, who lived in the next town. Often Noel would join them Sunday night. From the moment he entered the house, he felt like he was in enemy territory. Evelyn's parents either ignored him or lectured him on bottle feeding, childproofing, car seats, etc. They would constantly criticize him while making a big fuss over what a great mother Evelyn was.

One Sunday, his father-in-law made a joke about whether Noel knew the difference between a baby bottle and a beer bottle. Noel was furious because he realized Evelyn must have shared with her parents that they had recently argued over a six-pack Evelyn found in the refrigerator. She had warned Noel not to drink while tending the baby, which he had found insulting. Noel knew that it didn't sit well with his in-laws that he was the one tending the baby full-time. And he knew that her parents' approval was very important to Evelyn. So he suspected she was putting him down in an effort to gain favor with them. In the Love Lab, we helped the couple talk about this issue, and it turned out he was right. Evelyn was bad-mouthing Noel and sacrificing her "we-ness" with her husband.

Once Evelyn realized what she was doing, and how it was affecting Noel and their marriage, she was able to change. She brought the baby to her parents' home less often, so that they saw their granddaughter mostly on Noel's home turf. When her mother expressed concern that the baby wasn't getting enough to eat, Evelyn piped up that Noel had just taken her to the pediatrician, who declared her perfectly plump and healthy. When her father suggested that the baby needed a heavier snowsuit, Evelyn told him that Noel knew better than anyone what was best for their daughter. At first, Evelyn's parents were miffed by her new attitude. But as time went on, they came to accept the change. And Noel and Evelyn found that their marriage flourished. They finally developed a sense that they were a team. They had mastered the task of building "we-ness."

EXERCISE 1: IN-LAW PROBLEMS

If you are having ongoing problems with a family member, fill out this brief questionnaire. It will focus you on these relationships so that you can determine whether your sense of "we-ness" as a couple needs to be strengthened when it comes to a particular relative. You should both jot down your answers to this form on separate paper.

1. Think of your relationship with various members of your spouse's family. If you feel that your partner isn't necessarily on your side in any of these relationships or that there are ongoing issues with a particular family member, check off the appropriate box.
- ❒ Spouse's mother
- ❒ Spouse's stepmother
- ❒ Spouse's father
- ❒ Spouse's stepfather
- ❒ Spouse's brother(s) _____
- ❒ Spouse's sister(s) _____
- ❒ Other family member _____

Describe the successes so far:

_____
_____
_____
_____

Describe the conflicts that remain:

_____
_____
_____
_____

2. Think about your spouse's relationship with your kin. If you feel that your spouse isn't necessarily on your side in any of these relationships or that there are ongoing issues with a particular family member, check off the appropriate box.

☐ Mother
☐ Stepmother
☐ Father
☐ Stepfather
☐ Brother(s) _____
☐ Sister(s) _____
☐ Other family member _____

Describe the successes so far:

_____
_____
_____
_____

Describe the conflicts that remain:

_____
_____
_____
_____

Now get together with your spouse and read over each other's responses. Discuss what can be done to increase the amount of support and solidarity you are getting from each other. Try not to be defensive if your spouse perceives a problem and you don't. Remember that much about relationships has to do with perception. So, for example, if your wife believes that you side with your own mother against her, that's something you need to work on in your marriage, even if you don't agree with her perception of the situation.

Money, Money, Money

The task: Balancing the freedom and empowerment money represents with the security and trust it also symbolizes.

Whether their bank account is teeming or they're just scrimping by, many couples confront significant conflicts over finances. Often such disputes are evidence of a perpetual issue, since money is symbolic of many emotional needs—such as safety and power—and goes to the core of our individual value systems. But when a simpler, solvable financial problem arises, the key to resolving it is to first understand a marriage's task in this area. While money buys pleasure, it also buys security. Balancing these two economic realities can be work for any couple, since our feelings about money and value are so personal and often idiosyncratic.

I find that solvable financial differences are usually the province of newlyweds. That's because as a marriage goes on, these issues either become resolved successfully or develop into perpetual problems about money's symbolic meanings. However, long-term couples may also find themselves facing a solvable money issue as their circumstances change. Differences of opinion over job changes, financing the children's education, planning for retirement, and caring for elderly parents are common sources of friction in midlife.

The solution: Some clearheaded budgeting is called for. Below are some simple steps you can take to get a handle on how much you'd like to spend—and on what. Keep in mind, though, that managing complex financial matters is beyond the scope of this book. If you need extra help with financial planning and investing, you'll find plenty of resources online or at your local library or bookstore. What's most important in terms of your marriage is that you work as a team on financial issues and that you express your concerns, needs, and fantasies to each other before coming up with a plan. Make sure you don't end up with a budget that forces martyrdom on either of you. This will only build resentment. You'll each need to be firm about items that you consider nonnegotiable.

STEP 1: ITEMIZE YOUR CURRENT EXPENDITURES

Use a form like the one that follows to record how you have spent your money over the last month, six months, or year, whichever time frame is most appropriate to your situation. You may be able to do this just by reviewing your financial statements. Also consider using budgeting software or an Internet resource—you can find plenty of options by searching online for "family budget worksheet."

Expenditures
Food
    Groceries
    Eating out or takeout
Mortgage or rent
    Vacation rentals
    Remodeling
    Property taxes
    Condo maintenance fees
Home office supplies
Utilities
    Electricity
    Gas
    Heat
    Water
Landline phone

Cell phone
TV provider
Internet
Household maintenance
    Housecleaning
    Laundry
    Dry cleaning
    Supplies and equipment (vacuum, bathroom cleaner, etc.)
Clothes
Personal care (haircuts, manicures, sundries)
Car
    Gas
    Maintenance and repairs
    License renewal, registration
    Insurance
    Parking, tolls
    Payments
Other transportation
    Bus, train, ferry fares
Trips
    Business
    Visiting family
    Other vacations
Recreation
    Babysitters
    Dates (movies, plays, concerts, sports)
    Home entertainment (video, streaming, CDs)
Health
    Insurance premiums
    Doctor
    Dentist
    Pharmacy
    Health club membership
    Other (eyeglasses, massages, counseling, etc.)
Appliances and electronics (TV, computer, tablet, cell phone)
Gifts
Charitable contributions

Interest on loans, bank charges, credit cards
Life insurance
Investments and savings (stocks, etc.)

STEP 2: MANAGE EVERYDAY FINANCES

1. Write down every expense from the list above that you consider essential for your sense of happiness and well-being.
2. Look carefully at your income and assets. Now try to create a budget that allows you to manage everyday finances and other "essentials" based on your means.
3. Come up with a plan for paying bills on a regular basis. Determine who handles and keeps track of bill-paying.
4. Discuss your separate lists and plans with each other. Look for common ground between your two approaches. Decide on a workable strategy that allows both of you to meet your "essential" needs. Agree to sit down and revisit your plan in a few months to make sure it's working for both of you.

STEP 3: PLAN YOUR FINANCIAL FUTURE

1. Imagine your life five, ten, twenty, or thirty years from now. What would be your ideal circumstance? Think of things you want (house, and so on) and the kind of life you would ideally like to lead. Also think through the kinds of financial disasters you would most want to avoid. For example, some people's greatest financial fear is not having enough money to retire. Others fear not being able to fund a child's college education.
2. Now list your long-term financial goals, taking into account what you most desire and what you most fear. For example, your goals might include buying your own home, having a well-funded retirement account, or not having to work more than one job.
3. Share your lists with each other. Look for similarities in your long-term goals. Discuss your perspectives.
4. Come up with a long-range financial plan that will help you

both meet your goals. Be sure to revisit this plan every so often—say, every year—to make sure you're still in agreement.

Following these steps has helped couples with a wide variety of financial differences come up with workable solutions. For example, Linda loved stylish clothes and working out at the health club near her office. Devon considered both of those frivolous wastes of money. He far preferred to spend his money on lunches out with friends and two skiing vacations every year. To Linda, his pleasures were overly indulgent. After they each filled out the form, they could see exactly how much money they had. They talked about their finances as a couple and arrived at a temporary compromise budget. Neither of them wanted to give up on their favorite pleasures, so they decided that they would open three savings accounts, one for each of them plus a joint account. They agreed to put a portion of each paycheck into their joint account to save for their children's education and other major expenses down the road. Then they individually would save for gym memberships and ski trips. They decided that in six months they would talk over this arrangement again to determine whether their new budgeting system was working for both of them.

Tina and Gene had a different dilemma. Their oldest son, Brian, was just two years away from college. Although they had saved enough for him to attend the local community college, Tina wanted to send him to the more rigorous (and more expensive) state university, which offered more advanced science courses. Brian had always been an exceptional student. His dream of becoming an aerospace engineer seemed like a realistic goal. But to pay the higher tuition this would entail, Gene would have to postpone his dream of buying a lake house. Although Gene cared deeply about his son's education, he also worried that if they didn't buy a home now, they'd get priced out of the market and would never realize his lifelong dream. Gene wanted Tina to go back to work full-time so that they could afford the college tuition and the country home. But Tina was resisting because her very elderly mother lived with them and depended on Tina for her daily care.

Gene thought it was time for Tina's sister to take over her mother's care. But Tina's sister worked full-time and said she wasn't able to do that. The other option was to put her mother in a nursing home, but Tina was dead set against such a decision. Gene and Tina were having almost daily fights over the issue.

When Tina and Gene filled out the budgeting form, a simple solution did not present itself. But the process of looking through their expenditures together transformed the emotional climate between them. Rather than arguing about the issues, they felt like a team again. They made lists of the various pieces of information they needed to find out about student loans and scholarships. In the end, Gene accepted that he would have to postpone his dream for a few more years. Tina did go back to work, but only on a part-time basis. Gene was able to shift his work hours so that he could be home with his mother-in-law while Tina was away. And Brian spent two years at the less costly community college before transferring to the state flagship university.

The problems and solutions encountered by these couples are unlikely to match yours. The point is that whatever your disagreement over finances, you'll defuse the tension by working as a team to devise a plan you both can accept, even if it doesn't give you everything you want right now.

Housework

The task: Creating a sense of fairness and teamwork.

Joanne was fed up. For months she had been asking Greg not to throw his dirty laundry on the bedroom floor. For months he kept forgetting, just like he kept forgetting to vacuum the carpet and wash the dishes every night, even though he agreed that these were his jobs. Both of them worked full-time, but Joanne usually got home first and would end up picking up after Greg. As she ran the vacuum or scraped hardened cereal out of his dirty bowl, she would be seething. When he got home, she'd give him the silent treatment or make sarcastic remarks about being the unpaid maid. He'd insist that the problem was that she was a terrible nag. "Maybe if you'd leave me alone about it, I'd be more likely to do it," he'd tell her.

Greg didn't realize how damaging his attitude toward housework was to his marriage until the day he arrived home to the sound of banging from the bedroom. He walked in to find his wife, still in her business suit, nailing his dirty boxer shorts to the oak floor. "They've been there for three days," she told him. "So I figured you wanted to make them a permanent part of the decor."

Joanne and Greg eventually divorced, so I'm not suggesting that you find the solution to housekeeping conflicts at the nearest hardware store! The point is that men often don't realize how deeply women care about keeping their home in order. There are certainly exceptions to the gender differences in this area, but as a general rule, in the Odd Couple spectrum of cleanliness, women skew more toward the fastidious Felix and men toward slovenly Oscar.

When a husband doesn't do his agreed-upon share of the housework, the wife usually feels disrespected and unsupported. Inevitably this leads to resentment and a less satisfying marriage. The "slacker" husbands I talk to aren't being deliberately rude. They just don't understand why housework is such a big deal to their wives. Many were raised in homes where their father did no housework even if Mom worked. A husband may claim he agrees it's unfair for his wife to work a second shift when she gets home while he sits back, but old ways die hard. On some level, many men still consider housework to be a woman's job. When the husband "helps," he feels he should be applauded—but instead his wife keeps demanding he do more, which makes him defensive and likely to do less.

A major cause of this unfortunate dynamic is that most men, like Greg, tend to overestimate the amount of housework they do. This has been documented by British sociologist Ann Oakley. I know this is true in my own home. When I complain that I'm doing all of the housework, my wife says, "Good!" because she knows that means I'm actually doing half.

The solution: By now the key to resolving this issue should be clear: men have to do more housework! Sometimes men shirk their responsibility in this department due to a lack of motivation. Let's face it—no one wants to trudge out the recycling in the snow. So maybe this little fact will spark a husband's enthusiasm for domestic chores: *women find a man's willingness to do housework extremely erotic.* When the husband does his share to maintain the home, both he and his wife report a more satisfying sex life than in marriages where the wife believes her husband is not doing his share. The benefits to these marriages extend beyond the bedroom. In these relationships, the women also have significantly lower heart rates during marital arguments, which means they are less likely to begin a discussion harshly and so avoid triggering that whole downward spiral of conflict involving the four horsemen and flooding that leads to divorce.

I'm not suggesting that every husband must do a straight 50 percent of the housework if he wants to save his marriage and see his sex life improve. The key is not the actual amount he does but his wife's subjective view of whether it's enough. For one couple this could indeed mean an even split of chores. But in another marriage the wife may be just as satisfied if he takes care of some chores she hates—like cleaning the bathroom or vacuuming—or even if he agrees to budget for a weekly housekeeper to lighten both their loads.

The best way to figure out how much housework a husband needs to take on is for the couple to talk over the following list. By itemizing exactly who does what, you'll finally have an objective basis for determining who *should* do what.

Use the list to describe to each other first your perception of how things are currently handled and then how you would like them to be. This list extends beyond actual cleaning to other domestic chores—like managing family finances and various aspects of child care—that can also cause conflict if either partner considers the distribution of labor to be unfair.

You may find that certain patterns emerge. As I said, men often believe that they are doing a larger share of domestic chores than is actually the case. In many marriages the husband does more of the "brute strength" tasks like washing the car or mowing the lawn, or the abstract jobs like financial planning that don't have to be done on a daily basis or on a strict timetable. The wife carries more than her share of the mindless, daily drudge work—like cleaning and picking up—which leaves her resentful.

Who Does What List

CAR CARE

Car maintenance (oil change, registration, etc.)	Now:	Ideal:
Refilling gas tank	Now:	Ideal:
Car insurance	Now:	Ideal:

CARE OF THE HOME

Remodeling	Now:	Ideal:
Home maintenance	Now:	Ideal:
Buying furniture	Now:	Ideal:
Buying appliances	Now:	Ideal:
Watering houseplants	Now:	Ideal:

CHILD CARE

Preparing meals and lunches	Now:	Ideal:
Supervising homework	Now:	Ideal:
Bathing	Now:	Ideal:
Bedtime	Now:	Ideal:
Discipline (determining and implementing)	Now:	Ideal:
Caring for sick child	Now:	Ideal:
Dealing with child's emotions	Now:	Ideal:
Interacting with schools	Now:	Ideal:
Planning birthdays	Now:	Ideal:
Shopping	Now:	Ideal:

CHILDREN'S SCHEDULING AND TRANSPORTATION

Making doctor appointments	Now:	Ideal:
Transportation to and from doctor	Now:	Ideal:
Transportation to and from school/day care	Now:	Ideal:
Transportation to and from playdates/after-school activities	Now:	Ideal:
Attending teacher conferences	Now:	Ideal:

Scheduling and attending   Now: Ideal:
   special events

COMMUNICATIONS
Keeping in touch with family/friends   Now: Ideal:
Taking phone messages   Now: Ideal:
Returning phone calls or e-mails   Now: Ideal:

ENTERTAINMENT
Planning get-togethers with friends   Now: Ideal:
Making dinner reservations   Now: Ideal:
Planning "date nights"   Now: Ideal:
Prepping home for parties   Now: Ideal:
Choosing travel destinations   Now: Ideal:
Reserving travel tickets   Now: Ideal:
Planning romantic vacations   Now: Ideal:
Planning family vacations   Now: Ideal:
Planning romantic weekends   Now: Ideal:

FINANCES
Financial planning   Now: Ideal:
Managing investments   Now: Ideal:
Bill-paying   Now: Ideal:
Taxes   Now: Ideal:
Handling legal matters   Now: Ideal:
   (e.g, wills, living trusts)

FOOD
Planning menu   Now: Ideal:
Grocery shopping   Now: Ideal:
Cooking   Now: Ideal:
Doing dishes/running dishwasher   Now: Ideal:
Emptying dishwasher   Now: Ideal:

HEALTH
Coordinating medical care   Now: Ideal:
Managing health insurance   Now: Ideal:

HOUSECLEANING, REGULAR
General tidying up   Now: Ideal:
Making beds   Now: Ideal:
Cleaning kitchen, general   Now: Ideal:
Vacuuming   Now: Ideal:

Sweeping	Now:	Ideal:
Washing floors	Now:	Ideal:
Cleaning bathrooms	Now:	Ideal:
Taking out garbage and trash	Now:	Ideal:
Recycling	Now:	Ideal:
Laundry	Now:	Ideal:
Folding laundry	Now:	Ideal:
Putting away clean clothes	Now:	Ideal:
Putting out clean towels	Now:	Ideal:

HOUSEWORK, PROJECTS

Home repairs	Now:	Ideal:
Washing/waxing floors	Now:	Ideal:
Washing windows	Now:	Ideal:
Changing lightbulbs	Now:	Ideal:
Appliance repairs	Now:	Ideal:
Defrosting and cleaning refrigerator	Now:	Ideal:
Yard and garden work	Now:	Ideal:
Other:		
_____	Now:	Ideal:
_____	Now:	Ideal:
_____	Now:	Ideal:

Now you should have a clear sense of which tasks you currently share and which fall into each partner's domain. Depending on what you consider ideal, it may be time to reallocate domestic tasks so that the load is more equitable. Remember, the actual quantity of housework the husband completes is less important than whether his wife considers him to be pulling his weight. What is critical, however, is that the husband attend to chores without his wife having to ask ("nag") and that he be flexible in what duties he takes on, depending on her needs. For example, if he sees that she's especially tired one night, does he volunteer to wash the dishes even though it's her turn? This conveys that all-important honor and respect. Helping his wife in this way will turn her on more than any "adults only" video. Of course, if in your relationship the sex roles are reversed when it comes to household chores, the rules still apply.

Becoming Parents

The task: Expanding your sense of "we-ness" to include your children.

"A child is a grenade. When you have a baby, you set off an explosion in your marriage, and when the dust settles, your marriage is different from what it was. Not better, necessarily; not worse, necessarily; but different." So wrote Nora Ephron in *Heartburn*, her roman à clef about the breakup of her marriage to journalist Carl Bernstein. Virtually every study that has looked at how people make the transition from couplehood to parenthood confirms her view. A baby sets off seismic changes in a marriage. Unfortunately, most of the time those changes are for the worse. In the year after the first baby arrives, 67 percent of wives experience a precipitous plummet in their marital satisfaction. (For the husband, the dissatisfaction usually kicks in later, as a reaction to his wife's unhappiness.) There are wide-ranging reasons for this deep disgruntlement, including lack of sleep, feeling overwhelmed and unappreciated, the profound responsibility of caring for such a helpless little creature, and juggling mothering with a job.

The big mystery is not why 67 percent of new mothers feel so miserable, but why the other 33 percent just seem to sail through the transition to motherhood unscathed. (In fact, some of these mothers say their marriage has never been better.) Thanks to the 130 couples we followed from their newlywed stage to as long as nine years afterward, I now know the secret to keeping a marriage happy and stable even after the "explosion." What separates these blissful mothers from the rest has nothing to do with whether their baby is colicky or a good sleeper, whether they are nursing or bottle-feeding, working or staying home. Rather, it has everything to do with whether the husband experiences the transformation to parenthood along with his wife or gets left behind.

Having a baby almost inevitably causes a metamorphosis in the new mother. She has never experienced a love as deep and selfless as what she feels for her child. Almost always, a new mother experiences nothing less than an utter reorientation of meaning in her life. She discovers she is willing to make enormous sacrifices for her child. She feels awe and wonder at the intensity of her feelings for this fragile little being. The experience is so life-altering that if her husband doesn't go through it with her, it is understandable for distance to develop between them. While the wife is embracing a new sense of "we-ness" that includes their child, the husband may still be pining for "just the two of us." So he can't help but begrudge how little time she seems to have for him now, how tired she always is, and how often she's preoccupied with feeding the baby. He resents that they can't ride their bikes to the beach anymore because the baby is too small to sit up in a back carrier. He loves his child, but he wants his wife back. What's a husband to do?

The answer to his dilemma is simple: He can't get his wife back—he has to follow her into the new realm she has entered. Only then can their marriage continue to grow. In marriages where the husband is able to do this, he doesn't resent his child. He no longer feels like only a husband but like a father, too. He feels pride, tenderness, and protectiveness toward his offspring.

How can a couple ensure that the husband is transformed along with his wife? First, the couple need to ignore some popular bad advice. Many well-meaning experts recommend that they consider marriage and family a balancing act, as if their lives are a seesaw with the baby on one end and the marriage on the other. Couples are counseled to spend some time away from the baby and focus on their marriage and outside interests: talk about your relationship, your job, her job, the weather, anything but the baby at home. But marriage and family are not diametrically opposed. Rather, they are of one cloth.

Yes, the couple should spend time away from the baby occasionally. But if they are making this transition well together, they will find that they can't stop talking about the baby, nor do they want to. They might not even get through that first meal without calling home—at least twice. Too often, such couples are made to feel as if they have done something wrong because they have made their own relationship seemingly secondary to their new roles as parents. The result is that they feel all the more stressed and confused. But in fact, they have done something very right.

The important thing here is that they are in it together. To the extent that both husband and wife make this philosophical shift, the parent-child relationship and the marriage thrive.

Here are some more tips to help couples stay connected as they evolve into parents:

Focus on your marital friendship. Before the baby comes, make sure that you really understand each other and your respective worlds intimately. The more of a team you are now, the easier the transition will be. If a husband knows his wife, he will be in better tune with her as she begins her journey to motherhood.

Don't exclude Dad from baby care. Sometimes, in her exuberance, a new mother comes off as a know-it-all to her husband. While she agrees, in theory, that they should share the baby's care, she casts herself into a supervisory role, constantly directing—if not ordering—the new father and even chastising him if he doesn't do things exactly her way: "Don't hold her like that," "You didn't burp him enough," "The bath water's too cold." In the face of this barrage, some husbands are more than happy to withdraw, to cede the role of expert to their wives and accept their own ignorance. The sad result is that they do less and less and therefore become less and less accomplished and confident in caring for their own child. Inevitably, they begin to feel more excluded.

The solution is simple. The new mother must back off. She needs to realize that there's more than one way to burp a baby. If she doesn't like her husband's way, she should remember that the baby is his child, too, and will benefit from experiencing more than one parenting style. A few baths in tepid water are a small price for an infant—and a marriage—to pay for the father's ongoing commitment to his family. If the mother feels her husband's approach is really unsafe, she should direct him to their pediatrician or a baby-care guide. Some small, well-timed doses of gentle advice-giving are fine (don't forget to use a softened start-up), but lectures and criticism will backfire.

Feeding time can be especially difficult for the new dad. Penis envy may well be a Freudian myth, but breast envy is alive and well in almost every home where the wife is nursing an infant. Fathers can't help but feel jealous when they see that beautiful bond developing between their wife and baby. It's as if the two have formed a charmed circle that he just can't enter. In response to this need, some baby-gear websites actually offer devices that allow men a close approximation of the nursing experience. There is, for example, an attachment that you can strap onto your chest that delivers warm milk to the baby through plastic breasts! But most couples don't need to resort to extra equipment to help the man feel included. Instead, they can find a role for the husband in the ritual of breastfeeding. For example, it can be the husband's job to carry the baby to the mother at feeding time. He can be the official "burper." He can also make it his custom to sit quietly with his wife and child during feeding times, perhaps gently stroking the baby's head or singing softly.

Let Dad be baby's playmate. Some men have admitted to me that they don't feel much connection with their child until the baby gets older and can walk, talk, and play. Unfortunately, by then their distance from family life has created fissures in their marriage. The reason men may take longer to "bond" with their children is that, as countless studies have confirmed, women tend to be more nurturing toward children while men are more playful. And since most men assume you can't really play with a helpless baby, they don't feel engaged by their child for much of the crucial first year.

But dads who spend time with their young babies will discover that infants are not "blobs" who do nothing but cry, nurse, poop, and sleep. Even newborns can be great playmates. Babies begin to smile at a mere three weeks. They can track movements with their eyes even earlier than that. Soon they are chortling, kicking their legs in delight. In short, the father who gets to know his babies by bathing, diapering, and feeding them will inevitably find that they love to play with him and that he has a special role in their lives.

Carve out time for the two of you. Part of the transition to parenthood entails placing a priority (albeit usually second place) on the marriage itself. So you should use a babysitter, relative, or friend to get some time alone with each other. But remember, you haven't failed if you end up spending a lot of your "dates" discussing the baby—you've succeeded. As the baby grows into a toddler and then becomes school-aged, you'll find that your conversations when you're alone together won't always gravitate toward your child and your role as parents.

Be sensitive to Dad's needs. Even if he is a good team player and is making the philosophical shift toward parenthood along with his wife, the man is still going to feel somewhat deprived by the baby's overwhelming and seemingly endless need for her. Even if, intellectually, he understands that the baby's demands supplant his own in priority, he's going to miss his wife. The more his wife acknowledges what he has given up and lets him know how central he still is to her life, the more understanding and supportive he will be able to be. If she never has any time for just the marriage, he will have a tendency to withdraw from the relationship.

Give Mom a break. For all the daily wonders a mother experiences during the newborn stage, she is also likely to be exhausted, whether she is also working outside the home or the baby is her full-time job. It will help their marriage if her husband is able to modify his work hours so that she has time to take a break and reconnect with the outside world.

Sex

The task: Fundamental appreciation and acceptance of each other.

No area of a couple's life offers more potential for embarrassment, hurt, and rejection than their sexual relationship. In recent years, sexual satisfaction in marriage has become a research focus of mine because so many couples complain about a decline in passion. In the most common scenario, the husband desires sex significantly more frequently than the wife. For example, in a study of couples who had a toddler at home, we found that the husbands wanted intercourse an average of six times more often. This was true whether both partners rated their sex life as fabulous or virtually nonexistent. In other words, even among couples who were satisfied with their erotic life, the husbands wanted more sexual intercourse.

What is the key to sexual satisfaction in a long-term relationship? In our study of couples with young children (a time in most marriages), we found that those whose sex life good to great made sex a priority rather than considering it the last obligation on a long to-do list. These couples talked about their sex life, ensured they had one-on-one time together, and put the relationship first, despite the competing demands of work and children. They also found sexual satisfaction through diverse methods, not just intercourse. In short, they had high levels of trust and were attuned to each other in and out of the bedroom. These results indicate that valuing and supporting the friendship between partners is the key to long-term satisfaction, sexual and otherwise. For this reason, your sex life is likely to improve as you incorporate the lessons of the Seven Principles into your daily lives.

A significant obstacle to a happy sex life, however, is difficulty communicating about the topic clearly. Often couples "vague out," making it hard to decipher what they're actually trying to tell each other. Here's a classic example from a couple we taped in our lab:

EMILY: Think about your feelings two and a half and three years ago, and how we dealt with the problem and how we felt. I mean, think. It was much more a problem then in my eyes than it is now.

NOAH: I think we're more secure together now than we were then. I don't know. I would say the actual problem we haven't dealt with anymore, any differently since then, I don't believe. I don't know if we've really changed.

EMILY: Do you feel any differently about it, though?

NOAH: How do you feel?

EMILY: Well, I guess I feel that the problem two and a half and three years ago, I viewed it as something that could ruin our marriage. I was real worried about us not making it. I don't really worry about that anymore.

NOAH: I never considered it a threat to our marriage. I know you did, but I never did.

EMILY: Okay. And maybe I'm feeling more secure now, is why I don't.

The "problem" this couple is discussing is that he has always wanted sex more frequently than she does. In this snippet of conversation, she is trying to get him to agree that it's not a problem anymore. She wants his reassurance. He thinks the problem still exists, but he avoids telling her that directly.

So often when a husband and wife talk to each other about their sexual needs, their conversations are like this—indirect, imprecise, inconclusive. Frequently both partners are in a hurry to end the discussion, hopeful that they will miraculously understand each other's desires without much talk. They rarely say things like "I love it when you stroke my breasts for a long time the way you did last night" or "I really need you every day" or "Morning is my favorite time for making love," and so on. The problem is that the less clear you are about what you want, the less likely you are to get it. Sex can be such a fun way to share with each other and deepen your sense of intimacy. But when communication is fraught with tension, then frustration and hurt feelings too often result.

The solution: Learn to talk to each other about sex in a way that lets each partner feel safe. This will enhance the experience for both of you. For example, research consistently shows that women have more orgasms when couples are able to talk comfortably about this topic. To get started, take this quiz to get a sense of how you're feeling about your current sex life.

QUIZ: QUALITY OF SEX, ROMANCE, AND PASSION IN THE RELATIONSHIP

For each item, check the one box below that applies to your relationship right now:

I WOULD SAY THAT:

1. ❏ A. Our relationship is romantic and passionate.
   ❏ B. Our relationship is becoming passionless—that is, the fire is going out.

2. ❏ A. My partner is verbally affectionate and compliments me.
❏ B. My partner is not very verbally affectionate or complimentary toward me.

3. ❏ A. My partner regularly or often tells me, "I love you."
❏ B. My partner rarely tells me, "I love you."

4. ❏ A. My partner expresses respect and admiration toward me.
❏ B. My partner rarely expresses respect and admiration toward me.

5. ❏ A. We do touch each other tenderly a fair amount.
❏ B. We rarely touch each other these days.

6. ❏ A. My partner courts me sexually.
❏ B. My partner does not court me sexually.

7. ❏ A. We do cuddle with each other.
❏ B. We rarely cuddle with each other.

8. ❏ A. We still have our tender and passionate moments.
❏ B. We have few or no tender or passionate moments.

9. ❏ A. We often kiss each other passionately.
❏ B. We rarely or never kiss each other passionately.

10. ❏ A. My partner surprises me with romantic gifts.
❏ B. My partner rarely or never surprises me with romantic gifts.

11. ❏ A. Our sex life is fine.
❏ B. There are definite problems in this area.

12. ❏ A. The frequency of sex is not a problem.
❏ B. The frequency of sex is a problem.

13. ❏ A. Being able to just talk about sex, or talk about sexual problems, is not a serious issue between us.

❐ B. Being able to just talk about sex, or talk about sexual problems, is a serious issue between us.

14. ❐ A. Differences in desire are not a big issue in this relationship.
    ❐ B. Differences in desire are a big issue in this relationship.

15. ❐ A. The amount of emotional connection during sex is not a problem.
    ❐ B. The amount of emotional connection during sex is a problem.

16. ❐ A. My partner is satisfied with our sex life.
    ❐ B. My partner is not satisfied with our sex life.

17. ❐ A. I do feel romantic toward my partner.
    ❐ B. I do not feel very romantic toward my partner.

18. ❐ A. I feel passionate toward my partner.
    ❐ B. I feel passionless—that is, my own fire is going out.

19. ❐ A. My partner is romantic and passionate.
    ❐ B. My partner is passionless—that is, the fire is going out in my partner.

20. ❐ A. The satisfaction I get from sex is not a problem.
    ❐ B. The satisfaction I get from sex is a problem.

21. ❐ A. We have made sex and romance a priority in this relationship.
    ❐ B. We have not made sex and romance a priority in this relationship.

22. ❐ A. I definitely know how to turn my partner on sexually.
    ❐ B. I do not really know how to turn my partner on sexually.

23. ❐ A. My partner definitely knows how to turn me on sexually.
    ❐ B. My partner does not really know how to turn me on sexually.

24. ☐ A. I feel desired by and sexually desirable to my partner.
☐ B. I do not feel desired by and sexually desirable to my partner.

25. ☐ A. Overall we can and do talk easily and comfortably about our sexual needs.
☐ B. Overall we do not talk, or we do not talk comfortably, about our sexual needs.

26. ☐ A. Overall we know and respect each other's sexual fantasies.
☐ B. Overall we do not know or do not respect each other's sexual fantasies.

27. ☐ A. Overall we are good sexual partners.
☐ B. Over all we are not very good sexual partners.

Scoring: Add up all of the times you answered "A."

27: Congratulations! The quality of sex, romance, and passion in your life together is as good as it gets.

20–26: The quality of sex, romance, and passion in your relationship is pretty good right now, but talking more directly about your sex life would likely improve it. Read on to see how to accomplish this in an effective, positive, and gentle manner.

11–19: The quality of sex, romance, and passion in your relationship could stand some real work. But the situation probably isn't critical yet. You are hardly alone—many couples have difficulty in this area. The ideas and tips below will help you learn to talk more effectively to each other about your sexual needs and desires.

0–10: Currently, the quality of sex, romance, and passion seems to be a very serious issue between you. The advice in this chapter will be helpful, but it may be more beneficial to first review chapter five (nurturing your fondness and admiration) and chapter six (turning toward each other) before concentrating on specific sexual issues.

Five Ways to Make Sex More Personal and Romantic

The goal of sex in a long-term relationship is to have fun, heighten closeness, and feel valued and accepted in this very tender area of your marriage. Here are some of the ways the couples we've worked with have enhanced the experience.

1. REDEFINE WHAT YOU MEAN BY "SEX."

Although romance and sex are intimately connected, you'd never know that from strolling the aisles of your local bookstore. Instead, you'll usually find that advice books on how to enhance and improve your relationship are kept in a separate section from books on sex. The latter are called sex "manuals," and they can get very technical about anatomy and physiology. But they rarely talk about sex in the context of the relationship (communication, handling conflict, etc.). Meanwhile, the books on relationships rarely talk explicitly about sex. Unfortunately, this separation reflects what goes on in most couples' bedrooms. When sex becomes about technique rather than passion and communication, the result is sexual anxiety. Men worry about their erections. Women worry about achieving orgasm. Both become self-conscious, and it all becomes difficult to talk about.

Instead of isolating sex from the rest of your relationship, try a change in attitude. Stop thinking that sex is about orgasm and consider *everything positive that happens between you as part of sex*. This notion comes from insights offered by respondents to *The Hite Report*, researcher Shere Hite's groundbreaking, best-selling survey of female sexuality. Many of the women Hite interviewed complained that their men likened achieving orgasm to a touchdown ("the Big O"). This goal-oriented approach to love-making can cause a great deal of sexual dysfunction because if that objective isn't reached, then there's the sense that something is "wrong." The women told Hite they wished their men would be more present and just enjoy the sensations of pillow talk, touching, caressing, kissing, and so on. That's why I suggest to couples that they consider all positive interactions to be sex. Foreplay occurs every time you turn toward each other in some little way throughout the day. (At the Gottman Clinic, we even offer T-shirts and mugs with the slogan "Every Positive Thing You Do in Your Relationship Is Foreplay.") This perspective greatly reduces anxiety about sexual dysfunction and performance and makes the entire experience more pleasurable. Not focusing on orgasm as the goal helps couples see that sex, the physical part of connection, is all about just that: connection.

2. LEARN HOW TO TALK ABOUT "IT."

It is common for couples to want to discuss their sex lives but not know how to express themselves without sounding critical or feeling embarrassed. So here are some ground rules:

Be gentle and positive. Because most people feel so vulnerable about whether they are attractive to their spouse and a "good" lover, the key to talking about sex is not to criticize your partner. There really is no reason to be judgmental because you aren't talking about something *bad* in your relationship. You are brainstorming and sharing your perspective on *how to make a good thing better*. A conversation about lovemaking that starts with one partner criticizing the other is going to end faster than a "quickie." Nothing is guaranteed to make your spouse want to touch you less than if you say, "You never touch me." It's better to say, "I loved when we kissed last weekend on the big couch. I'd love more of that, it makes me feel so good." Likewise, instead of, "Don't touch me *there*," you'll get a better response if you say, "It feels extra good when you touch me *here*."

Be patient with each other. Individuals vary widely on how comfortable they are discussing sexual matters frankly. Based on upbringing and background, many people still have feelings of shame connected to enjoying sex and therefore find it difficult to acknowledge, much less discuss, their sexual needs and desires, even (or especially) with their life mate. If you are in this situation, my advice is to go slowly. It may be best to start by each of you talking about your feelings concerning sex itself—what messages you received about it as children, your conflicts about it, etc., before delving into the specifics about what you or your partner likes best sexually. Such a discussion can be very powerful for your relationship and enhance your emotional intimacy and sense of safety with each other.

Don't take it personally. I know this sounds contradictory because sex is so intimate, but to an enormous degree, what turns your partner on or off isn't about you! Sexual proclivities are so deeply entrenched and idiosyncratic that the goal of lovemaking is to explore what works for each of you. It isn't an implied criticism of your attractiveness, sexual virility, lovemaking skill, or innermost being if your partner likes it harder, softer, more or less kinky, with or without lingerie or dirty talk, etc. Try to have the same attitude a professional cook has about preparing food. A chef isn't insulted if a customer isn't in the mood for polenta tonight or has an aversion to olives. Instead he or she makes accommodations that will satisfy the customer's palate.

Compromise. It is up to both of you to decide what feels okay and safe and what doesn't. Sexuality is incredibly malleable, so it really is possible to make accommodations to each other's desires that will be pleasurable to both of you. For example, Mike wanted to have sex several times a week, but Lynne thought once every other week was enough. As a result, Mike felt frustrated and rejected. Over time he became more insistent that they increase the frequency. He'd bring home books and all sorts of erotica in an effort to turn Lynne on. But this just made her feel pressured, which backfired. As Mike's frustration grew, Lynne's desire dwindled. By the time they came to our workshop, Lynne and Mike had no idea how they could work out this issue. We suggested they shift their focus from sex to sensuality and that the person with the least interest (currently Lynne) be put in charge of the couple's sensual experience. Since Lynne loved massages, we suggested she select a book on the topic that appealed to her and use massage to direct their sensual evenings, which entailed no sex per se, but plenty of holding and touching. Gradually, Lynne's sexual desire heightened, and eventually they began to have sex about twice a week.

3. CHART YOUR SEXUAL LOVE MAPS.

I've found that a successful blueprint for gathering information on your partner's sexual maps is to frame questions in two general ways:

What felt good last time?

Can you recall some good moments of sex between us?

What did you feel about our nonsexual affection, touching, caressing, kissing, or massage?

What did we do that turned you on?

What did we do that made you feel closer to me?

What made you feel relaxed?

What made you feel ready for touch and sensuality?

What made you feel connected to me?

What made you in touch with your body?

What made you able to surrender and let go?

What do you need to make sex better?

What do you need to put you in the mood?

Do you like feeling that we have "all the time in the world"?

How do you feel about giving or receiving a quickie?

What should I do if you feel too tired or too busy for sex, or are not in the mood?

If I am really horny but you are not feeling sexy, do you feel comfortable just saying no? What do you need from me in order to feel comfortable saying no?

If you are on the fence about having sex and I am very horny, what do you need from me? Are you okay with me trying to get you in the mood? If so, how should I do that?

What makes sex more like lovemaking to you?

What are good fantasies or thoughts for you?

What would be a good sex ritual?

What would be good to do for gourmet, fantasy date sex?

(For a more extensive and explicit list of questions to enhance your sex maps, see our book *What Makes Love Last?* And also check out the info at www.gottsex.com.)

4. HAVE ONGOING CONVERSATIONS ABOUT SEXUAL INTIMACY.

Your sex life will benefit if you keep your sexual maps up to date. This requires talking about the experience from time to time as a way of taking each other's sexual "temperature." Doing so keeps you attuned to each other's needs and any misunderstandings or new negotiations you need to make to keep you both feeling loved and satisfied. For example, here is a conversation between a happily married couple who are lying in bed at the end of the day. The husband tries to initiate sex, and the wife rebuffs him. But rather than giving each other the silent treatment or expressing anger, they talk it out, using the sort of conflict-resolution skills presented in the previous chapter.

JED: How are you doing, baby? (*Hoping to hear "I'm happy. You're great. Let's have sex."*)

JANE: Not very well, actually.

JED: Tell me all about it. (*Disappointed because he'd been wanting to make love.*)

JANE: I need a lot more touching. Lately you haven't touched me very much at all. I have been feeling lonely and sad.

JED (*Thinking "Oh, no, it's all my fault again. I'm sorry I asked."*): Tell me more about that.

JANE: Well, we used to cuddle in the mornings, and lately you have been getting up at 4 a.m. and working on your client presentation. So we never cuddle now. I miss that a lot.

JED (*Thinking "She's right. I've been really obsessed with that work project."*): You're right, I have been totally obsessed. That really sucks for you.

JANE: Do you really have to do that? Every morning?

JED: No, I don't. I'll stay in bed and cuddle, also because I love cuddling, too, it's so sweet. It's very peaceful.

JANE: That'd be great. What about you? What do you need from me?

JED: Well, when you said I didn't touch you very much, my first thought was, "That's bull. I put my arms around her last

Sunday and she brushed me off. That hurt. I do touch her a lot, so this is all her fault, not mine. That was my first defensive thought, anyway. I'm glad I stifled that, though."

JANE: Well, that Sunday you put your arm around me because you wanted sex, right?

JED: Yes, I guess that's true, mostly. (*Feeling a little embarrassed.*)

JANE: I have a tough time wanting to make love when I haven't been touched in a while nonsexually.

JED: Really? ("*I would want to have sex with her at any time, any place, unless I'm hungry.*")

JANE: Really.

JED: I don't have that problem.

JANE: I know you don't, but I need to feel close to you first, not feel lonely. Do you get that?

JED: I do, I see. I'm not like that about sex, but I do understand. Okay, I get what you need.

JANE: And I gather you need me to say yes more of the time when you initiate?

JED: That would be sweet.

JANE: Okay, I can do that, if you touch me more nonsexually.

JED: Thanks for making me more aware of that.

JANE: You're welcome.

5. LEARN HOW TO INITIATE SEX—AND TO REFUSE IT GENTLY.

Many couples are uncomfortable discussing how to initiate sex and also don't know how to say, "Sorry, I'm not in the mood" in a way that doesn't feel hurtful or rejecting. It is also difficult to cope with being turned down. I hope the following advice makes it easier.

The key to making "yes" and "no" feel less loaded is to have an agreed-upon *ritual* in your relationship for navigating sex. (And remember, "sex" can be any positive connecting a couple does.) A ritual is an approach, either verbal or nonverbal, that you both expect, can count on, and look forward to. It makes asking for sex explicit and routine. I know of one couple who have a pair of Korean dolls on their mantle. When one wants sex, he or she puts one of the dolls in a prone position. The partner signals interest by repositioning the other doll as well. Of course, a ritual doesn't need to be so elaborate or particularly creative. A couple's ritual for initiating cuddling and intercourse may be for one partner to rub the other's back in a circle when they get into bed. The partner can then roll over and continue the physical connection or politely decline.

One ritual for requesting sex that I find especially effective comes from noted sex therapist Lonnie Barbach. She suggests that couples use a scale from 1 to 9 to indicate how amorous each of them is feeling, with 1 meaning "Not at all amorous," 5 meaning "I'm convince-able," and 9 meaning "Let's do it!" So, if your partner approaches and you're not in the mood, you can say, "I love you and you are extremely sexy, but right now I'm at 1." If you're not sure, you could say, "Right now I'm a 5. So let's kiss and see where it goes."

Here are some other rituals used by couples I've worked with:

Just saying straight out, "I want to make love."
Kissing the partner's neck and saying, "I really want you."
Putting your arms around your partner and asking if he or she
    would like to make love.
Leaving a partner a note saying you want to make love tonight.
Sending the partner a sexy e-mail or text during the day.
Lighting candles in the bedroom.
Suggesting taking a bath together.

Refusing Sex Gently

If you're not in the mood, let your partner down softly. Here are ways to say no that won't sting so much. Put them in your own words, of course!

"I usually would love having sex with you, but I need to take a
    rain check. Right now I'm really not in the mood. But I still
    find you very attractive."
"I'm sorry, honey, but it's not the right time for lovemaking for
    me. But I still love you a lot, and you are very attractive."

"I'm just too wiped out. But I definitely want a rain check so I have something to look forward to."

Coping with "No"

Whatever a couple's ritual for initiating sex, it's imperative that there be no negative consequences if the partner says "no." That can be easier said than done. Often when (usually) the wife says, "Not tonight" (again), the husband responds with hurt, frustration, even anger. His reaction is understandable, but it is also likely to reduce how often his wife says yes. To underline that point, here are the results of an experiment in which I used game theory to model the likely frequency of sex between a hypothetical couple. Jim is always interested in having sex; Mary not so much. My calculations determined that if Jim complains, sulks, or otherwise subjects Mary to a "negative payoff" whenever she declines his overtures, they end up having sex about once every three weeks. But if he actually rewards her "no" with a small positive payoff (perhaps he expresses understanding or asks what *she* would like to do), their rate soars to four times a week. Counterintuitive as it sounds, the results suggest that *husbands who reward their wives for saying no will end up having a lot more sex*!

Of course, the exact frequency of sexual encounters between a particular couple is impossible to predict. The point is that, for both husbands and wives, the more you can hear, understand, and respect your partner's "no" about any marital issue, the more "yes" there will be in your relationship.

In this chapter I've tried to give you practical advice to help you solve some common marital problems. But sometimes, no matter how diligently you try to end a conflict, it just can't be done. If that's the case, you are dealing with a perpetual problem. Avoiding or breaking out of gridlock over such a problem is one of the chief challenges all couples face. My next principle will show you just how to save—or protect—your marriage from your irreconcilable differences.

11

Principle 6:
Overcome Gridlock

*Y*ou want to have children; he doesn't. She wants you to attend church with her; you're an atheist. He's a homebody; you're ready for a party every night. All couples have some irreconcilable differences. But when partners can't find a way to accommodate these perpetual disagreements, the result is *gridlock*. When couples gridlock over issues, the image that comes to my mind is of two opposing fists. Neither can make any headway in getting the other to understand and respect their perspective, much less agree with it. As a result, they eventually view the partner as just plain selfish. Each becomes more deeply entrenched in his or her position, making compromise impossible.

While couples can gridlock over momentous issues, like deciding if they will pass a particular religion on to their children, it's not uncommon to reach loggerheads over differences that would seem ridiculously trivial to anyone outside of the relationship, like punctuality or even which way to fold napkins. Usually these issues reflect basic differences in personality or lifestyle preferences. Whether they seem important or petty to outsiders, all gridlocked disagreements share four characteristics. You'll know you've reached gridlock if:

1. You've had the same argument again and again with no resolution.
2. Neither of you can address the issue with humor, empathy, or affection.
3. The issue is becoming increasingly polarizing as time goes on.
4. Compromise seems impossible because it would mean selling out—giving up something important and core to your beliefs, values, or sense of self.

As with most difficulties, the best approach to coping with gridlock is to avoid it in the first place. Fortunately, the more adept you become at following the other six principles, the less likely you are to gridlock over intractable differences. As you come to know and trust each other, you will find that disagreements that once would have overwhelmed you are more easily handled, especially if you make use of the exercises in this chapter concerning hidden dreams. A significant key to preventing gridlock is also to be on the lookout for those small moments where you "miss" each other's needs. If either of you is feeling a lot of hurt over seemingly minor slights, you may want to spend some extra time on strengthening your fondness and admiration (chapter 5) and practice turning toward each other (chapter 6). Not acknowledging and talking out these small moments can make a relationship more vulnerable to gridlock over significant issues.

When couples are able to sidestep gridlock, they come to treat their perpetual problems as they would a pesky allergy or bad back. They know the difficulty won't ever go away, but they manage to keep it from overwhelming their life together. Of course, when you're in the midst of gridlock, it may seem impossible that you could manage the conflict as readily as, say, a trick knee. But you *can* do it. Remember that you don't have to solve the problem to get past gridlock. Neither of you has to "give in" or "lose." The goal is to be able to acknowledge and discuss the issue without hurting each other.

What Dreams Are Made Of

To navigate your way out of gridlock, you have to first understand that no matter how seemingly insignificant the issue, gridlock is a sign that you each have dreams for your life that the other isn't aware of, hasn't acknowledged, or doesn't respect. By dreams I mean the hopes, aspirations, and wishes that are part of your identity and give purpose and meaning to your life. Dreams can operate at many different levels. Some are very practical (such as wanting to achieve a certain amount of savings), but others are profound. Often these deeper dreams remain hidden while the more mundane ones ride piggyback and are easier to see. For example, underneath the dream to make lots of money may be a need for security.

Our deepest dreams are frequently rooted in childhood. You may long to re-create some of your warmest memories of family life from your youth—such as having dinner together every night without interruptions from the TV or text messages. Or, you may feel the psychological need to distance yourself from painful childhood memories by not duplicating the same patterns or activities. For example, you may resist having family dinners if the evening meal in your childhood home was often the setting for hostility between your parents that left you with indigestion.

Here is a list of some common "deep" dreams expressed by couples I've worked with.

1. A sense of freedom
2. Feeling at peace
3. Exploring who I am
4. Adventure
5. A spiritual journey
6. Justice
7. Honor
8. Consistency with my past values
9. Healing
10. Having a sense of power

11. Dealing with growing older
12. Exploring a creative side of myself
13. Getting over past hurts
14. Asking God for forgiveness
15. Exploring an old part of myself I have lost
16. Having a sense of order
17. Being productive
18. Getting my priorities in order
19. Exploring the physical side of myself
20. Being able to compete and win
21. Traveling
22. Atoning
23. Ending a chapter of my life—saying good-bye to something

All of these dreams are beautiful. None of them are inherently bad for a marriage. But a dream can cause problems if your spouse doesn't respect it or you keep it hidden. Under these circumstances, either you may have open battles over the issue, or it may go underground and only be expressed symbolically. In the latter case, the couple may think they are at loggerheads over whether to go out to dinner every Sunday night, but the bottom-line issue has to do with something much deeper than a restaurant meal. Sunday night holds a special place in both of their hearts, stemming from their childhoods. Her dream is to eat out because her family did that every Sunday, a treat that made her feel special. But for her husband, a restaurant meal was always much less of a treat than having his very busy mother cook for the family—something she only did on Sundays. So the question of a restaurant versus a home meal is really symbolic of what makes each of them feel loved.

When Dreams Are Respected

Why do some couples cope so gracefully with these sorts of issues while others get bogged down? The difference is that the happy couples are aware of each other's dreams and consider helping each other realize them to be one of the goals of marriage. "We want to know what the other person wants in their life," says Justine, who is happily married to Michael. But she could just as well be talking for all emotionally intelligent couples. In satisfying relationships, partners incorporate each other's goals into their concept of what their marriage is about. These goals can be as concrete as wanting to live in a particular kind of house or to attain a certain academic degree. But they can also be intangible, such as longing to feel safe or wishing to view life as a grand adventure.

Shelley wants to go to college. Malcolm's hefty paycheck allows her to do that. But he yearns to quit his high-pressure marketing job because his dream is to be his own boss and build boats. In a happy marriage, neither spouse insists that the other give up their dream or attempts to manipulate them. They work it out as a team, taking into account each other's wishes and desires. Maybe Malcolm decides to keep at the grind till Shelley finishes school. Perhaps Shelley studies part-time or suspends her studies for an agreed-upon length of time. Practicality might demand that one or both of their dreams be put on hold for a while. Whatever they decide to do isn't really the issue. The point is that their concept of their marriage incorporates supporting both of these dreams. The way they go about making such decisions—with mutual respect for and acknowledgment of each other's aspirations—is part of what makes their relationship so meaningful to them.

A Horse Named Daphne

When either spouse isn't aware of or doesn't fully appreciate the importance of supporting his or her partner's dreams, gridlock is almost inevitable. That was the root cause of the severe marital problems between Ed and Luanne, a Seattle couple who were interviewed in my Love Lab for a TV news program. When Ed and Luanne were in the lab together, you could see that their fondness and admiration were still there. But they were experiencing enormous stress over Luanne's nine-year-old horse, Daphne, with whom she often competed in horse shows.

Before they were married, Ed was very taken with Luanne's

horse. But now that he was confronted with the monthly bills for Daphne's care and maintenance, she became a source of tension between him and his wife. He wanted Luanne to sell the horse so that they could save money. The more he and Luanne argued over selling Daphne, the more he feared, deep down, that she cared for the horse more than she did for him and their marriage.

The couple talked out this problem in three fifteen-minute sessions, snippets of which were aired on the show. In between those sessions, my team and I coached them, using the sorts of techniques you'll find in this chapter. Luanne was told not to give up on her dream and to make sure that Ed understood that he came first in her heart. We helped Ed understand that helping Luanne realize her dream to compete in horse shows with Daphne was part of his role as her spouse. He also needed to accept Luanne's influence when it came to making financial decisions. By the end of the three sessions, Ed and Luanne had made a major leap forward in their marriage. When Ed told Luanne he would support her decision to keep Daphne, her wide smile lit up the screen.

Eventually, Luanne sold Daphne in order to lease a younger horse (though she still visited Daphne). She continued to compete in horse shows, and Ed continued to support her desire to do so.

When Dreams Are Hidden

For Ed and Luanne, it was apparent that a dream was the root cause of their conflict. The challenge was to respect the dream and each other's needs. But for many couples, the dream that is at the core of the conflict is not so obvious. Only by uncovering this dream can the couple get out of gridlock.

Take the case of Katherine and Jeff. They were happily married until Katherine became pregnant. Suddenly, it seemed to Jeff, her Catholic faith took on a much more central role in her life. He himself was an agnostic. When he found out that she had been talking with her father about having the baby baptized, he was livid. He did not want his child to have any kind of formal religious instruction.

By the time Katherine and Jeff discussed this conflict in my lab, they had clearly become gridlocked. I could tell that their marriage was in serious danger because they were emotionally distant from each other. Even while discussing the highly personal issues of faith and family, they didn't raise their voices, cry, smile, or touch each other. They were able to talk intellectually about their difference of opinion, but they were emotionally disengaged. And since their problem was really an emotional one—concerning their feelings about families, parenthood, and religion—no amount of careful intellectual analysis would be able to resolve it.

At their next session, I suggested that instead of trying to solve the issue, they should just listen to each other talk about what religion symbolized to them. This was the only way to get to the hidden dreams that were fueling the conflict. Katherine went first. She described how her faith had carried her through very hard times. Her parents went through a rancorous divorce. For ten years, her father had no contact with the family. Her mother became so depressed that Katherine couldn't depend on her. She felt completely unloved and alone until she turned to the Church, which embraced her. Not only did she feel a kinship with her fellow worshippers but she felt comforted by prayer. When all the chips were down, feeling God's love brought her deep comfort. Katherine started crying as she remembered those hard times and the solace she found in religion.

Jeff explained that he had been an agnostic his entire life. In contrast to Katherine's dysfunctional family, his was very strong and loving. When he went through hard times, he always turned to his parents. He wanted his child to feel the same trust in him and Katherine. He feared that if their son was "indoctrinated" into the Church, this would interfere with that bond; the child would be trained to turn to God instead of his parents.

Jeff and Katherine had opposing dreams: He envisioned them as a happy family that would supply all the love and support their children needed. He saw religion as a threat to their deep connection. Katherine viewed religion as a vital support system that she wanted to ensure was there for her children.

The key to ending gridlock for Jeff and Katherine was (and is for all couples) to discuss openly why their position was so important to them—and in particular to open up about the history behind their position and what it meant to them. We call this sort of discussion the "Dreams Within Conflict" approach to gridlock. It not only helps to defuse the problematic issue but also increases your sense of intimacy and connection.

When Katherine and Jeff used this approach to openly discuss their dreams, the mood in the room changed dramatically. Jeff told Katherine that he loved her. It finally sank in to him that her desire to baptize their baby came out of her deep love for their child—for *his* child. He realized it made "perfect sense" that out of this love she would want to protect the baby from ever feeling the pain she had experienced. This helped him reconnect with his own deep feelings for Katherine, which had gotten buried under all of the bitterness and anger.

In the first session, no emotion had passed between the couple. But this time, you could see the compassion on Jeff's face as he listened to his wife recount her childhood. When she cried, he handed her tissues and encouraged her to keep talking. Katherine listened just as intently to his side of the story.

Now that the real issues were out in the open, Katherine and Jeff were able to talk about raising their son in a way that honored both their visions. Jeff told her he wouldn't oppose the baptism. He himself would always be agnostic, but it was okay with him if the child received rudimentary training in Catholicism. However, he still opposed intensive religious study, because he feared the Church might impose ideas on the child. Katherine was able to accept this compromise.

Deep issues like these are unlikely to be declawed in just one session. But Jeff and Katherine made an important first step. They turned toward each other and respectfully acknowledged each other's dreams for their child. They agreed to seek further counseling to build on the success of the lab session. Will this issue ever go away or be resolved in their relationship? Probably not. But they have begun to learn to live with it peacefully.

Become a Dream Detective

If you've reached gridlock on any issue in your marriage, big or small, you need to identify which dream or dreams are fueling the conflict. One good indicator that you're wrestling with a hidden dream is that you consider your spouse to be the source of the marital difficulty. If you find yourself saying, for example, that the problem is simply that he is a slob or she is irresponsible or overly demanding, that's a sign of a hidden dream. It may indicate that you don't see your part in creating the conflict because it has been hidden from view.

Uncovering a hidden dream is a challenge. The dream is unlikely to emerge until you feel that your marriage is a safe place to talk about it. That's why it's important to begin by working on the first three principles, outlined in chapters 4, 5, and 6, in order to strengthen your friendship with your mate.

**Keep working on your unresolvable conflicts.
Couples who are demanding of their marriage are
more likely to have deeply satisfying unions than
those who lower their expectations.**

Often, deeply personal dreams go unspoken or underground because we assume they must in order to make the relationship work. It's common for both partners not to feel entitled to their dreams. They may see their own desires as "childish" or "impractical." But such labels don't end the longing. So if the relationship doesn't honor the dream, conflict will almost inevitably ensue. In other words, when you bury a dream, it just resurfaces in disguised form—as a gridlocked conflict.

EXERCISE I: DETECTING DREAMS

This exercise will give you plenty of practice in uncovering hidden dreams without, at first, focusing on your own relationship. Below are six examples of common gridlocked conflicts. Read each one, and think about what dreams may be hidden inside each partner's perspective. Make up a brief story or narrative that explains each partner's position. In each case, imagine that this is your position and that it is very hard for you to yield. Think of what your stance means to you and the roots of this dream. Imagining other people's dreams will help you unlock the door to those causing gridlock in your own marriage.

This is a creative exercise that has no right or wrong answers. We've included suggested dreams and stories for the couples. But try not to look at our stories about these couples' dreams until you've come up with your own. You'll get far more out of this exercise if you do it yourself.

Brandon and Ashley

BRANDON: I think my wife is too neat and tidy. I find myself constantly trying to find things after she has cleaned up. I think she is being inconsiderate and overly controlling, and I'm tired of it.

His Dreams Within This Conflict Might Be: I want to feel free in my own home. My mother was very concerned with appearances and kept the house overly neat, with the furniture covered with plastic. She nagged me all the time to clean up. My wife's neatness and nagging make me feel the way I did when I was a kid. To me, a messy home means comfort and freedom from criticism.

ASHLEY: I like a certain amount of order and neatness in our home. I find myself constantly cleaning up my husband's messes. I think he is being inconsiderate, and I am tired of this.

Her Dreams Within This Conflict Might Be: When the house is a mess, it takes me back to the chaos of my youth. As a child, there was nothing I could count on. For example, I never knew who, if anyone, would be making sure I got to school and back. My dad would forget to pick me up, and I hated him for that sometimes. Then I would get home, and there would often be no dinner and no clean clothes. It fell on my shoulders to create all the order and sense of responsibility for my younger siblings. I resented having to do all that. My dream is to provide a much healthier family environment for my kids and family. To me, order means predictability, security, and peacefulness. I want that for my kids.

Kyle and Nicole

KYLE: My wife is very emotional and claims that I am far too unemotional. This difference between us makes me feel that she is overreactive and out of control at times, perhaps overly sensitive. I think that being rational is usually the best approach to strong emotional situations, not getting more emotional. My wife claims that I am hard to read and too distant.

His Dreams Within This Conflict Might Be: I grew up in a family where everyone was a debater. We loved to argue with one another. My dad always asked a question, challenged me, and then took a contrary position to mine. It was no holds barred, and we all loved it. But getting emotional was illegal in this debating contest. Once someone got emotional, the argument was over. So staying in emotional control was highly prized in my family. It still is. So maybe I should be more emotional, but it's not in my makeup. My dream is to be strong. I think of being emotional as a weakness.

NICOLE: I am a very emotional person, and my husband is far too unemotional. This difference between us makes me feel that my partner is cold and "fake" at times, not really present. Many times I have no idea what he is feeling. I am frustrated by this difference between us.

Her Dreams Within This Conflict Might Be: I am just an emotional person, and that's all there is to it. I think that's what life is all about, feeling things, being in contact, responding. That's what "responsible" ought to mean, "response-able," or able to respond. That's the highest value for me. I respond to everything around me, to great art, architecture, children, sports, sad movies, everything! To be emotional just means being alive. This is the way I was raised, and I'm glad.

My dream is to share my emotions with the person I love. If I can't, the marriage is doomed to seem dead, fake, and lonely.

Ava and Thomas

AVA: My husband is overly jealous, especially at parties. I think that social occasions are a time to meet new people, which I find very interesting. But my husband gets shy and withdrawn. He claims that I flirt at parties, but this isn't true at all. I find the accusation insulting, and it makes me angry. I don't know how to reassure him, and I'm tired of not being trusted.

Her Dreams Within This Conflict Might Be: I really do not flirt, nor do I have any interest in anyone but my spouse. It's just that parties are my only way of satisfying my gregarious and wild side. I really don't want to be responsible for anyone else when I go to a party. My dream is to feel the freedom to explore.

THOMAS: At parties and other places, my wife looks at other men and acts flirtatious. I find this upsetting and demeaning. I have brought this up repeatedly but cannot get her to stop.

His Dreams Within This Conflict Might Be: I have always wanted to be able to feel that I was "enough" for someone special in my life. That is my dream: to feel truly attractive and desirable to my partner. I want my partner to be interested in me, in knowing me and finding out what I think, what I am like inside. I would find it incredibly romantic if I could go to a party with my wife and she didn't even notice that there was another man there, had eyes only for me, and was totally satisfied spending hours with just me.

Melissa and Liam

MELISSA: My husband likes to have sex much more often than I do. I don't know what to do when he keeps approaching me for sexual intimacy. I don't know how to say no in a gentle way. This pattern makes me feel like an ogre. I don't know how to deal with this.

Her Dreams Within This Conflict Might Be: I was sexually mistreated long ago. I had no control over this, and it was quite horrible, but it did happen. I know my partner is not to blame for many of the feelings I now have. But I feel that sex can be okay only if it is on my terms. In my marriage there has been a lot of healing and gentleness, but I probably will never get over these feelings of having gone through a real trauma. My dream is to have sexual closeness on my terms only.

LIAM: I like to have sex much more often than my wife. I keep getting my feelings hurt when she turns me down. This pattern makes me feel unattractive and unwanted. I don't know how to deal with this.

His Dreams Within This Conflict Might Be: My dream is to have my partner initiate sexual encounters with me and somehow be "swept away" by passion, I guess to really be totally attracted to me even though I don't think I'm much to look at. For me, having sex is the route to feeling deeply connected and fully accepted by the other person.

Ethan and Brittany

ETHAN: I think that my wife is far too stingy when it comes to money and doesn't believe in spending enough on just enjoying life and having fun. I also resent not having more personal freedom and control when it comes to money.

His Dreams Within This Conflict Might Be: Life is too short to just save for the future all the time. I know that a certain amount of that is necessary, but I want to have some sense that I am not living just for tomorrow. I don't want to feel that life is passing me by. And that's what I often feel, that I am not special enough to "waste" money on. I want to feel special and very alive. Where this comes from is, I suppose, always having to scrimp when I was poor. But now we make a good income, and I don't have to live like that anymore.

BRITTANY: I think that my husband is impractical when it comes to money and spends far too thoughtlessly and selfishly.

Her Dreams Within This Conflict Might Be: I want to enjoy life, but within limits. To me, the problem with the world is greed. People never seem to be able to have enough "stuff" or get enough money.

Just look at Americans on vacation, with all their things, campers, motorcycles, boats, cars. I don't want to want things. I want to be satisfied with just a small amount of things and a small amount of money. I honestly don't need very much to be happy. So I see myself as kind of like a monk, who has a purpose in life, and I do have that. A monk can be satisfied with very little, contented, counting all the blessings in life, and there are so many. So I believe in saving and spending very little. To me, that's how one should lead a moral life. Where does this come from? I think it comes from my father, who also was very frugal. Thanks to him, our family always did well, and when he died, my mom was well provided for. I respect what he accomplished.

Amanda and Mason

AMANDA: My husband likes to stay in much closer touch with our families than I do. To me, family connections are great sources of stress and disappointment. I have broken away from my family, and I want much greater distance.

Her Dreams Within This Conflict Might Be: It took me a great deal of effort to get away from a very dysfunctional family. My parents were very cold and distant. My sister wound up in a mental hospital, and my brother became a drug addict. I was the only one who escaped—by becoming very distant from my family and very close to my friends. Friendships have always meant a lot to me and continue to be very important. But I am wary of being close to my husband's family. I see a lot of dysfunctional patterns, and they scare me. My dream is for us to form our own family traditions and maintain our own independence.

MASON: I like to stay in much closer touch with my family than my wife does. To me, family connections are very important. My parents have always been there for me during very important challenges. Now, as they are getting older, I want to be there for them. The Bible says, "Do not abandon us when our strength has fled." I take that obligation very seriously.

His Dreams Within This Conflict Might Be: To me, a feeling of an extended family has always been very important. I can recall many a Sunday when our home would be filled with twenty or thirty relatives. The coffee and pastries would keep coming all afternoon, and there would be lots of good stories, card playing, and laughter. Then there would be great food for dinner. My dream is to maintain this feeling of community, closeness, and great comfort.

Working on a Gridlocked Marital Issue

Now that you have had some practice uncovering dreams, you're ready to address an area of gridlock in your relationship. Understand that working on these issues will take time. You may find that when you first begin to recognize and acknowledge your dreams, the problems between you seem to worsen rather than improve. Be patient. Acknowledging and advocating for your dreams is not easy. The very nature of gridlock means that your dreams appear to be in opposition, so you've both become deeply entrenched in your positions and fear accepting each other's influence and yielding.

STEP 1: EXPLORE THE DREAM(S)

To get started, choose a particular gridlocked conflict to work on. Then write an explanation of your position. Don't criticize or blame your spouse. Use the statements made by the couples above as your guide—notice that they don't bad-mouth each other. Instead, they focus on what each partner needs, wants, and is feeling about the situation. Next, write the story of the hidden dreams that underlie your position. Explain where these dreams come from and why they are so meaningful to you.

Once you both understand which dreams are fueling the gridlock, it's time to talk about them. Each person gets fifteen minutes as the speaker and fifteen minutes as the listener. Do not try to solve this problem. Attempting to do that now is likely to backfire. Your goal is simply to understand why each of you feels so strongly about this issue.

Speaker's job: Talk honestly about your position and what it means to you. Describe the dream that's fueling it. Explain where the dream comes from and what it symbolizes. Be clear and honest about what you want and why it is so important. Talk as if you were explaining your dream to a good friend or neutral third party. Don't try to censor or downplay your feelings about your dream in order to avoid hurting or arguing with your spouse. If you find this difficult, review the advice in chapter 9 about softening your start-up. Some of the same approaches hold: namely, to make "I statements" and to talk only about *your* feelings and needs. This is not the time to criticize or argue with your partner. How you feel about your spouse in relationship to this dream is a satellite issue that should not be addressed right now.

Listener's job: Suspend judgment. Don't take your spouse's dream personally even though it clashes with one of yours. Don't spend your time thinking up rebuttals or ways to solve the problem. Your role now is just to hear the dream and to encourage your spouse to explore it. Here are some supportive questions to ask. You don't have to use these verbatim, but put the thought and spirit behind them into your own words.

THE DREAM CATCHER'S MAGIC QUESTIONS

- "What do you believe about this issue? Do you have some values, ethical ideas, or other beliefs that relate to your position on this issue?"
- "What are all the things you feel about this issue?"
- "What does your position mean to you?"
- "What is your ideal dream here?"
- "Tell me the story of your dream. Does it relate to your history or childhood in some way? I'd like to understand what it means to you."
- "What do you want? What do you need? If I could wave a magic wand and you'd have exactly what you needed, what would that look like?"

Don't:

GEORGIA: I've always dreamed of going on a mountain-climbing expedition to Mount Everest.

NATHAN: First of all, we can't possibly afford something like that. Besides, I can't think of anything more stressful than mountain climbing. I get vertigo standing on a table.

GEORGIA: Forget it.

Do:

GEORGIA: I've always dreamed of going on a mountain-climbing expedition to Mount Everest.

NATHAN: Tell me more about what it means to you to climb a mountain. What would it do for you?

GEORGIA: I think I would feel exhilarated, like I was at the top of the world. As a child, I was always told that I was weak and couldn't do anything. My parents were always saying, "Careful, careful." I think climbing a mountain would be the most liberating thing I could do. I'd feel such a sense of accomplishment.

If you can, tell your partner that you support his or her dream. That doesn't necessarily mean that you believe the dream can or should be realized. There are three different levels of honoring your partner's dreams—all of which are beneficial to your marriage. The first is to express understanding of the dream and be interested in learning more about it. For example, Nathan could support Georgia's decision to take a course in mountain climbing and listen with enthusiasm when she talks about it, even if he has no interest in taking the course with her. The second level would be to actively enable the dream; in this case, Nathan could offer to help Georgia finance a mountain-climbing trip. The third level would be to become a part of the dream, to come to enjoy mountain climbing himself.

Acknowledging and respecting each other's deepest, most personal hopes and dreams is key to saving and enriching your marriage.

You may find that you're able to "go all the way" with some of your partner's dreams while with others you can't get past the first level of understanding and interest. That's okay. The bottom line in getting past gridlock is not necessarily to become a part of each other's dreams (although your marriage will be more enriched to the extent that you can) but to honor these dreams. After all, you don't want the kind of marriage in which you triumph at the expense of crushing your partner.

STEP 2: SOOTHE

Discussing dreams that are in opposition can be stressful. Pay attention to how you are each reacting to the conversation. Alert your partner if you feel signs of stress (for example, your heart begins to pound). Remember that if flooding occurs, the conversation will get nowhere. So be sure to use repairs if either of you becomes upset. If flooding does occur, stop for at least twenty minutes, and spend the time in any activity that calms you down. (For extra help, see "Soothe Yourself and Each Other" on page 179.)

STEP 3: REACH A TEMPORARY COMPROMISE (THE TWO-CIRCLE METHOD)

Now it's time to begin the ongoing task of making peace with this issue, accepting the differences between you, and establishing some kind of initial compromise that will help you continue to discuss the problem amicably. Understand that your purpose is not to solve the conflict—it will probably never go away completely. Instead, the goal is to defang the issue, to try to remove the hurt so that the problem stops being a source of great pain.

The way you start this process is by using the circle exercise on page 185 ("Finding Common Ground"). You define the minimal core areas that you cannot yield on. To do this, you need to look deep into your heart and try to separate the issue into two categories:

Nonnegotiable areas. These are the aspects of the conflict that you absolutely cannot give on without violating your basic needs or core values.

Areas of flexibility. This category includes all parts of the issue where you can be flexible, because they are not so "hot" for you. Try to make this category as large as possible and the first one as small as possible.

Share your two lists with your spouse. Working together, and using the skills you learned in chapter 9, come up with a temporary compromise. Try it for about two months, and then review where you stand. Don't expect this to solve the problem, only to help you both live with it more peacefully.

For example, Sally believes in living for the moment—she tends to be spontaneous and loose with her money. Gus's main goal in life is to feel secure. He moves slowly and carefully toward decisions and is very frugal. These differences lead them to clash when Sally insists that they buy a mountain cabin. Gus immediately says no—they can't afford it. Sally feels confident that they can.

For a year they gridlock over this issue. Whenever they try to discuss it, they become embroiled in a shouting match. Gus lets Sally know he considers her an irresponsible dreamer who always wants to squander the money they work so hard to earn. Sally accuses Gus of wanting to squash all the fun and joy out of her life.

To overcome the gridlock, Gus and Sally first have to explore the symbolic meaning of their positions on the cabin. In their first conversation to try to work on this issue, Sally says that her dreams are to pursue pleasure, to be able to truly relax, and to feel unity with nature, all of which she can realize by having a cabin. Although she also fears that Gus wants to turn her into a drone who's living just for tomorrow, she doesn't say this to him now. (She has said it frequently in the past.) Instead, she focuses on what she desires, not her anger and fears connected to Gus.

When it's Gus's turn to talk, he tells her that saving money has a lot of symbolic meaning for him. He longs to feel financially secure because he fears being destitute in his old age. He remembers seeing his grandparents suffering because they were so poor. His grandfather ended up in a low-quality nursing home that Gus believes took away his dignity. One of his big goals in life is not to feel humiliated when he is old. Gus is also furious at Sally because he believes she is reckless and has a childish need for immediate gratification, which is a threat to his well-being and the life he's trying to build. However, he doesn't hurl those accusations at her this time. Instead, he sticks to explaining and describing his dream of financial security and its roots in his childhood.

Once Sally and Gus have discussed the symbolic meaning of their positions, a transformation takes place. Rather than seeing each other's dreams as threats, they see them for what they are: deep desires held by someone they love. Although their dreams are still in opposition, they are now motivated to find some common ground, to find a way to respect and perhaps even accommodate both of them. Here's how they do this:

1. They define the minimal core areas that they cannot yield on. Sally says she must have a cabin. Gus says he must save $30,000 in order to feel financially secure.
2. They define their areas of flexibility. Sally says she can settle for a small cabin on just a couple of acres, rather than the larger retreat she had envisioned. She can also be flexible on the timing of acquiring a cabin. She would like to buy one right now, but can wait a few years as long as she feels Gus supports the decision and they work toward it together. Gus says he can be flexible about how quickly he must save his $30,000 as long as he knows that they are consistently working toward that goal by saving a specific amount from each of their paychecks.
3. They devise a temporary compromise that honors both of their dreams. They will buy a small cabin, but not for another three years. Meanwhile, they will devote half of their savings to a down payment and half to a stock fund. In a couple of months, they will review this plan and decide if it's working.

Sally and Gus realize that their underlying perpetual problem will never go away. Sally is always going to be the visionary, imagining a life filled with cabins and adventurous trips, and Gus is going to worry about their financial security, their retirement fund, and so on. But by learning how to cope with their differences, they can avoid gridlock on any specific conflicts their fundamental differences trigger.

Here are a few other examples, using some of the couples from the "Detecting Dreams" exercise above, that show how you can learn to live with your differences through this process. While none of these conflicts are likely to mirror yours exactly, they should give you an idea of how couples with entrenched differences of opinion can overcome gridlock.

Brandon and Ashley
Gridlocked problem: Housecleaning—she wants him to be neater, he wants her to leave him alone about it.

1. Detect and Discuss the Dreams Within the Conflict
Ashley's Dream: A sense of order and security at home
Brandon's Dream: A sense of freedom in his own home

2. Soothe
They agree to take a break by enjoying a hot bath together, with candles and music they both love.

3. Reach a Temporary Compromise (Two-Circle Method)
Nonnegotiable areas:
Ashley's: She can't abide dirty clothes left out, not in the hamper, or a dirty bathroom.
Brandon's: He can't abide having to clean up his papers right after he's finished with them.

Areas of flexibility:
Ashley's: She can live with some clutter as long as there isn't any dirt.
Brandon's: He can cope with cleaning up clothes, dishes, and bathrooms as long as he doesn't have to straighten up all the time.

Temporary compromise: They will both take responsibility for keeping bathrooms and kitchens clean. She will not bug him about his clutter more than once a week. But if he doesn't deal with it by then, she will pile it up and put it all on the floor of his home office.

Ongoing conflict: Ashley will always hate clutter; Brandon will always hate orderliness.

Kyle and Nicole
Gridlocked problem: Very different comfort levels with expressing emotions

1. Detect and Discuss the Dreams Within the Conflict
Nicole's Dream: Being emotional is part of her self-identity and part of what gives meaning to her life.

Kyle's Dream: He sees being emotional as a weakness.

2. Soothe
They read aloud the relaxation instructions on pages 181–182 as they monitor their own heart rates. They wait until both their heart rates are back to baseline before continuing.

3. Reach a Temporary Compromise (Two-Circle Method)
Nonnegotiable areas:
Nicole's: She cannot stop reacting with great passion to life.

Kyle's: He cannot become a highly emotional person just to please her.

Areas of flexibility: They both accept that their spouse cannot change a basic personality trait.

Temporary compromise: They will be respectful of their differences in this area. He will be receptive to her need to talk about and share feelings. She will accept when he cannot do this.

Ongoing conflict: They will continue to have very different approaches to expressing emotion.

Ava and Thomas

Gridlocked problem: She enjoys spending time with other people at parties, while he wants her to stay with him.

1. Detect and Discuss the Dreams Within the Conflict

Ava's: To feel free and be able to explore by meeting new people at social events

Thomas's: To be the center of her attention

2. Soothe

She is soothed by his reassurance that he has no desire to control her or determine who her friends are. He is soothed by her insistence that she is not interested in any man but him. They take a half hour to meditate, an activity they both enjoy.

3. Reach a Temporary Compromise (Two-Circle Method)

Nonnegotiable areas:

Ava's: She must have the freedom to enjoy herself and meet new people.

Thomas's: He cannot abide her dancing with or touching other men, even in a friendly way.

Areas of flexibility:

Ava's: She doesn't have to be completely separate from her husband at parties.

Thomas's: He can tolerate her talking with other men for a few minutes.

Temporary compromise: They will stay together at parties for about half the time. The other half she can go off and mingle by herself. But she will not dance with or touch other men—and if he tells her he's upset by her behavior, she'll stop.

Ongoing conflict: Ava will always want to socialize more than Thomas is fully comfortable with.

Now see if you can outline your own problem in the same way. First write a clear statement of what the issue is and which dream(s) is fueling it. Then note which areas are nonnegotiable for each of you and which you are able to be flexible about. Finally, write out a temporary compromise that you agree to try for a brief period of time. It will be helpful if you also write a brief description of your ongoing conflict to confirm that you both understand that it remains unresolved—but you can live with it.

STEP 4: SAY "THANK YOU"

It may take more than one session to overcome gridlock on issues that have been deeply troubling to your marriage. These sessions can be stressful, no matter how diligently you attempt to accept each other's viewpoint without judgment. The goal here is to re-create the spirit of thanksgiving, in which you count your blessings and look inward to express gratitude for all you have. This may be particularly difficult to do after talking about gridlocked marital conflict, but that's all the more reason to make the effort. To be sure you end on a positive note, offer your partner three specific thank-yous. (For suggestions, turn to the "I Appreciate" list on pages 74–76.)

Follow these four steps, and you'll be able to move out of gridlock on your perpetual problems. Be patient with the process and each other. By their very nature, these problems are tenacious. To loosen their grip on your marriage will take commitment and faith on both your parts. You'll know you're making progress when the issue in question feels less loaded to you both—when you can discuss it with your sense of humor intact, and it no longer looms so large that it crowds out the love and joy in your relationship.

12

Principle 7:
Create Shared Meaning

*W*e used to have a yuppie marriage," says Helen. "By that I mean it was very superficial. We got along okay and really loved each other, but I didn't feel that connected to Kevin. It was like we were roommates who made love." Helen, a "devout feminist," had always prided herself on her independence. At first she thought it was great that she and Kevin had their own lives—separate careers, interests, and friends. But the longer they were married, and especially after they had children, the more she felt something was lacking. She didn't want to give up her strong sense of individual identity, but she wanted more from her marriage. After attending our workshop, she realized what it was: she wanted to feel more like she and Kevin were a family.

If your marriage adheres to my first six principles, there's a good chance that your relationship is stable and happy. But if you find yourself asking, "Is that all there is?" your situation may be similar to Helen and Kevin's. What may be missing is a deeper sense of shared meaning. Marriage isn't just about raising kids, splitting chores, and making love. It can also have a spiritual dimension that has to do with creating an inner life together—a culture rich with symbols and rituals, and an appreciation for your roles and goals that link you and that lead you to understand who you are as a family.

Usually we think of culture in terms of large ethnic groups or even countries where particular customs and cuisine prevail. But a culture can also be created by just two people who have agreed to share their lives. In essence, each couple and each family create its own microculture. And like other cultures, these small units have their customs (like Sunday dinner out), rituals (like a champagne toast after the birth of each baby), and myths—the stories the couple tell themselves (whether true, false, or embellished) that explain their sense of what their marriage is like and what it means to be part of their group.

Paula and Doug viewed themselves as the "runts" of their respective families. Both were considered the least intelligent, attractive, or likely to succeed of their siblings. But as it turned out, all of their brothers and sisters ended up unmarried or divorced, while Paula and Doug formed a happy, stable marriage; held steady jobs; and raised great kids in a loving home. Part of their marriage's culture, the story they tell themselves about themselves, is what a great team they make, how feisty they are, how they thumbed their noses at all the naysayers and succeeded against the odds.

Developing a culture doesn't mean a couple sees eye to eye on every aspect of their life's philosophy. Instead there is a meshing. They find a way of honoring each other's dreams even if they don't always share them. The culture that they develop together incorporates both of their dreams. And it is flexible enough to change as husband and wife grow and develop. When a marriage has this shared sense of meaning, conflict is much less intense and perpetual problems are unlikely to lead to gridlock.

It is certainly possible to have a stable marriage without sharing a deep sense of what is meaningful about your lives together. Your marriage can "work" even if your dreams aren't in sync. The last chapter showed you just how to navigate your way around perpetual problems so that you can live with them rather than ending up gridlocked. It is important to accept that you each will probably have some dreams that the other doesn't share but can respect. You may, for example, adhere to different religions but have enough respect for each other's spiritual journey to bridge the differences in your faiths.

But it is also true that a rewarding marriage is about more than sidestepping conflict. The more you can agree about the fundamentals in life, the richer, more profound, and, in a sense, easier your marriage is likely to be. You certainly can't force yourselves to have the same deeply held views. But some coming together on these issues is likely to occur naturally if you are open to each other's perspective. *A crucial goal of any marriage, therefore, is to create an atmosphere that encourages each person to talk honestly about his or her convictions.* The more you speak candidly and respectfully with each other, the more likely there is to be a blending of your sense of meaning.

At our workshop, Helen and Kevin were able to focus on the spiritual side of their lives together by talking over some of the questions you'll find later in this chapter. For the first time, they spoke earnestly about their own families, their family histories, values, and symbols. When they returned home, Helen took out her family's old photo album and showed Kevin pictures of her great-grandparents who had come to America from Ireland. She told him the story she had heard countless times about her great-grandparents' marriage—how they had become engaged before her great-grandfather left for America. He then remained true and devoted to her great-grandmother during the four long years it took to save up enough money to bring her over, too. The message of this story, she had come to understand, was that loyalty is one of the backbones of marriage and family life. Until now she had never expressed that to Kevin so directly.

He himself reminisced about some of his own family's tales—especially about his grandmother who single-handedly ran a general store in rural Kansas and almost went broke because she was always giving away free food to poor neighbors during the Depression. The townspeople all knew that she reserved a certain amount of her goods for the town's needy families, who would come by every Monday night at closing time. "My dad always said that we Monahans tend to be generous to the point of being foolish," he told Helen. "But he always said it in a way that let you know he was very proud that we were like that." Kevin told Helen how that perspective had infused his own adulthood—from his insistence that they make large charitable contributions to the size of the Christmas tips he gave out.

That conversation marked a turning point in Kevin and Helen's marriage. From then on they talked frequently about values like loyalty and generosity that had been instilled in them by hearing family stories as children. Over time, as they heard each other's family chronicles and passed them on to their children, these tales wove together into the ongoing story of the new family they were creating. Helen accepted and incorporated the stories and values of the Monahans that were important to Kevin into her own life, and he did the same for her heritage.

As I said, the more shared meaning you can find, the deeper, richer, and more rewarding your relationship will be. Along the way you'll also be strengthening your marital friendship. This in turn will make it even easier to cope with any conflicts that crop up. That's the beauty of the Seven Principles. They form a feedback loop that ensures that as you work on each principle, it becomes easier to work on the others.

The Four Pillars of Shared Meaning

In my work with couples, I've come to identify four critical mainstays of shared meaning. When couples build these together, they enrich their relationship and family life.

PILLAR ONE: RITUALS OF CONNECTION

It is a sad fact that less than a third of U.S. families eat dinner together regularly, and more than half of those that do have the television on. This effectively ends conversation during dinner. Creating rituals in your marriage (and with your children) can be a powerful antidote to this tendency to disconnect. A ritual is a structured event or routine that you each enjoy and depend on and that both reflects and reinforces your sense of togetherness. Most of us are familiar with rituals from our childhood, whether going to Midnight Mass on Christmas Eve, lighting Kwanzaa candles or the menorah, sharing pumpkin pie at Grandma's Thanksgiving, attending family reunions, etc. However, it's common for people not to discuss what these traditions symbolize to them. In his book *The Intentional Family,* sociologist William Doherty highlighted the importance of couples creating rituals that are intentional and meaningful. By recognizing the ongoing value and significance of the rituals you each bring to your relationship, and the new ones you create together, you further your identity as a family.

Rituals don't necessarily have to derive from your respective childhoods and family histories. You can create your own. If you wished your family had gone on outings together on the weekends, you may want to incorporate that into your weekly routine. Or if you wish a bigger deal had been made out of the spiritual side of Christmas, you may decide to attend Midnight Mass together every year. New rituals are likely to develop naturally as you go through life together as a couple. For example, at the Thanksgiving dinner that Julie and I have been sharing with a small, core group of friends for thirteen years, we always go around the table and each of us recounts what we are grateful for in the past year. These stories have grown longer and more personal over the years, and Julie and I look forward to this heartwarming ritual of connection.

Baking family birthday cakes together became an important ritual for Nick and Halley and their children. As a toddler, their son developed an allergy to eggs, so they could not buy him a birthday cake at any of the local bakeries. Instead, for every family member's birthday, Nick and Halley would bake an egg-free cake. Eventually their son outgrew his egg allergy, but the family ritual of home-baked birthday cakes remained. The ritual gave them a chance to come together and celebrate birthdays in a warm, home-based way.

The hallmark of rituals of connection is that they are not haphazard. They are structured, scripted traditions that you can depend on. You know how events will play out and that you will have each other's attention and connect in a manner you both find meaningful. For example, Julie and I are very proud of a ritual of connection we call our "annual honeymoon." Once a week for the past fifteen years we have stayed in the same room at the same bed-and-breakfast in a beautiful area one hundred miles from our home. We bring along our kayak, visit art galleries and artists' studios, and hike the trails. We spend the week catching up, dreaming together, and, yes, sometimes fighting and clearing the air over any issues we had ignored due to busy-ness. It is always romantic, magical, and special.

Many couples could also benefit from developing rituals around lovemaking and talking about it. People often think that sex should be spontaneous and is best if it isn't planned. But if you ask couples when sex was best, they usually say it was early in their relationship, during courtship. Back then, romantic dates were planned, thought was devoted to what to wear, what perfume or cologne to use, the music and wine, etc. Returning to those rituals of planning for romance and sex can heighten the experience for both partners.

To get a sense of how well you create a sense of shared meaning through rituals, answer the following questions. If you find that you don't see things the same way, consider this discovery an opportunity to create a ritual of connection that will be deeply meaningful to both of you.

RITUALS OF CONNECTION QUESTIONNAIRE

Read each statement and circle T for "true" or F for "false."

1. We see eye to eye about the rituals that involve family dinnertimes in our home. **T F**
2. Holiday meals (like Thanksgiving, Christmas, Passover) are very special and happy times for us (or we both hate them). **T F**
3. End-of-the-day reunions in our home are generally special times. **T F**
4. We see eye to eye about the role of TV in our home. **T F**
5. Bedtimes are generally good times for being close. **T F**

6. During the weekends, we do a lot of things together that we enjoy and value. **T F**

7. We have the same values about entertaining in our home (having friends over, parties, and so on). **T F**

8. We both value, or both dislike, special celebrations (like birthdays, anniversaries, family reunions). **T F**

9. When I become sick, I feel taken care of and loved by my spouse. **T F**

10. I really look forward to and enjoy our vacations and the travel we do together. **T F**

11. Spending our morning time together is special to us. **T F**

12. When we do errands together, we generally have a good time. **T F**

13. We have ways of becoming renewed and refreshed when we are burned out or fatigued. **T F**

Scoring: Give yourself 1 point for each "true" answer. If you score below 3, your relationship could stand some improvement in this area. Turn to the shared-meaning exercise that begins on page 272, and focus on the "rituals" section.

PILLAR TWO: SUPPORT FOR EACH OTHER'S ROLES

Our sense of our place in the world is based to a great extent on the various roles we play—we are spouses, perhaps children and/ or parents, and workers of one kind or another. From the standpoint of marriage, our perspective on our own roles and our mate's can either add to the meaningfulness and harmony between us or create tension.

Your marriage will feel more profound to the degree that your expectations of each other—what you feel your partner's place in your family ought to be—are similar. We're not talking here about seemingly superficial issues like who washes the dishes; we're talking about your deep expectations of yourself and your spouse. For example, both Ian and Hilary believed that a husband should be a protector and provider and the wife more of a nurturer. Chloe and

Evan believed in an egalitarian marriage in which the spouses supported each other emotionally and financially. Because in both of these marriages husband and wife had a similar philosophy about their roles, their marriages worked. Of course, were Ian married to Chloe and Hilary to Evan, there'd be enormous friction.

Having similar views about parenting—for example, the values you consider important to pass on to your children—also adds to a marriage's meaning. So do questions about the kind of interaction you should now have with your parents and siblings. Do you consider them part of your family or outsiders you keep your distance from? Even your views of what it means to work—and the significance you attach to your own work—can deepen your sense of connection with your spouse. In other words, to the extent that you feel similarly about these issues, your marriage will be strengthened.

None of this means that you should (or, for that matter, *could*) see eye to eye on every philosophical or spiritual aspect of life. For example, couples who are in the same line of work may draw different meanings from it. Johnny is passionate about being a scientist. His work as a geologist forms a significant part of his identity and colors how he sees the world. He feels personally inspired by the scientific approach with its emphasis on objectivity and analysis, and he takes great pride in being a geologist. If you ask him what he is, he will say he is a geologist first. His wife, Molly, is also a geologist, but she doesn't identify quite so profoundly with her profession. She sees herself as a woman first, rather than as a scientist. Yet they connect in so many other areas that this difference is not a sticking point.

ROLES QUESTIONNAIRE

To get a sense of how well you create shared meaning by supporting each other's roles, read each of the following statements and circle T for "true" or F for "false."

1. We share many similar values in our roles as parents. **T F**
2. We share many similar values in our roles as spouses. **T F**
3. We have many similar views about what it means to be a good friend to others. **T F**
4. My partner and I have compatible views about the role of work in one's life. **T F**
5. My partner and I have similar philosophies about balancing work and family life. **T F**
6. My partner supports what I see as my basic mission in life. **T F**
7. My partner shares my views on the importance of family and kin (sisters, brothers, moms, dads) in our life together. **T F**

Scoring: Give yourself 1 point for each "true" answer. If you score below 3, your relationship could stand some improvement in this area. Turn to the shared-meaning exercise that begins on page 272, and focus on the "roles" section.

PILLAR THREE: SHARED GOALS

Part of what makes life meaningful are the goals we strive to achieve. While we all have some very practical ambitions—like earning a certain income—we also have deeper, more spiritual aspirations. For one person, the goal may be to find peace and healing after a tumultuous, abusive childhood. For another, it may be to raise children who are good-hearted and generous. Many times, we don't talk about our deepest goals. Sometimes, we haven't even asked ourselves these questions. But when we start, it gives us the opportunity to explore something that can have a profound impact on ourselves and our marriage.

Not only will you increase the intimacy of your marriage by sharing your deepest objectives with your spouse, but to the extent that you work together to achieve shared goals, they can be a path toward making your union even richer. For example, both Emilie and Alex were committed to volunteer work for their church. Once their kids were grown, they decided they wanted to leave a spiritual legacy to their community. So he joined the board of directors of the religious school, and she started an adult education program at the church for people who wanted to become reacquainted with their faith. "I would have done this on my own," says Emilie. "But feeling in partnership with Alex about the importance of giving something back to my community and my church has made it an even more rewarding experience. I feel renewed not just in my faith but in my marriage as well."

SHARED GOALS QUESTIONNAIRE

To get a sense of how well you create shared meaning through goals, read each of the following statements and circle T for "true" or F for "false."

1. We share many of the same goals. **T F**
2. If I were to look back on my life in very old age, I think I would see that our paths had meshed very well. **T F**
3. My partner values my accomplishments. **T F**
4. My partner honors the personal goals I have that are unrelated to our marriage. **T F**
5. We share many of the same goals for others who are important to us (children, kin, friends, and community). **T F**
6. We have very similar financial goals. **T F**
7. We tend to have compatible worries about potential financial disasters. **T F**
8. Our hopes and aspirations, as individuals and together, for our children, for our life in general, and for our old age are quite compatible. **T F**
9. Our life dreams tend to be similar or compatible. **T F**
10. Even when they are different, we have been able to find a way to honor our life dreams. **T F**

Scoring: Give yourself 1 point for each "true" answer. If you score below 3, your relationship could stand some improvement in this area. Turn to the shared-meaning exercise that begins on page 272, and focus on the "goals" section.

PILLAR FOUR: SHARED VALUES AND SYMBOLS

Values and beliefs form the final pillar of shared meaning in a marriage. These are philosophical tenets that guide how you wish to conduct your lives. For some people, values are deeply rooted in religious conviction. But couples who are not religious may also have a belief system that determines their perspective on life and informs the choices they make.

Often, a couple's shared values and beliefs are represented by symbols, which can be actual objects or intangible. Religious icons like a crucifix or mezuzah are obvious symbols of faith a couple may display in their home. They represent values if their meaning is discussed, made personal, and agreed upon. But there are more personalized symbols as well. For Jenna and Spencer, their dining room table held special significance. They had saved up for many years to have it custom made by a local carpenter who was an expert carver. Every time they set it for family celebrations, its charm and strength spoke to them of the beauty and stability of their own marriage. Another family kept a statuette of a baby angel on the mantel in memory of their first baby, who was stillborn. The angel commemorated the baby but also represented their own resilience and deep love and support for each other, which had gotten them through this tragedy and allowed them to go on to have a large, happy family.

Abstract symbols are no less significant to a marriage. Even a home itself can be of great symbolic meaning to a couple. They may view it not only as the place where they eat and sleep but as the spiritual center of their lives together—the place where they consummate their love, where their children were conceived and grew, and so on. Family stories also tend to be richly symbolic and reflect deeply entrenched values. Helen's story about her great-grandparents who kept their love alive even when separated by an ocean symbolized the family's deep sense of loyalty. Every time that story was retold (and almost by definition, family stories do get told over and over again through the years), it was symbolic of the great value they place on loyalty.

In my own home, we have a wall covered with pictures of our

ancestors. The family stories associated with these relatives embody values we share as a couple. For example, there is a picture of my great-grandfather, a kosher butcher who was known for his generosity. Every week he would give away 10 percent of his meat to needy families of all religions, including gypsies. He actually had a spy network that alerted him to which families were hungry, and the meat would then magically appear on their doorstep. I often would tell our daughter that he embodied the kind of caring and giving that we value and aspire to emulate.

SHARED VALUES QUESTIONNAIRE

To get a sense of how well you create shared meaning through values, read each of the following statements and circle T for "true" or F for "false."

1. We see eye to eye about what home means. **T F**
2. Our philosophies of what love ought to be are quite compatible. **T F**
3. We have similar values about the importance of peacefulness in our lives. **T F**
4. We have similar values about the meaning of family. **T F**
5. We have similar views about the role of sex in our lives. **T F**
6. We have similar views about the role of love and affection in our lives. **T F**
7. We have similar values about the meaning of being married. **T F**
8. We have similar values about the importance and meaning of money in our lives. **T F**
9. We have similar values about the importance of education in our lives. **T F**
10. We have similar values about the importance of fun and play in our lives. **T F**
11. We have similar values about the significance of adventure. **T F**
12. We have similar values about trust. **T F**
13. We have similar values about personal freedom. **T F**

14. We have similar values about autonomy and independence. **T F**
15. We have similar values about sharing power in our marriage. **T F**
16. We have similar values about being interdependent, being a "we." **T F**
17. We have similar values about the meaning of having possessions, of owning things (like cars, nice clothes, books, music, a house, and land). **T F**
18. We have similar values about the meaning of nature and of our relationship to the seasons. **T F**
19. We have a similar level of sentimentality and need to reminisce about things in our past. **T F**
20. We have similar views about what we want in retirement and old age. **T F**

Scoring: Give yourself 1 point for each "true" answer. If you score below 3, your relationship could stand some improvement in this area. In the following shared-meaning exercise, focus on the "values" section.

EXERCISE: USING THE FOUR PILLARS TO CREATE MEANING

This four-part exercise offers a list of questions for you to answer and discuss. There is a section for each of the four pillars of shared meaning: rituals, roles, goals, and values. This questionnaire is not designed to be completed in an evening or even a month. Consider it a starting-off point for many future discussions and fireside chats.

To make the best use of this exercise, focus on the pillar that most needs bolstering in your relationship. Take the questions one at a time. You can even write your thoughts about each question in a notebook. Then read and discuss each other's entries. Talk about your differences on this issue as well as your areas of common ground that you can build upon. Find ways to honor both of your values, philosophies, and dreams. Although in many areas you may have separate needs, find ways to be supportive of each other's. Where you differ fundamen-

tally, focus on being respectful, on honoring the differe
you. (If this leads to an argument, work through the ex
chapters concerning Principles 4, 5, and 6, even if you've
so.) If you like, you can write your own family constitution
plain your areas of agreement about meaning and philosop

Pillar One: Creating Rituals of Connection

Agree on at least two important rituals of connection that you'd like to
add to your relationship or focus on more. See the list below for ideas.
Meaningful rituals can be created around Big Days (such as an anniversary) or more everyday interactions—such as how sex between you is
initiated or how you start your mornings. For each ritual you choose,
discuss why it is meaningful and important to you. Talk about whether
it was celebrated during your childhood and if so whether you enjoyed
your family's approach. Then iron out the specifics of how you would
like this ritual to unfold between you. Who should be responsible for
which aspects?

RITUALS AROUND CELEBRATIONS
  Birthdays
  Anniversaries
  Thanksgiving
  Christmas
  New Year's Eve
  Passover
  Ramadan
  Easter
  Kwanzaa
  Sabbath
  Graduation and other rites of passage

RITUALS AROUND RECREATION
  Date night
  Planning getaways and adventures
  Romantic evenings out
  Dinner at home

Hosting parties

Vacations (how do we decide, where do we go, when do we go)

RITUALS OF COMMUNICATION

Expressing pride in each other

Communicating daily appreciations

Discussing relationship issues

Dealing with misfortune or bad news

Expressing our needs

Discussing stressful events

SEXUAL RITUALS

Initiating lovemaking

How we gently refuse lovemaking

How we talk about lovemaking

RITUALS AROUND EVERYDAY LIVING

How we stay healthy

Morning routines and leave-taking

End-of-day reunions

How we renew ourselves when we are fatigued or burned out

Bedtime routines

Falling asleep together

Dealing with illness

Pillar Two: Roles

The more you can talk frankly to each other about your deeply held views about your roles in life, the more likely you are to reach a consensus that makes sense and comes naturally to your family. On separate pads answer the questions below; then share your thoughts with each other. (You don't have to answer every question. Skip the ones that aren't relevant to your life.)

I. How do you feel about your role as a husband or wife? What does this role mean to you? How did your father or mother view this role? How are you similar and different? How would you like to change this role?

2. How do you feel about your role as a father or mother? What does this role mean to you? How did your father or mother view this role? How are you similar and different? How would you like to change this role?

3. How do you feel about your role as a son or daughter? What does this role mean to you? How did your father or mother view this role? How are you similar and different? How would you like to change this role?

4. How do you feel about your role as a worker (your occupation)? What does this role mean to you? How did your father or mother view this role? How are you similar and different? How would you like to change this role?

5. How do you feel about your role as a friend to others? What does this role mean to you? How did your father or mother view this role? How are you similar and different? How would you like to change this role?

6. How do you feel about your role in your community? What does this role mean to you? How did your father or mother view this role? How are you similar and different? How would you like to change this role?

7. How do you balance these roles in your life?

8. What are all the ways that your relationship already supports you in the roles you play?

9. What else can your relationship do to support you in the roles you play?

Pillar Three: Goals

Write some thoughts about each question, and then share these thoughts with your partner before discussing what your common goals are.

1. Write a "mission statement" for your life. List the missions that matter to you most.

2. Does your relationship support each of your missions? How? How does it not support them?
3. If you were to write your own obituary, what would you like it to say?
4. What goals do you have for yourself, your partner, your children?
5. What do you want to accomplish in the next five to ten years?
6. What is one of your life dreams that you want to fulfill?
7. What legacy do you want to leave?
8. Are there meaningful activities that could be great sources of energy and pleasure for you but that keep getting postponed or crowded out by more immediate, but less significant, concerns?

Pillar Four: Values

The following questions will help you talk to each other about the significance of symbols in your marriage.

1. What symbols (such as photos or objects) show who our family is in the world, what we value about being members of this family?
2. Which family stories do you consider sources of pride that you consider central to your traditions and symbolic of your values?
3. What does a home mean to you? What qualities must it have? What was the experience of home like for each of you during childhood?
4. What objects or activities symbolize to you a meaningful and well-lived life? Some examples are being charitable, wearing a crucifix, lighting a candle for deceased ancestors. Do you feel that you express your philosophy of life to the degree you'd like?

Feeling a sense of unity with your spouse on the deepest issues is unlikely to occur overnight. Exploring together is really an ongoing, lifelong process. The goal shouldn't be to agree on every aspect of what is profoundly meaningful to you, but to have a marriage where you are both open to each other's most dearly held beliefs. The more you create a marriage where these convictions can be readily divulged, the more joyous will be the life that you share.

Afterword:
What Now?

*N*o book (or therapist) can solve all of your marital problems. But learning the Seven Principles really can change the course of your relationship. Even making just a small and gentle shift in the trajectory of your marriage can have a dramatic, positive effect over time. The catch, of course, is that you have to build on the change and keep it going. Improving your marriage is a kind of journey. Like all voyages, it begins by suspending disbelief, taking one small step, and then seeing where you are and taking the next step. If you get stuck or take a few missteps, reread portions of this book with an eye toward charting where your marriage is now. Then you'll be able to figure out how to help it along in the right direction.

Here are some general strategies that you can incorporate into your daily life to move your relationship forward every day.

The Magic Six Hours

When we followed up on couples who attended our Seattle workshops, we wondered what would distinguish those couples whose marriages continued to improve from those whose marriages did not. Would we find that the successful group had dramatically overhauled their lives? Far from it. To our surprise, we discovered that they were devoting only an extra six hours a week to their marriage. Although each couple had their own style of spending these extra six hours, some clear patterns emerged. In general, these couples were giving their marriages a concentrated refresher course in the Seven Principles. The approach works so phenomenally well that I've come to call it the Magic Six Hours. Here's how you can do it, too:

Partings. Make sure that before you say good-bye in the morning you've learned about one thing that is happening in your spouse's life that day—from lunch with the boss to a doctor's appointment to a scheduled phone call with an old friend.

Time: 2 minutes a day × 5 working days
Total: 10 minutes

Reunions. We recommend a hug and a kiss that lasts at least six seconds. The six-second kiss is worth coming home to. Also, be sure to engage in a stress-reducing conversation at the end of each workday for at least 20 minutes (see page 97).

Time: 20 minutes a day × 5 days
Total: 1 hour 40 minutes

Admiration and appreciation. Find some way every day to communicate genuine affection and appreciation toward your spouse. Genuinely say, "I love you."

Time: 5 minutes a day × 7 days
Total: 35 minutes

Affection. Show each other physical affection when you're together during the day, and make sure to always embrace before going to sleep. Even if on occasion your goodnight kiss just lasts for microseconds, think of it as a way to let go of any minor irritations that have built up over the day. In other words, always lace your kiss with forgiveness and tenderness for your partner.

Time: 5 minutes a day × 7 days
Total: 35 minutes

Weekly date. This just-the-two-of-you time can be a romantic way to stay connected. Ask each other open-ended tions that let you update your love maps and turn toward each other. Think of questions to ask your spouse (like "Are you still thinking about redecorating the bedroom?" "Where should we take our next vacation?" or "How are you feeling about your boss these days?").

Time: 2 hours once a week
Total: 2 hours

State of the union meeting. Select one hour a week to talk about your relationship *this week*. Keep this time sacred. Begin by talking about what went right. Then give each other five appreciations you haven't yet expressed. Try to be specific. Next, discuss any issues that may have arisen. Use gentle start-up and listen nondefensively. Move to problem solving with the two-circle method described on p. 185. If there was a regrettable incident, process it using the exercise on p. 188. End by each of you asking and answering, "What can I do to make you feel loved this coming week?"

Time: 1 hour a week
Grand Total: Six hours!

As you can see, the amount of time involved in incorporating these changes into your relationship is quite minimal. Yet these six hours will help enormously in keeping your marriage on track.

Remember, working briefly on your marriage every day will do more for your health and longevity than working out at a health club.

Marital Poop Detector

perts" claim that a significant cause of unhap-
e is that husbands and wives have overblown
ach other. By lowering these expectations, the
argument goes, you become less likely to feel disappointment. But
Donald Baucom of the University of North Carolina has debunked
this idea by studying couples' standards and expectations of each
other. He has found that people with the greatest expectations for
their marriage usually wind up with the highest-quality marriages.
This suggests that by holding your relationship to high standards,
you are far more likely to achieve the kind of marriage you want
than you are by looking the other way and letting things slide.

Our research on newlyweds confirms what Baucom found.
The couples we studied who adjusted to elevated levels of negativity (irritability, emotional distance) in their marriage ended up less
happy or satisfied years later. Those who refused to put up with
lots of negativity—who insisted on gently confronting each other
when, say, contempt or defensiveness threatened to become pervasive, wound up happy and satisfied years later.

These findings suggest that every marriage ought to be
equipped with a built-in early-warning system that lets you know
when your marital quality is in jeopardy. I call this system the Marital Poop Detector because it's really a way of recognizing early
whether something just doesn't smell right!

Someone once said that to men the five most frightening
words in the English language are, "Let's talk about our relationship." Truth is, those words can be just as frightening to plenty of
women. The best way to conquer this fear is to talk about issues
in your relationship while they are still minor, before they build up
steam and become combustible. A Marital Poop Detector lets you
do that.

Usually one member of a couple tends to take the lead in sniff-
ing out trouble. More often than not it is the wife. When her husband gets cranky or withdrawn, she calls him on it and finds out

what's wrong. But there's no reason why you both can't perform this function in your marriage.

Here is a list of questions to ask yourselves once a week. It will guide you in assessing how your relationship is faring. Just remember to discuss these concerns using a softened start-up and without being critical of your spouse. The best approach is to say something like, "Hey, I really feel out of touch with you. What's going on?" (Be careful not to address any issues right before bedtime. This could interfere with your sleep.)

Instructions: Use this questionnaire to assess how things went in your marriage today (or lately) and whether you want to bring up any issues. Check as many as you think apply. If you check more than four, think about talking things over gently with your partner, within the next three days.

1. I have been acting irritably.
2. I have been feeling emotionally distant.
3. There has been a lot of tension between us..
4. I find myself wanting to be somewhere else.
5. I have been feeling lonely.
6. My partner has seemed emotionally unavailable to me.
7. I have been angry.
8. We have been out of touch with each other.
9. My partner has little idea of what I am thinking.
10. We have been under a great deal of stress, and it has taken its toll on us.
11. I wish we were closer right now.
12. I have wanted to be alone a lot.
13. My partner has been acting irritably.
14. My partner has been acting emotionally distant.
15. My partner's attention seems to be somewhere else.
16. I have been emotionally unavailable to my partner.
17. My partner has been angry.
18. I have little idea of what my partner is thinking.
19. My partner has wanted to be alone a lot.

20. We really need to talk.
21. We haven't been communicating very well.
22. We have been fighting more than usual.
23. Lately small issues escalate.
24. We have been hurting each other's feelings.
25. There hasn't been very much fun or joy in our lives.

Forgive Yourself

After working through the Seven Principles, it is probably very clear to you that there is no such thing as constructive criticism. All criticism is painful. Unlike complaints—specific requests for change—criticism doesn't make a marriage better. It inevitably makes it worse. What causes a spouse to be chronically critical? We have discovered that there are two sources. The first is an emotionally unresponsive partner. If Natalie keeps complaining to Jonah about leaving his towel on the bathroom floor and he just ignores her, eventually she is likely to start criticizing him—calling him a slob instead of politely reminding him to hang it up. This change in Natalie's approach is understandable, but it is hardly helpful to her marriage since her criticism will make Jonah even less responsive. The only way out of this cycle is for both of them to change—which won't be easy. It takes courage to be less critical of an unresponsive mate, and it takes courage to turn toward a partner who's always harping on your flaws. But both changes are necessary to end the cycle.

The other source of criticism in marriage comes from within. It is connected to self-doubt that has developed over the course of one's life, particularly during childhood. In other words, it begins as criticism of oneself. Aaron cannot really appreciate or enjoy his own accomplishments. When he has a setback in his business, he feels deep down that he is worthless. When his business is successful, he doesn't allow himself to be proud. There's a voice inside him that says this is not good enough. He continually searches for approval but cannot enjoy it or even accept it when it is offered.

What happens when Aaron marries Courtney? Since he has

trained his mind to see what is wrong, what is missing, and not to appreciate what is there, it's difficult for him to rejoice in what's right with his wife or their marriage. So instead of appreciating Courtney's wonderful qualities, including her wry humor, her loyalty, and the deep emotional support she offers him when he is in danger of losing his job, he focuses on what he considers her flaws—that she is highly emotional, somewhat awkward socially, and not as meticulously clean around the house as he'd like.

The story of Aaron and Courtney reflects what goes wrong 85 percent of the time in marriages. If you consider yourself inadequate, you are always on the lookout for what is not there in yourself and your partner. And let's face it: anyone you marry will be lacking in certain desirable qualities. The problem is that we tend to focus on what's missing in our mate and overlook the fine qualities that *are* there—we take those for granted.

If you recognize yourself in the description of the self-critic, the best thing you can do for yourself and your marriage is to work on accepting yourself with all of your flaws. As I look back on my own life, I realize that forgiving myself for all of my imperfections has made an immense difference in my role as a husband and father.

One route toward this forgiveness may be your personal spiritual beliefs. Many religious traditions include prayers of gratitude that focus our attention on the many blessings in our lives. Whatever your perspective on religion, there is an important message here for long-term relationships. Expressions of thanksgiving and praise are the antidotes to the poison of criticism and its deadly cousin, contempt. The following exercise will start you on this path.

AN EXERCISE IN THANKSGIVING

STEP 1. For one week, try to be aware of your tendency to criticize. Instead shift your focus toward what is right. Notice what you have and what others contribute. Search for reasons to praise. Begin with simple things. Praise the world. Appreciate your own breathing, the sunrise, the beauty of a rainstorm, the wonder in your child's eyes.

Utter some silent words of thanksgiving (to no one in particular) for these small wonders in your day. This will begin to shift your focus away from the negative.

STEP 2. For an entire week, offer your spouse at least one genuine, heartfelt praise each day. Notice how this exercise affects your partner and yourself. If you are able, extend the exercise one more day. Then another. Expand the exercise to others in your life as well— for example, to your children. When you meet someone new, look for what is special about this person. Appreciate these qualities. Remember, this all has to be genuine and heartfelt. Don't be phony. Notice these positive qualities. Enjoy them. Try to tell people what you notice and genuinely appreciate about them. Just find one feature for each person. Ignore the shortcomings.

As you stretch the period of thanksgiving one day beyond a week, and then another day, and another, you'll receive a great gift: You will become less critical of yourself. Grace and forgiveness will enter your world. This is what the spiritual "Amazing Grace" is all about. You begin to enjoy your own accomplishments, rather than consider them inadequate.

One of the most meaningful gifts a parent can give a child is to acknowledge his or her own mistake, to say, "I was wrong here" or "I'm sorry." This is so powerful because it also gives the child permission to make a mistake, to admit having messed up and still be okay. It builds in the forgiveness of self. Likewise, being able to say "I'm sorry" and mean it is a pretty great gift to give your spouse— and yourself as well. The more you can imbue your relationship with the spirit of thanksgiving and the graceful presence of praise, the more profound and fulfilling your lives together will be.

Index

290

humor, sense of, 42
husbands
    and baby care, 220–21
    changes in roles of, 123–25
    emotionally intelligent, 123–25
    and housework, 212–17
    learning to yield, 125–28
    and parenthood, 218–22
    playing with baby, 221
    sensitivity to needs of, 221–22
    see also men

immune system, and health, 6–7
influence, 115–36
    "anything you say, dear," 116
    changes in, 123–25
    compromise in, 184–87
    decision making in, 116, 117
    escalation of conflict in, 119–20
    exercises, 130–36
    and friendship, 121
    gender differences in, 117,
        121–23
    Gottman Island Survival Game,
        133–36
    learning to yield in, 125–28
    negativity in, 117
    power sharing in, 116, 117,
        128
    questionnaire, 128–29
    and religion, 118–19
    resistance in, 117, 118–20
    yielding to win in, 129–32
in-laws
    exercise in problem solving
        with, 205–7
    solving problems of, 201–7
"innocent victim" stance, 37

intelligence, emotional, 4–5, 21,
    27, 45, 54, 119, 121, 123–25,
    240
Intentional Family, The
    (Doherty), 264
interests, common, 17
Internet, 92–93, 195–99, 208
"I" statements, 11–12, 13, 167–68,
    190, 251
    "I appreciate," 74–76, 168, 178,
        259
    "I feel," 176
    "I need to calm down," 176

Jacobson, Neil, 13, 98

Kelly, Joan, 18
Kiecolt-Glaser, Janice, 3, 7
killer cells, 7
knowledge, strength in, 54–56

Lawson, Annette, 18
Levenson, Robert, 43, 158
life expectancy, 6, 7
listening
    active, 11–14, 97–98
    and stonewalling, 38–39
Love Lab, 1–2, 6, 24–25, 26, 30,
    68, 162, 182, 204, 240, 241,
    277
love maps, 53–66, 113, 124
    exercises, 58–65
    knowledge and strength in,
        54–56
    questionnaire, 56–58
    sexual, 230–31
    20 questions game, 58–60
    Who am I?, 62–65

ABOUT THE AUTHORS

JOHN M. GOTTMAN, a leading research scientist on marriage and family, is emeritus professor of psychology at the University of Washington; executive director of his laboratory, the Relationship Research Institute; and cofounder of the Gottman Institute. He held an NIMH research scientist career award for twenty years. Dr. Gottman is the author of more than two hundred professional journal articles and forty-two books, as well as the recipient of numerous prestigious awards for his extensive contributions to marriage and family research. He was recently named by *Psychotherapy Networker* as one of the ten most influential psychotherapists in the past quarter century. He graduated magna cum laude from Fairleigh Dickinson University with a B.S. in mathematics-physics. He obtained his M.S. in mathematics at the Massachusetts Institute of Technology, and his Ph.D. in clinical and developmental psychology from the University of Wisconsin. Dr. Gottman frequently gives public lectures and appears on popular media to explain research findings to the general public in understandable and useful everyday language. As cofounder of the Gottman Institute, Dr. Gottman conducts several intensive weekend workshops per year for clinicians and for couples in Seattle, as well as small group retreats and intensive marathon couples therapy at his home on Orcas Island, all based on his scientific research on how long-term happy and stable relationships work. Contact the Institute at www.gottman.com and gottmanprivateretreats.com or at its toll-free number, (888) 523-9042.

NAN SILVER is a former editor in chief of *Health* magazine and coauthor, with Dr. Gottman, of *What Makes Love Last?* and *Why Marriages Succeed or Fail*. Visit her at nansilver.net.